West European Politics since 1945

The political structure of the European Community, which Britain is joining in 1973, can best be understood against the background of the national political systems which created and shaped it. This book gives a full but clear account of the political forces at work in Europe after 1945, particularly in France and Germany, the two 'hereditary enemies' whose reconciliation made the Common Market possible.

In describing each phase of the movement towards West European unity—the Schuman Plan of 1950 which produced the Coal and Steel Community, the Rome Treaties of 1957 which led to the European Economic Community and Euratom, and the negotiations for British membership in the Sixties and Seventies—Roger Morgan first analyses developments within France, Germany and the other states concerned, and then examines their effects on Europe as a whole. Similarly the parts played in the growth of European unity by Robert Schuman, Konrad Adenauer, General de Gaulle, Willy Brandt and others are described in the context first of these statesmen's place in their national political systems and then of their attitudes towards the institutions of Europe. The influence of the USA and the Soviet Union on Western Europe and Europe's relations with the Third World are also critically assessed.

Written primarily for students of contemporary history and international politics this study sheds light both on the process of European integration and on the broader themes of Europe's political life; it also provides the reader with a basis for assessing the likely developments in Europe's institutions.

Dr Roger Morgan is currently Deputy Director of Studies at the Royal Institute of International Affairs.

West European Politics since 1945

The Shaping of the European Community

Roger Morgan
Deputy Director of Studies,
Royal Institute of International Affairs

B. T. Batsford Ltd
London

First published 1972

© Roger Morgan, 1972

Printed by Bristol Typesetting Co Ltd
Barton Manor, St Philips, Bristol
for the publishers
B T BATSFORD LTD 4 Fitzhardinge Street, London WIH OAH

ISBN 0 7134 1122 8 (HARD COVER)

ISBN 0 7134 1123 6 (PAPER BACK)

Preface

The plan of this book requires a word of explanation. The political structure of post-war Western Europe has been shaped by a process of interaction between the national systems—of which the French and West German have been by far the most important—and the supra-national institutions of the European Communities. In order to bring out the nature of this interaction, each of the main time-periods—the late forties, the fifties and the sixties—has been analysed in four chapters, dealing respectively with France, Germany, the other four member-states of the European Communities and the Community institutions themselves. Chapter 14, covering the shorter period from 1969 to 1971, is correspondingly divided into four sections. This procedure—somewhat analogous to the system of weighted voting in the Community's Council of Ministers—reflects the preponderant influence of France and Germany in the politics of European integration up to 1971.

This study has been partly written since I joined the staff of the Royal Institute of International Affairs, though most of the material was assembled during my earlier teaching in British and American universities. I am very grateful to Andrew Shonfield, formerly Director of Studies and now Director of Chatham House, for making it possible for me to complete a piece of work I had begun before I came to the Institute; and likewise for several stimulating conversations about European affairs, of which he may find some traces in the pages that follow. I am also grateful to my wife Annette for a discussion of Europe which we have pursued since the time of the Messina Conference (see Chapter 9), and for her devoted support and encouragement during the writing of this book; to Carola Piggott for typing the book so cheerfully and efficiently, and for her many valuable editorial comments and suggestions; and to Rena Fenteman for reading the proofs and making many improvements, and to Helen Roy for compiling the index. Full responsibility for any remaining errors of fact or judgement must be placed on the author's personal obstinacy.

Roger Morgan
July 1972

Contents

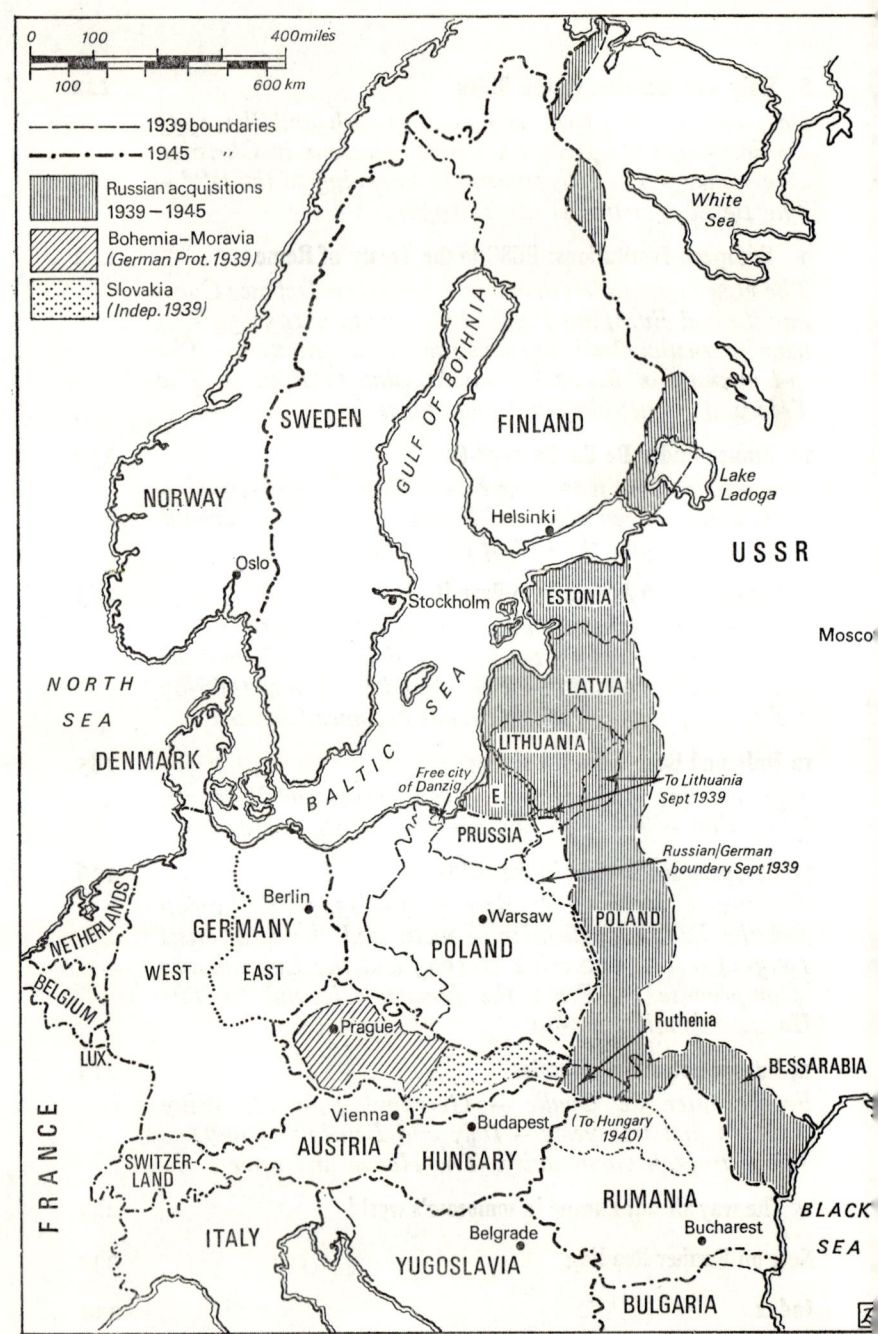

White
Sea

SWEDEN

FINLAND

NORWAY

GULF OF BOTHNIA

Helsinki

Lake
Ladoga

USSR

Oslo

Stockholm

ESTONIA

Mosco

NORTH
SEA

BALTIC SEA

LATVIA

LITHUANIA

To Lithuania
Sept 1939

DENMARK

Free city
of Danzig

E.
PRUSSIA

Russian/German
boundary Sept 1939

NETHERLANDS

Berlin

GERMANY

Warsaw

POLAND

BELGIUM

WEST   EAST

LUX.

Prague

Ruthenia

BESSARABIA

FRANCE

Vienna

Budapest

(To Hungary
1940)

SWITZER-
LAND

AUSTRIA

HUNGARY

RUMANIA

BLACK
SEA

ITALY

Belgrade

Bucharest

YUGOSLAVIA

BULGARIA

Soviet gains in the Second World War

Six original members of European Economic Community

ICELAND
•Reykjavik

NORTH
SEA

NORWAY

Oslo•

SWEDEN

FINLAND

Helsinki•

Stockholm•

BALTIC
SEA

Moscow•

USSR

UNITED
KINGDOM

DENMARK

Dublin
EIRE

London•

Copenhagen•

WEST
Berlin

EAST

Warsaw•

POLAND

ATLANTIC

NETHERLANDS

GERMANY

BELGIUM

Bonn•

Prague•

CZECHOSLOVAKIA

OCEAN

Paris•

LUXEM-
BOURG

Vienna•

Budapest•

RUMANIA

SWITZ-
ERLAND

AUSTRIA

HUNGARY

Bucharest•

BLACK

FRANCE

Belgrade•

YUGOSLAVIA

BULGARIA

SEA

ADRIATIC SEA

Sofia•

ITALY

Rome•

Tirane•

ALBANIA

GREECE

TURKEY

SPAIN

Corsica

PORTUGAL

•Madrid

Sardinia

Athens•

Lisbon•

Sicily

MEDITERRANEAN SEA

•Malta

Crete

0   100   500 miles

100   800 km

The EEC and its neighbours

Abbreviations

CDU	Christlich-Demokratische Union
CFDT	Conféderation Française Démocratique du Travail (Christian trade union organisation)
CGT	Conféderation Générale du Travail (Communist trade union organisation)
CRS	Compagnies Républicaines de Sécurité (French riot police)
CSU	Christlich-Soziale Union (Bavarian CDU)
ECSC	European Coal and Steel Community
EDC	European Defence Community
EEC	European Economic Community
EPC	European Political Community
FDP	Frei-Demokratische Partei
FO	Force Ouvrière (Socialist trade union movement)
GDR	German Democratic Republic
MLF	Multilateral Force
MRP	Mouvement Républicain Populaire (Christian Democrats)
NATO	North Atlantic Treaty Organisation
OEEC	Organisation for European Economic Co-operation
RPF	Rassemblement du Peuple Français (Gaullists)
SED	Sozialistische Einheitspartei Deutschlands (Socialist Unity Party of East Germany)
SFIO	Section Française de l'Internationale Ouvrière (Socialists)
SPD	Sozialdemokratische Partei Deutschlands
UDSR	Union Démocratique et Socialiste de la Résistance (centre-left party during the Fourth Republic)

1 Europe in the Post-War World

The Europe of the Six

Europe in 1945 represented, in the much-quoted words of Winston Churchill, 'a charnel-house, a rubble heap, a breeding ground for pestilence and war'. The aim of this book is to explain how the devastated Europe of 1945 has become, by the 1970s, economically prosperous, socially stable and, in political terms, a force to be reckoned with: a force able to stand independently—at least as far as the economic and monetary aspects of politics are concerned—and to make the two world powers, the United States and the Soviet Union, take notice of it.

The title speaks of 'Western Europe', and this requires a closer definition. What is the justification for taking the original six member states of the European Economic Community— France, West Germany, Italy and the three members of the Benelux Union (Belgium, the Netherlands and Luxembourg) —and for presenting an account of their activities and their relations as a study of 'Western Europe'?

The first answer is that these six states are the ones that took the lead in giving concrete expression to their own feeling that they constituted a unity. The institutions set up by the Six —the Coal and Steel Community of the early 1950s and then, later, Euratom and the European Economic Community —are the most substantial embodiment of the idea that the states of Europe are committed to a common destiny, and can only solve their problems by acting together. As we shall see, many other international institutions of post-war Europe represent common action of various kinds—either close unity between a small number of states like the Benelux Union itself, or a distinctly less intense degree of cooperation among a much larger number of states, as represented by the Council of Europe. The European Communities set up by the Six, however, represent a degree of mutual commitment to integration which gives these states the right to be regarded as the true pioneers of a united Europe.

What the Six had in common, as we shall see, was a roughly similar level of economic development; a high degree of disillusionment with the sovereign state, a form of political organisation which by 1945 had brought them to a common catastrophe; a range of domestic political forces which were at least broadly alike; and a realisation that they had to work together because they were geographically contiguous.

In broader terms, this Europe, of course, only represents the western half of a truncated continent: the biggest single result of the Second World War, as far as Europe was concerned, was the advance of Soviet power into the heart of what had previously been considered Western Europe, the centre of Germany. This meant that a number of indisputably European states—Poland, Czechoslovakia, Hungary and the Balkan states of Yugoslavia, Bulgaria and Roumania, not to mention the eastern and central parts of Germany itself—no longer took part in the political affairs of the West. Either they were fully annexed by the Soviet Union, like the former Baltic states and parts of Poland, Czechoslovakia, Roumania and Germany, or they were subjected to régimes basically dependent on Soviet power for their existence. In either case, an externally-imposed unity engulfed them, that was not to give way to any significant diversity for some years after the War. When the ' European idea ' was first preached in the 1920s by such pioneers as Count Coudenhouve-Kalergi or Aristide Briand, they took for granted the unity of a Europe going to the western frontiers of the Soviet Union; and forty years later President de Gaulle was to speak of Europe's natural limits as being the Atlantic to the west and the Urals to the east. However, during most of the period covered by this book, from the late 1940s to the mid-1960s, there was no question of the states of Eastern Europe playing any independent part as actors in international affairs. Relations with Eastern Europe did indeed have a large influence on the politics of the West—particularly, as we shall see, over the ever-present problem of the reunification of Germany—but the area where the active initiatives could be taken and significant achievements carried out was normally Western Europe alone.

The Europe to be analysed here was fairly sharply delimited to the north and south as well. To the north lie a group of states —the United Kingdom and the Scandinavian countries—that until the 1960s were only prepared to link their fortunes to a limited degree with those of the other Western European states. Although the United Kingdom and the Scandinavian states shared the commitment of Western Europe to the values of liberal democracy, and although they were prepared to cooperate in increasing degrees in such organisations as the Council of Europe, their position after 1945 did not impel them—as the other West European states were impelled—towards fuller integration. Britain, committed by tradition to the affairs of Europe only at moments of severe crisis, had become more of an island than ever as a result of her freedom from invasion during the Second World War, when the rest of Europe had been swallowed up by the Nazi flood, and her foreign policy after 1945 was dominated by her relations with the United States and with the evolving Commonwealth; she also feared, as did the Scandinavian states, that her relatively high standard of living would be threatened if she joined in too close a union with her less fortunate Western European neighbours. Although, as we shall see, the policies of Britain towards the Continental states, and their own policies towards her, were vital factors in the development of Western Europe, and although by the 1960s Britain had come to accept the view that her destiny was indeed linked to that of the Continent, we shall find that the evolution of British politics, like those of Scandinavia, play only a marginal part in our story, corresponding with the geographically and psychologically marginal place these countries occupied.

To the south, again, are states with somewhat different characteristics from those of the hard core of Western Europe. Spain and Portugal in 1945, thanks to their basically undemocratic constitutions, found themselves—particularly in the case of the former, where Franco's victory in the civil war had alienated the sympathies of much of Western Europe—isolated from the mainstream of events. To these political peculiarities must be added the fact that they were economically much more backward than their neighbours to the north; their relative lack of heavy industry, and the generally low standard of living of their populations, put them in a class apart, and for these reasons their rôle in the development of the central political issues of Europe was very slight—though again there were signs of a *rapprochement* as the 1960s proceeded. Another pair of small states at the opposite

end of the Mediterranean—Greece and Turkey—were involved
to some degree in the main currents of European politics, and
became members of such organisations as the Council of Europe
and the North Atlantic Treaty Organisation, but again their
economic under-development, political instability and preoccupa-
tion with limited political issues such as Cyprus, made their participation in Western European affairs only marginal.

This book thus concentrates on the affairs of the Six, though
it should again be underlined that these have often been crucially
influenced by the policies of outside powers—both European
states such as Britain, or the states of Eastern Europe, and the
two super-powers—America and Russia—whose centres of
gravity lie essentially outside Europe.

We have talked so far of 'Western Europe' and of the Six as
a unity, as if the Six already formed a united bloc, responding
as one to the challenges of the outside world and linked in solving their domestic problems. To some extent, compared with the
other areas mentioned above, this picture is accurate. They have
indeed shown their willingness to advance together towards unification, and their more venturesome spokesmen have suggested
that full unity is the ultimate goal: for some, like President de
Gaulle, this unity was to be one which preserved the individual
characteristics and freedom of action of each state, and one which
produced a Europe consciously and emphatically independent
of the outside world; while for a European like Jean Monnet, the
Europe to be created was a fully united federal one, whose relations with the United States were to be marked not by full independence but by interdependence. For both schools of thought,
however, and for the many variants in between, 'Europe' always
represented some form of union of the Six.

Nonetheless, it would be misleading to write the history of
post-war Western Europe as though the movement towards integration was its only theme, or as though this movement had gone
forward in a harmonious manner, uninterrupted by any reassert-
ions of conflicting national interests. It is true that in 1945 the
Second World War had bled the old nation-states of Europe
white. It is also true that the statesmen who faced the task of
political reconstruction in each of these states all shared the
realisation that the nineteenth-century creed of nationalism had
now run to the end of its disastrous course, and had to be

replaced by something new. This conviction left its traces in the
wording of all the new constitutions of Western Europe—those
of the Fourth French Republic of 1946, of the Italian Republic
of 1947, and of the West German Federal Republic of 1949—
—each of which made explicit provision for sovereign powers to
be transferred to a future United States of Europe. It is true again
that the industrialists, bankers and others responsible for
economic policy in post-war Europe, being on the whole convinced that the nation-state could no longer provide an adequate
framework for this reconstruction, turned instead to new institutions of economic cooperation on an international level, and
accepted the principle that Europe's economic future must be
planned in common.

Yet despite these widespread convictions of the early post-war
period in Europe, the concept of the nation-state nevertheless
retained considerable vitality—this concept had after all dominated the political history of Europe for at least five centuries—
and once the critical situation of the immediate post-war years
had been overcome, nationalism began to revive. We have already
suggested how the impact of the Second World War on Britain
had been to strengthen and consolidate the view that the nation-
state could appropriately and successfully take charge of the most
diverse aspects of the nation's economic and social life, and could
also appear to offer the best framework for post-war reconstruction and social reform. Not surprisingly, among the states of the
Continent as well, the one where the idea of national independence raised its head most insistently was France, the Continental
state that shared with Britain a long tradition of national independence, political and military power, and also colonial involve-
ments outside Europe. Although France had been severely shaken
economically and politically by the Second World War, and
although many of her post-war statesmen were leaders of the
movement towards European integration—Monnet and Schuman
being outstanding examples—we shall find many occasions when
the reassertion of national independence by France herself chal-
lenged the progress of the institutions she had helped to create.
The paradigms of this go from France's hesitation in accepting
supra-national economic planning by OEEC in the late 1940s,
through her more dramatic and influential rejection of the European Defence Community and its twin the European Political

Community in 1950-54, to the series of blows against the supra-
national structure of the European Economic Community de-
livered by President de Gaulle during the 1960s.

France, however, has by no means been alone in reasserting
national interests against 'European' ones: her main European
partner, West Germany, has also—if not to the same extent—
shown examples of the same process. Thus, for instance, Chancellor Adenauer's policy of linking the Federal Republic intimately
with the organisations of Western unity was subject to perpetual
challenge by the Social Democrats and Free Democrats, who
argued that this policy would destroy any hope of reunification
with East Germany. Again, on various occasions from 1956 until
the end of his chancellorship in 1963, Adenauer himself occasionally adopted lines of policy that ran contrary to those of the
North Atlantic Treaty Organisation and even (for instance in
his Franco-German treaty of January 1963) those of EEC. Since
Adenauer's time, again, Germany in the late 1960s has been
strong enough in economic and financial terms to stand out against
the overwhelming consensus of her European partners in policy
on these matters—most notably in the international monetary
crises of November 1968 and later, when she stoutly rejected the
majority European view that her currency should be revalued.

Examples of national interest dominating policy at the expense
of European interests can also be found in the actions of the
other members of the European Community, and they remind
us of the fact that this Community—despite all the progress it
has made in limiting the traditional freedom of action of nation-
states—remains a fragile construction whose total collapse is perhaps not impossible, if the forces of nationalism reassert themselves as they occasionally appear likely to do.

There is no denying, in fact, that the countries of Europe, as
well as the basic underlying interests they have in common—
economic progress, political stability, military security against
attack—also have certain interests which vary to a considerable
degree from from one state to another. The military threat from
the Soviet Union, for instance, naturally appears more pressing to
West German policy-makers situated immediately next to the
Red Army, and with their former capital half under hostile occupation and exposed to the risk of being cut off except from the
air, than it does to their counterparts in Paris. Again, if one thinks

of the problem of enlarging the existing Community, the Dutch have an obvious interest in bringing in one of their major trading partners, Britain, but have much less interest in bringing in the Danes who might compete with them as agricultural producers; whereas Germany, a net importer of agricultural produce, might have a strong interest in bringing in Denmark, and relatively less interest—at least on economic grounds—in bringing in Britain.

These differing political and economic interests, which are in fact those of the political electorates in each of the countries concerned, are bound to be reflected in the policies adopted by their governments. Despite all the hopes of the European pioneers that there would one day be a European Parliament endowed with real authority and elected directly by the voters of each town and village in Europe, a politician's road to power is still essentially a national one, and the Minister who comes to office in Bonn, Paris or Rome will have to think first of the electorate of his own country, and only second—in the event of a conflict of interest—of the European interest to which he may ideally be committed. The history of Western European politics since the war is a story of the interaction between two underlying forces: on the one hand, the drive towards unity and integration; and on the other, the forces welling up from each national political system, arising from a change of government, perhaps, or from the result of a national election, that have sometimes boosted the integration movement along, and sometimes interrupted it (as did the French election of 1951, or the consequences of the constitutional crisis in the same country in 1958).

The political behaviour of Western Europe's leaders since 1945 fits neither into the traditional notions of ' power politics ', according to which national policy-makers pursue their ' national interest ' as they see it, unencumbered by any feeling of loyalty to a larger international community; nor into the pattern of behaviour prescribed in the visions of the early pioneers of European unity, who thought that sovereign power would be drained away from national capitals towards the centre to such an extent that national interests would be totally downgraded, or at the most would be the subject of amicable arbitration by the government of a United States of Europe.

The true nature of political decision-making in the capitals of Western Europe since 1945—and also in Brussels and the

B

other embryonic capitals of what may be the Europe of the future—has been a mixture of these two styles. Just as there have clearly been moments when European statesmen have sacrificed their short-run national interest for the sake of 'making Europe', so there have clearly been occasions when deadlock or even bitter conflict at the 'European' level can only be explained by processes at work within the national systems of the participating states.

This is the reason why this book alternates between analysing movements and events at the European level, and examining the forces at work at the 'lower' level of the main national systems: only a dual analysis of this kind can bring out the nature of the process of interaction which has made post-war Western Europe what it is. A further dimension, which must equally be borne in mind, is that of the pressures on Western Europe from the super-powers outside, and the different ways in which the European states responded to them.

The first factor that needs to be made clear, in order to set the scene for a discussion of the political and economic forces at work in Western Europe, is the way in which this area—the area within which Christian Democracy, Social Democracy and the other main forces were to operate—was limited and defined by the outcome of power relationships at the end of the Second World War.

This outcome—the division of Europe into the two spheres of influence of the two super-powers—did not simply result from a crude carve-up at the Yalta Conference or any other conference, as President de Gaulle was to allege in the 1960s: it resulted from a much more complicated interplay of military and diplomatic factors in the closing stages of the Second World War, which have to be described to explain why the Cold War in Europe took the form it did in the early post-war years.

The beginnings of the Cold War 1945-47
The confrontations between the Soviet Union and the Western powers, in the course of which the conflicting nature of their aims became quite clear, and which revealed the existence of what Churchill in 1946 was to call 'the Cold War', took place in an almost continuous series of diplomatic encounters. There was the conference of Foreign Ministers in Moscow in October-November, 1943 (the three major powers being represented by Cordell

Hull, Anthony Eden and Vyacheslav Molotov) and this was followed by the 'summit' meeting at Tehran in November-December, which brought all the three war-time leaders—Roosevelt, Churchill and Stalin—face to face for the first time. The inter-Allied discussions on the future of Europe, and particularly the future of Germany, were continued in the European Advisory Commission set up at this time, whose deliberations were followed by two further summit conferences in the closing months of the war: the Yalta Conference in February 1945 and the Potsdam Conference in July-August (by which time Roosevelt had been replaced by Truman, and Churchill by Attlee). After Potsdam, there were no further conferences at the summit level for ten years—when the 'Geneva spirit' of 1955 appeared to symbolise the thawing of the Cold War after the death of Stalin—but there were several meetings of the Council of Foreign Ministers established at the end of the war; and it was at one of these meetings—in Moscow in March and April, 1947—that the division of the world into two blocs, and the institutionalisation of the Cold War, were so obvious that they could no longer be denied.

The international meetings of these four years (1943-47) revealed the objectives of the major powers concerned, and it was the clash of these designs—particularly those of the United States and the Soviet Union—that shaped the framework within which Western Europe was to develop. What were these basic objectives? It may be instructive, in trying to understand what the major powers in 1945 really wanted, to compare the situation at the end of the Second World War with that a quarter of a century earlier, after the First. In 1919, at the time of the Paris Peace conference that was to lay down the lines of a new world, there was one power with very concrete objectives (France, obsessed by the need for economic reparations from Germany, and military security against her); one with rather abstract and sweeping objectives (the United States, whose President, Woodrow Wilson, dreamed of setting up a totally new international order); and a third whose position tended to oscillate between these two points of view (Britain, whose leader, Lloyd George, was often as down to earth in his demands as Clemenceau but who also at times spoke the optimistic language of Woodrow Wilson). The interaction between the territorial, economic and

military demands of France, and the broader approach represented by the United States, with Britain hovering awkwardly
between them, powerfully influenced the outcome of the Paris
Peace Conference—the Treaty of Versailles signed on 28 June
1919.

The peace ' settlement ' which emerged in the immediate aftermath of 1945 was in many ways very different from that of 1919:
for one thing, the victorious Allies could not agree—and have
still not agreed—on the terms of a treaty to be signed with their
main enemy Germany, though they did agree to sign treaties with
her minor allies Hungary, Finland and Roumania. The post-1945
' settlement ' in Europe, therefore, was more of a settling-down
to the facts of a new world but—like that of 1919—it also bore
the marks of conflicting national ambitions. In 1945, as in 1919,
one of the major powers had quite concrete and realistic objectives: this was the Soviet Union, whose policy after 1945 was
not unlike that of France after 1919. Again, there was one power
whose aims were broad, sweeping and on the whole optimistic:
in 1945, as in 1919, this was the United States, and in many ways
Roosevelt, the initiator of the United Nations Organisation, had
played a rôle similar to that of Woodrow Wilson, the founder
of the League of Nations. And again, without stretching the
parallel too far, we can say that Britain in 1945—a power greatly
reduced in strength with goals sometimes as material as those of
Russia, and sometimes as abstract as those of the United States—
played a part roughly like that she had played in 1919. (A further
point of comparison that may be made, without carrying it too
far, is that in 1945, as in 1919, there was one potentially quite
important power excluded by her temporary weakness from any
effective say in the making of the peace: in 1919, the Soviet
Union—racked by civil war, foreign intervention and the chaos
of the early revolutionary years—did not take part in the Peace
Conference and later took her revenge on the West for the decisions made in her absence; in 1945, the rôle of the excluded but
potentially troublesome power-in-eclipse could be allocated either
to China, or else—so far as European affairs were concerned—
to France, whose leader, General de Gaulle, deeply resented the
fact that she had not been included in the Yalta Conference, and
regarded the decisions taken in France's absence as invalid.)

The view that the Soviet Union in 1945 had essentially clear-cut designs abroad may be surprising in view of the repeated assertions of the Soviet leaders that they regarded their country as the vanguard of world Communist revolution. Stalin, Molotov and the other Soviet leaders certainly argued as though their aim was the spreading of revolution abroad—even though they had abolished the Communist International as a gesture of wartime conciliation in 1943—and the fact that they looked on the world as Marxist-Leninists of course influenced their interpretation of what other powers (particularly the United States) were doing. There is, however, a good deal of evidence that Stalin in 1945 did not seriously expect or wish to spread revolution farther afield, any more than he had in 1927 when he advised the Chinese Communist Party against revolution, or in the 1930s when he had concentrated on building up an alliance of anti-fascist states against Germany. In 1945, he is on record as telling the Yugo-slav Communist leaders not to try to make a revolution, and at the same time he let it be clearly understood by the French and Italian Communist Parties that—powerful though they were— it would not be welcomed by the Soviet Union if they used their position to try to take over their countries. Simultaneously, Stalin was advising Mao Tse-tung to continue his alliance with Chiang Kai-shek (advice which Mao politely acknowledged, then dis-regarded—bearing in mind the lessons of 1927) and in 1946, when asked whether a Communist régime in Germany would be desirable, Stalin replied: ' Communism in Germany would be like a saddle on a cow '.

Like France in 1919, what the Soviet Union really wanted from the peace settlement were certain clearly defined benefits, that is to say, reparations for the damage done to her by the German invasion, security against any possible repetition of it, and thirdly (this one a less concrete objective), for her rank as a great power to be formally acknowledged by her status in international organisations. Russia needed reparations in 1945, as France did in 1919, because of the almost unimaginable des-truction carried out by the Germans after their invasion of the USSR in 1941. Between 1941 and 1945, about one-third of the economic resources of the Soviet Union had been destroyed, twenty-five million people (or about twelve per cent of the total population) had been turned out of their homes, or had them ravaged by the Germans, and about twelve million people (about six per cent of the total population—seven million soldiers and five million civilians) had met their deaths. These facts go a long way to explain the insistent Russian demand for restitution from Germany and from the satellite countries who had joined her in the attack, i.e. Austria, Finland, Roumania and Hungary. These states, like the eastern part of Germany, were now at the mercy of the Soviet Union, and the Russian demands for compensation were ruthlessly enforced. The main source of these for the USSR was of course Germany, and this aspect of what was called ' the German question ' will be discussed in more detail later on: here it is enough to emphasise that the need for reparations was one of the basic motives of Soviet conduct.

Russia's second main objective—again one that she had in common with the France of 1919—was security against any possible recurrence of the German invasion, whether this was to be feared from Germany alone or from Germany in combination with allies. As did France in 1919, the Soviet Union tried to guard against this danger by following three lines of policy: military alliances, territorial annexations and control over satellite buffer-states. In terms of alliance, the Soviet Union ended the war with treaties of friendship and mutual support signed with Britain in 1942, and with France in 1944, each of which was to last for twenty years. Their duration for that length of time showed that they were meant to be more than temporary agreements for war-time collaboration, and the USSR could expect them to be in some ways the equivalent of the Anglo-American guarantee to France in 1919—except that the latter had never in fact come into force because of the opposition of the United States Senate. As for the practical value of these alliances, Stalin could probably see by 1945 that the interests and aims of the Soviet Union and Britain were likely to prove incompatible and lead to controversy, but the treaty with France appeared to offer something of more practical value. De Gaulle had made the signing of this treaty in December 1944 a matter of considerable pomp and circumstance when he flew to Moscow for the signature accompanied by his Foreign Minister, Georges Bidault: the Franco-Soviet Treaty was the first independent act of French foreign policy after the establishment of de Gaulle's provisional government in liberated Paris. Even though France scarcely appeared likely to offer any worthwhile military support against a revival of German power, her diplomatic support in keeping Germany under control could be valuable to the Soviet Union, particularly if Britain and the United States agreed together in taking an unfriendly line towards Soviet demands.

The USSR's second line of action was the extension of her frontiers westwards: just as France in 1919 recovered Alsace-Lorraine from Germany, so the Soviet Union took advantage of her victory in 1945 to recover territories—from the Baltic to the Black Sea—that had been part of Tsarist Russia before 1917 but had been annexed by her neighbours—Finland, Poland and Roumania—during her period of crisis after the revolution. The Russians in 1945, of course, went farther than the French in 1919 in appropriating territory that had never belonged to them before—for instance, parts of East Prussia around the city of Königsberg (now renamed Kaliningrad), and the eastern tip of Czechoslovakia which gave Russia a strategically important common frontier with Hungary. The territories thus acquired by the Soviet Union included the areas through which Germany had attacked her in both World Wars—this was particularly true of the large area of Poland that she now recovered, encouraging the Poles to make up for the loss by moving westwards at the expense of Germany—and the motive for their annexation was very largely that of strategic security.

The third line of Russia's policy in the security field was again one in which she emulated the France of Poincaré, and even improved on what he had been able to do for his country. Whereas France in 1919 had limited her creation of a range of satellite- or buffer-states between herself and her dangerous neighbour to the half-hearted attempt to set up a separatist republic in the Rhineland and the even less serious attempt to detach south-west Germany and Bavaria from the Reich, the Soviet Union in 1945 firmly took control of a ring of states from Finland to Albania, using military force where necessary, and installed obedient satellite governments in all of them. Whether a state had been an ally of Nazi Germany (like Finland, Hungary or Roumania) or had been a victim of Nazi aggression (like Poland, Yugoslavia or Czechoslovakia), the process was the same. After a period of coalition government in which the Soviet occupying forces saw to it that the Communists gained leading positions, all the satellites were sooner or later transformed into one-party states, with governments entirely dependent on and subservient to the Soviet Union.

The third main objective of Soviet policy, along with reparations and security, was the unequivocal establishment of the Soviet Union as a great power in the eyes of the world, with all that this implied. In a sense, this goal represented a further dimension of national security: if the world regarded the USSR as a great power, she was in less danger of attack. There was also, however, the psychological motive: the Soviet Union had been excluded from the main decisions of world politics ever since her creation, from the Versailles Peace Treaty of 1919 to the Munich Agreement of 1938; she had fought her way out of a position of isolation, first by signing an opportunistic and short-lived treaty with Nazi Germany in 1939, and then by forming an alliance with the Western Powers after the German attack in 1941, and she was now concerned to establish the point that major decisions of world politics should no longer be taken without her. When the Russians insisted on having a predominant voice in the political future of Poland or Roumania (as they did when Churchill visited Moscow in October 1944, or again at the Yalta Conference in February 1945), or when they put pressure on Turkey to hand over territories on the eastern side of the Black Sea, or to allow the Soviet Union greater rights of naval passage through the Dardanelles, they were not only standing up for material Soviet interests, but asserting the more general point that the USSR was a power, quite literally, to be reckoned with. The same motive must have underlain the Soviet claims—made in 1945, though not very seriously pressed—to take over, under a United Nations mandate, the Italian colony of Libya, or to be given a large share of representation on the international governing body of the port of Tangiers. In the Mediterranean, as indeed in Persia—where the Russians were reluctant to relinquish their war-time zone of occupation in Azerbaijan—and again later throughout the Middle East, the Russians wished to establish their right to a share of influence.

In contrast with these Soviet requirements of compensation, security and an increase in national influence, the post-war goals of the United States were theoretical and even idealistic. It can be said, firstly, that President Roosevelt—right until his death in April 1945—hoped for a reasonable degree of understanding with the USSR, and for a world freed from the fear of war by the defeat of the dictators and the establishment of the United Nations; secondly, that United States public opinion, as represented in Congress, was extremely unwilling to embark on the arduous and expensive course of military confrontation with the Russians, and only agreed to commit American strength to the defence of Europe with some reluctance; and thirdly, that this process of standing up to Soviet pressure was in fact hastened by the change in leading political personnel after the death of Roosevelt.

As for the President himself, he was certainly not so naïvely over-optimistic as his predecessor Woodrow Wilson had been in 1919: it is clear from several of his statements that Roosevelt expected the Soviet Union to try to establish its control over Eastern Europe, and realised that this might have unpleasant consequences for the people of Poland and the other states involved. Roosevelt did, however, hope that the Soviet occupation of these areas would not be too harsh or too long-lasting, and he appears to have believed that the fundamental interests of the USSR and the Western Powers could be reconciled without too much conflict, suspicion, or the risk of war or any confrontation approaching it. He also shared the general American belief that with the elimination of the Axis dictatorships, one of the main causes of war in the world had been removed—democratic régimes, he felt, were much less war-like than dictatorships—and he thought that the weakening or the elimination of European colonial empires (including the British Empire) would also do away with a source of injustice and potential conflict in world affairs. Finally, Roosevelt appears to have expected the United Nations Organisation to develop into a functioning world peace system, representing an adaptation of the war-time alliance to the tasks of preventing war from recurring. He was determined that the United States should not turn its back on the United Nations (as it had on the League of Nations), and this was an important reason why the headquarters of the UN were established in New York rather than Geneva.

If the President had tried to take a different line in 1945—leaving considerable American forces in Europe in an attempt to stand up actively to Soviet pressure—he would have run against powerful currents of opinion at home. As in 1918, the American public assumed that once the war was over the problem of world peace would be solved, and therefore expected ' the boys to come home '. During the Yalta Conference, Roosevelt told Stalin that within two years of the war's end there would be no American troops left in Europe. The public pressure for such withdrawals was underlined in the congressional elections of 1946, which—exactly like those of 1918—produced a Republican majority committed to the cutting of taxes in general and foreign military expenditure in particular. The United States army was in fact reduced from above five million in May 1945 to less than half a million in March 1946: even though the administration may have felt able to carry out this massive demobilisation without a great sense of insecurity, because of the knowledge that the atomic bomb now existed as a reserve weapon, the figures reflect a strong public demand for a return to peace-time ' normalcy '. American opinion also assumed that peace treaties would be signed as soon as possible with the enemy states—treaties were in fact concluded by the end of 1946 with Italy, Roumania, Hungary and Finland—and that these written indications of a return to normality would be accompanied by the establishment of democratic régimes wherever possible.

It was the Soviet defiance of this American wish for liberal democratic régimes that provoked a tougher attitude on the part of Roosevelt's successors than the line he had taken himself. As early as the summer of 1945, when the Soviet Union was patently unwilling to allow a Western-type democratic régime to be established in Poland, President Truman and Byrnes, his Secretary of State, were protesting vigorously, together with the British Foreign Secretary, Ernest Bevin, at this breach of the Yalta Agreement, which had committed everyone to support democracy. By early 1946, Truman was writing impatiently to Byrnes, ' I'm tired of babying the Soviets ', and the scene was set for an increasingly tough American response to the threat which the Soviet Union now appeared to present.

If the aims of the Soviet Union were fairly concrete, and those of the United States still relatively abstract, those of the third major power—the United Kingdom—oscillated between the two. In this, Britain repeated her rôle of 1919, when Lloyd George, as we have noted, had sometimes appeared to be close to the down-to-earth realism of Clemenceau and at other times to be near the saintly idealism of Woodrow Wilson. In some ways, the

Labour government that came to power in Britain in 1945 continued the fairly realistic policy pursued by Churchill towards the Soviet Union: he had realised that she would be likely to extend her power quite considerably, and had tried to limit this expansion both by agreement with Stalin (the famous ' spheres of influence' agreement made in Moscow in October 1944) and by military firmness (as in Greece from 1944 onwards). Ernest Bevin, as Foreign Secretary, certainly had no illusions about possible Communist duplicity—he had contended successfully with Communist influences in the trade union movement for many years—and he stood up stoutly for traditional British interests in the Eastern Mediterranean that appeared to be endangered by Soviet pressure on Greece and Turkey. At the same time, the Labour government shared some of the hopes of Roosevelt and other Americans—outlined above—that the post-war world would be one of harmony and peaceful progress under the auspices of the United Nations. However, until Truman began to take a tougher line towards the Soviet Union in the course of 1946, the British government was at times seriously worried that residual American opposition to what the United States saw as British imperialism might bring the two super-powers together in a tacit or explicit understanding to keep Europe under their control—this might in practice have meant an American withdrawal from Western Europe, leaving the Soviet Union in a dominant position—and also to destroy what remained of Europe's influence in the world outside. The American commitment to the defence of non-Communist Europe, contained in the so-called Truman Doctrine promising immediate aid to Greece and Turkey in March 1947, was thus a most welcome turning-point from the British point of view.

Before this decisive crossroads in American foreign policy was reached—it meant an unprecedented long-term financial and military commitment in peace-time—disagreement between East and West mounted on a number of fronts.

The problem of Germany, as already mentioned, was the supreme cause of East-West friction. Soviet and Western interpretations of the war-time commitment to subject Germany to demilitarisation, decentralisation, denazification and democracy, led to a series of clashes in the Allied control organs for Germany. There was also the problem of reparations, already mentioned:

for the reasons indicated, the Russians went ahead and extracted enormous quantities of machinery and other material goods from their zone of occupation, and this unilateral pillage—continuing at a time when the Western powers were being forced to put money and resources *into* their zones, to keep the population alive—led to mounting tension. By the time of the meeting of the Conference of Foreign Ministers in Moscow in the spring of 1947, deadlock on the German question had been reached: the more spectacular East-West clashes that occurred later—the failure to agree on currency reform in the spring of 1948, the Berlin blockade that followed, and the setting-up of the two rival German states in 1949—all stemmed from the impasse registered at this conference. By 1947, the political régimes of the two parts of Germany had diverged almost beyond any hope of reconciliation: in the Soviet zone, the Social Democratic Party had been forced to merge with the Communist Party to form the Socialist Unity Party, whereas in the Western zones, a variety of political parties—Christian Democrat, Social Democrat and Free Democrat—had been brought into existence.

More broadly, throughout Eastern Europe, the Soviet Union was now using its military power to install political régimes that could be relied on to be subservient: as we have seen, the first stage in the process was for coalition governments to be established, with the Communist Party in a leading position, and this was followed by the removal of non-Communist leaders from the coalition, and finally even by the elimination of unreliable Communist leaders themselves—for instance, Gomulka in Poland or Anna Pauker in Roumania. The establishment of one-party systems in the political sphere was paralleled by the expurgation of possible centres of resistance elsewhere in society: Churches, trade unions and voluntary movements of all kinds were subordinated to the Communist régimes. What was taking place was a straightforward clash between the Soviet interest in establishing a band of reliable satellite states, and the Western belief that the ' democracy' upheld in the Yalta Agreement meant a liberal-democratic, Western-type democracy, and not the so-called ' people's democracy' imposed by the Russians. Western indignation at Soviet behaviour in Eastern Europe, and fear of the possibility of Russia trying to implant similar régimes farther West, mounted during 1946 and 1947, and—as we shall see—

became still more acute after February 1948, when the USSR imposed a Communist régime in Czechoslovakia, the one state in Eastern Europe that had hitherto preserved a genuine coalition government and a degree of independence.

In other regions of the world, too, Soviet behaviour gave cause for alarm: in Iran, as already mentioned, the Soviet Union refused to leave the zone of occupation in the northern part of the country, which had been allocated to her by inter-Allied agreement in 1942, and Soviet troops even tried to set up a Socialist Republic of Azerbaijan before they were pressed into leaving by a resolution of the United Nations Organisation in 1946. In the Far East, again, the uneasy coalition between Chiang Kai-shek and the Chinese Communists broke down by 1946, and a large-scale civil war—obviously a fight to the finish—was in progress by 1947.

What finally precipitated the Truman Doctrine of March 1947 —which may be taken as the first comprehensive statement from either side declaring that a state of 'cold war' existed—was Britain's economic weakness in the winter of 1946-47, which forced her to relinquish her military and economic support to Greece and Turkey. In February 1947, the British government announced that it could only keep up this support for a matter of weeks, and this induced a frantic reappraisal of policy in Washington, that resulted in Truman's statement of 12 March. The Truman Doctrine, telling the Soviet Union that further pressure on Greece and Turkey would meet with American resistance, and also threatening to apply this principle in other areas, too, if necessary, was a fairly sharp warning by the man who had told his Secretary of State a year earlier that he was tired of 'babying' the Russians. It is true that the speech was followed a few months later by a much more conciliatory statement by the new Secretary of State, Marshall, proposing an economic plan for the reconstruction of both East and West Europe, thus including the Soviet Union and her satellites in the offer of American aid. It has been argued that if the offer of the Marshall Plan had been made before the threat of the Truman Doctrine, the onset of the Cold War could have been averted, but this idea, though tempting, is implausible. The fact is that by 1947 both the Soviet Union and the United States were so distrustful of the other's intentions that little real hope for collaboration between them—whether on the German problem or on anything else—remained.

One basic feature of the development of the Cold War was that both sides exaggerated the other's intentions: on the one hand, the Soviet Union accused the United States of trying to establish anti-Soviet régimes in countries on the borders of the USSR, and reacted with corresponding alarm to such a prospect; on the other hand, the United States appeared to take seriously the theoretical Russian objective of spreading Communist revolution to the whole world, and regarded every increase in Soviet influence in any country, however small or however close to the USSR, as a step towards the fulfilment of this dangerous ambition. It is easy to see why both sides made statements that lent themselves to the worst interpretations. Stalin could hardly proclaim that he was taking over Poland as a means of gaining a buffer against German aggression, and he therefore had to proclaim that the establishment of Communism in Poland was part of a revolutionary process which by definition was likely to spread; while, on the other hand, Truman could hardly commit American money and troops to the defence of Greece and Turkey in the name of preserving the balance of power in the Eastern Mediterranean (such a concept would have sounded archaic and imperialistic to the American Congress), and, as he put it, he therefore had ' to scare the pants off Congress ' by portraying Soviet influence in Turkey and Greece as part of a world conspiracy which must be resisted globally. Both sides thus made statements which led to a built-in escalation of mistrust and hostility.

This is not to say that the Cold War was in itself unreal, a figment born of mutual fantasies and misperceptions. The Soviet Union and the United States *did* have conflicting interests in the post-war world; the Russians *did* spread their power over large areas of Eastern Europe, and *might* have been tempted to try to spread it farther west, if Stalin had not been so prudent, and if the American commitment to defend Western Europe had not come when it did. The fact was that most of the political leaders of Western Europe—Churchill, Attlee and Bevin in England, de Gaulle and Léon Blum in France, De Gasperi in Italy, and Adenauer in Germany—*did* regard their security as threatened by the USSR, and therefore warmly welcomed the American commitment when it came. The international framework of Western

Europe's development in the early post-war years was thus set by a confrontation between the two super-powers. Poland, Hungary and even Czechoslovakia, who might have participated more closely in the political evolution of Western Europe, were prevented from so doing by the Soviet Union—symbolically, the USSR insisted that Czechoslovakia and Poland drop their interest in the Marshall Plan in 1947—and the countries of Western Europe found themselves for a time dependent on American economic aid and political support. These factors profoundly influenced the development of the West European states, and the nature of the relations that grew up between them. We should also note, however, that the Soviet threat, except at the worst moments of the Cold War (the Berlin blockade of 1948-49, the Korean War of 1950) did not appear *overwhelmingly* massive and imminent. There were times when West Europeans became convinced that all the Soviet Union wanted was security within the zone of influence she had acquired as a result of the war. When this feeling came to dominate the Western European view of East-West relations—for instance, during the 'euphoric' period from 1953-56, between the death of Stalin and the Hungarian crisis, or again in the more relaxed atmosphere of the 1960s—the flavour of European politics, and the impetus towards Western unity, were to be importantly modified. The development of relations between the two super-powers—of which the early Cold War phase sketched in this chapter was the first instalment—thus continued to be a crucial dimension in the evolution of politics in the Western European area.

2 Post-War France 1945-50

The Liberation and after: France's political forces
The post-war period in France's political history can be said to
run from the Liberation in 1944 almost up to the parliamentary
election of 1951. The main turning-points on the way were de
Gaulle's resignation as head of the Provisional government in
January 1946, the adoption of the Fourth Republic's constitution
later the same year, and the withdrawal of the Communists from
the coalition government in May 1947.

France had three main political creeds, and a political force
incarnated by an individual: Socialism, Communism, Christian
Democracy and Gaullism. The country's political life in the post-
war years was marked by the mutual conflicts and consequent
weakening of the first three of these, and—as 1946 gave way to
1947—by the growing strength of the fourth.

The battlefield on which these struggles developed was defined
by three chronically urgent issues with which the French people
and their rulers had to deal. These were the problems of economic
and social reconstruction after the devastation of the war; the
question of the nature of the political régime to be adopted by
France (on this point, most Frenchmen agreed that they wanted
something really new, and the ironically named Radical Party,
as the chief representative of the discredited Third Republic, was
in eclipse); and the perpetual difficulty of how France should
try to protect herself and to influence the affairs of the outside
world—the problem of what foreign policy was appropriate in
a Europe where France's power and influence had been tragic-
ally reduced.

The Constituent Assembly elected in October 1945—the first
expression of the French popular will since the Liberation—was
dominated by the three parties of the left: Communist, Socialist
and Christian Democrat. The political parties representing
the pre-war forces associated with the Third Republic—the
Radical Party and the Conservatives—were reduced to extremely
small numbers, and the rising force of Gaullism was not yet
organised as a party. The election results were as follows:

Parties	Number of Seats
Communists and associates	160
Socialists and associates	146
Christian Democrats (MRP)	152
Radicals and associates	29
Democratic and Socialist Union of the Resistance	30
Right-wing parties and Independents	66

Our consideration of what these forces represented must begin with the Communist Party, the largest group in the new Assembly, and the one seated to the left of the President as he surveyed the parties arranged in front of him from left to right. Founded at the Congress of Tours in 1920, when the left-wing members of the old French Socialist Party had broken away under the impact of the Bolshevik Revolution, the Communist Party had seen a steady increase in its strength; it gained particularly from the swing to the left in the 1930s, which in 1936 brought into power the Popular Front government led by the Socialist Léon Blum and supported by the Communists. The latter had faithfully followed every change of direction in Moscow's policy—as Blum was sarcastically to remark, ' the Communists are not to the left, they are to the east '—moving from violent denunciation of the Socialists as traitors in 1930 into the Popular Front coalition with them when the rise of Hitler presented the Soviet Union and Europe with a new threat, and back again into neutrality between Nazi Germany and the Western Powers at the time of the Hitler-Stalin pact in August 1939. It was at this point that the Communist leader Maurice Thorez defied his call-up into the army and disappeared to Moscow, and the Communist Party as a whole was banned for its propaganda campaign against the French war effort. Only after 1941, when Hitler's attack brought the Soviet Union into the war, did the Communist Party take a leading part in the opposition to the German occupying forces. From then on, however, this rôle was a very active one indeed, and the Communists were the leaders of the resistance—and hence the political masters of large areas of France—in many regions, particularly in the south. Thanks to their record in the resistance (the years 1939-41 were easily forgotten) and to their claim to represent the authentic tradition of the French Revolution of

C

1789, the Communists had a strong appeal to the mood of the French people in 1945, dominated by a desire to make a clean break with the past. They, at least, could not be held responsible for the collapse of the Third Republic, and their programme— large-scale nationalisation of industry, extended social welfare benefits, and the promise of peace with the Soviet Union—won the Communists their leading position in the 1945 Assembly.

Next to the Communists, to the centre-left of the President, sat the French Socialist Party, led by the veteran Prime Minister of the 1936 Popular Front, Léon Blum. Although its 146 members were slightly outnumbered—to their surprise—by the Catholic MRP, the Socialist Party represented a force without which it was impossible to form a government. The party— standing for a range of policies broadly similar to those of the British Labour Party—had grown slowly but surely in strength since 1920. It took some time, in fact, to recover from the loss of its considerable left-wing element when the Communist Party broke away at the Congress of Tours—incidentally, taking with them the party's daily newspaper *l'Humanité*, which continued under its Communist direction to bear the inscription ' Founded by Jean Juarès '. Under steady pressure from the Communists to remain faithful to the old ideals of Marxism and intransigent opposition to capitalism, the Socialist Party in the 1920s had refused to take part in coalitions of the Centre left: Léon Blum, a brilliant lawyer, civil servant and literary critic who became the party's leader after the Congress of Tours, argued that it was right to *support* the governments led by left-wing Radicals like Herriot or Daladier, but he refused to *participate* in them. By the mid-1930s, with the rise of European Fascism and the swing to the left at the French election in 1936, Blum agreed that the moment had come for the Socialist Party to take the lead in forming a government, and he attempted the uneasy feat of governing with the support of the Communists to his left and Radicals to his right, until the second of his two coalition governments was overthrown in the spring of 1938. The Socialist Party was by this time badly demoralised—although Blum and other leaders believed in resistance to Hitler, there was a powerful pacifist wing under the leadership of Paul Faure, the party's General Secretary—and in the critical vote of support for Pétain and surrender in 1940, the majority of the Socialist parliamentarians voted to give the marshal a free hand to surrender to the Germans. This meant that many of the Socialist Deputies elected in 1945—Guy Mollet, Daniel Mayer and others who were to play a prominent part in the Fourth Republic—were new men, and only a small group of the pre-war leadership—Blum, Vincent Auriol and Jules Moch among them—remained.

From the Liberation until May 1947, the Socialist Party found itself—as in the Popular Front period—the centre of a tripartite coalition, linked on the left to the Communists and on the right to the MRP (who had now replaced the Radicals of the pre-war period). In terms of practical politics, co-operation with the MRP was easier than with the Communists: both the Socialists and the MRP agreed with much difficulty on a programme including the nationalisation of basic industries, and on the general lines of economic policy. In terms of political rhetoric, however, many of the Socialist old guard found the idea of unity with the Communists more appealing. The revolutionary myths of nineteenth-century France played a great part here: Communists and Socialists saw themselves as the heirs of the nineteenth-century Radicals in standing for rationalism against the clerical dogmatism of the Roman Catholic Church. The MRP, after all, even though its current leaders might stand for progressive social policies, was a *Catholic* party, and therefore—in the context of France's powerful political traditions—a party of the right.

This meant that many Socialists who were politically fairly right-wing—Guy Mollet, for instance—persistently argued at party congresses in favour of unity of action with the Communists, and spurned any idea of close association with the MRP. (Indeed, certain leaders of the MRP argued in 1945, when they took the decision to form their movement into a political party, that this step was only necessary because of the doctrinaire hostility of the Socialist Party to the Roman Catholic Church.) The breach with the Communists, when it came in 1947, was all the more bitter because of this attempt at unity after the war. (Incidentally, the Communist and Socialist trade union movements, which had also tried to collaborate, split apart with even greater vehemence when the great schism came in 1947, the Communist branch being much the larger.) On the other hand, collaboration with the MRP—which electoral mathematics later made necessary in one coalition government after another—was rendered more difficult for the French Socialist Party by its original enmity with the group with which it now had to ally.

The MRP itself—the third great block of Deputies facing the President of the new parliament—represented a novelty in French politics—a Catholic Party of the left. Throughout the history of the Third Republic—from the 1870s to the collapse in 1940—Catholicism had on the whole been a force of the right, opposed to the Republic that had dispossessed religious communities at the turn of the century, and that taught a militant anti-clericalism in state schools. In so far as Catholics took part in the politics of the Third Republic, they were very often to be found among the monarchists and conservatives of the extreme right, and only a small group of progressive Catholics—Christian Democrats— had made their appearance at the end of the Third Republic, at the election of 1936. Many Catholics, however, had taken an active part in the resistance, and several of those more politically inclined with relatively left-wing views (for instance, Georges Bidault, the President of the National Committee of the Resistance) subsequently felt that the time had come to reconcile the Church with politics by bringing a Christian point of view into life. As has been seen, the new MRP was very close to the Socialist Party in its support for the nationalisation of industry—particularly the expropriation of those industrialists who had collaborated with the Germans—and it also tried to implement its Christianity in political life by advocating greatly improved welfare services.

The Christian Democrats were also by nature ' Europeans ': it was on their initiative that the 1946 Constitution of France contained the commitment to relinquish national sovereignty to a future United States of Europe.

The MRP's success in the first post-war election—in October 1945—astonished everyone, including the party's own leaders. That a Catholic Party should win five million votes—even though many of them came from women voters who were granted suffrage for the first time—was a remarkable achievement. Not all these voters in fact shared the left-wing views of the party's post-war leadership: the collaboration of the MRP Deputies with the Communists, for example, in supporting the second draft constitution of October 1946, caused the Catholic faithful great alarm and, in the subsequent referendum, two MRP supporters out of three voted against the constitution. When the Gaullist movement became the RPF in April 1947, great numbers of the MRP voters switched to the more familiar right-wing allegiance represented by Gaullism: at the municipal elections in October, the MRP received only ten per cent of the votes, a drastic drop in relation to previous general election results. On two particular issues, the MRP—in contrast to its support for left-wing measures in the early post-war years—established itself as a party of the right. The first of these was the old quarrel about State aid for Church schools: when the French Socialist Party, loyal to its anti-clerical traditions, rejected the idea of public subsidies for Catholic schools, the initial reaction of the MRP was to argue that the Church should manage without State assistance of this kind. It was the Gaullist movement, however, which—by ardently championing the right of Church schools to receive State funds from 1947 onwards—forced the MRP (if it were not to lose the whole of its electoral support) to come out firmly on the same side. The other debated issue was colonial policy: partly by chance, it happened that the MRP provided the Minister for Colonial Affairs in a succession of post-war Cabinets, so that the party was associated with repression and colonial wars, first in Indo-China and then in North Africa. A further reason why the MRP upheld the rights of the French Empire so vigorously was precisely because their real interest lay in the construction of European unity: faced with accusations from the nationalist right wing in French politics that they were selling out France's national interests to Germany or to Italy, the MRP found it tactically useful to stress that they were among the stoutest defenders of France's rights in her colonial possessions overseas.

Moving to the right around the hemisphere of the French Assembly only a small remnant of the large Radical Party of the pre-war years was to be found in 1945. With the fall of France in 1940, and the discrediting of the Third Republic which the Radicals in 1945 vainly wished to restore (two-thirds of their voters deserted them on this issue in the first post-war election in October 1945), it could well be argued that the Radical Party had lost its *raison d'être*. Its rôle had indeed changed remarkably in the course of the twentieth century, making the word ' radical ' seem an anachronistic relic of its reckless youth. In the nineteenth century, the party had certainly been radical, representing the struggle of the French left wing for a democratic republican form of government against the monarchists and autocrats of the right (including the Church). However, from 1900 onwards the picture changed: the Radical Party became that which governed *par excellence*. It represented the dominant classes in French political society, the provincial *bourgeoisie* and the peasantry, and its central position in the political spectrum gave it an ideal base for tactical collaboration either with the left (the Socialists) or with the right (the traditional conservatives).

In 1945, however, the French people obviously wanted to reject what one writer had called ' the Republic of Pals ', that in which power had been held by a series of coalitions normally led by some more or less opportunist Radical politician. It is true that certain of the ' grand old men ' of pre-war Radicalism were still present in French political life: Edouard Herriot, Mayor of Lyons since 1907, and the man who as Prime Minister in 1924 had given diplomatic recognition to the Soviet Union, was re-elected to the post-war Assembly and—despite de Gaulle's taunts that he had remained on good terms with the Vichy government—was able to re-establish his political standing. There were other prominent Radicals in the post-war Assembly, among them men like Henri Queuille, who had been Minister of Agriculture in more than a dozen pre-war Cabinets; or Pierre Mendès-France, who had been a junior Minister in Blum's Popular Front government. New men with political aspirations —including Edgar Faure, René Mayer and Jacques Chaban-Delmas, all of them later Prime Ministers of France—also saw in 1945 that the Radical Party could still be the vehicle for an ambitious politician. The party was very little burdened by political doctrine: left-wing in political matters (that is, in favour of parliamentary sovereignty and opposed to the Roman Catholic Church), the Radicals remained right-wing in economic affairs: they opposed the post-war nationalisations, and kept a hand open to the more traditional conservatives on their right. When the tripartite coalition fell in 1947, as we shall see, the Radicals came into their own, and by 1948 Henri Queuille, an archetypal figure of the Third Republic, was the head of one of the longest-lived Cabinets of the Fourth.

Another small group in the 1945 assembly that was associated with the Radicals and had a good deal in common with them was the Democratic and Socialist Union of the Resistance (UDSR). As its name indicates, this group had sprung from the war-time resistance movement and, like most political forces in France after the Liberation, its programme was distinctly left-wing. Once the immediate post-war nationalisation of industry had taken place, however, the UDSR was to evolve, like the Radical Party, into a centre group with a tactically favourable position for joining coalitions either to the left or to the right. The left wing of the UDSR was represented by François Mitterand, who was to distinguish himself in 1954 by resigning from the Laniel government in protest against the deposition of the Sultan of Morocco, and later—in 1965—to challenge de Gaulle for the presidency of the Fifth Republic. The right wing of the UDSR was led by René Pleven, whose main contribution to the history of the Fourth Republic was to put forward the ill-fated European Army project of 1950, and who was later to confirm his right-wing sympathies by accepting ministerial office in the Fifth Republic.

Farther to the right again—occupying the seats on the extreme right of the 1945 Assembly—were the representatives of the traditional conservative wing in French politics. In 1945 they, in common with the Radicals, were diminished in number and reduced in political standing. Many politicians of the right wing had either collaborated with the German occupying forces or had been suspected of doing so: Flandin, a leader of the pre-war right who had been a Minister under the Vichy government, had been forced to leave political life, and even less eminent men such as Antoine Pinay, later to become Prime Minister, had been mildly implicated as a collaborator. There were others whose patriotic credentials were impeccable—Paul Reynaud, the last Prime Minister of the Third Republic (who had been put on trial by the Germans together with Léon Blum), Joseph Laniel and René Coty, later Prime Minister and President of the Republic respectively—but in the atmosphere of 1945, the right was very much on the defensive. It was only in 1951, with the foundation by Roger Duchet of the Nationa' ʾtre for Independents and Peasants, that the non-Gaullist in France was to assert itself as an effective force.

Problems and prospects 1945-47
In the first years after the Liberation—indeed

post-war period—France's economic and social difficulties were overpowering, almost blocking the view of governments that tried to look beyond them in the attempt to create a new political structure too. France's economic situation after the Liberation was desperately weak: even two years later, in 1946, economic output was 28 per cent below that of 1929, France's best pre-war year, and by early 1947 the position was in some ways even worse. There was a moment of hope in the spring of 1945, when Pierre Mendès-France, as Minister for Economic Affairs, proposed a drastic programme of economic measures, including a currency reform and a strict block on rises in prices and incomes. But de Gaulle thought this medicine too strong for the French people, and Mendès-France resigned.

After his departure, the chronic inflation—which was, in political terms, the most pressing of all France's economic problems—continued with increasing momentum. The index of retail prices (based on the 1938 figure of 100) had reached 308 by January 1945; by December of the same year, it had reached 497; and it went on rising. By the summer of 1947, official figures showed that the average urban worker in France spent three-quarters of his wages on food, and by this time the highly significant political convention had been established that the post of Minister of Food in every Cabinet was filled by a non-party official: none of the political parties wished to incur the unpopularity of being held responsible for the continually rising cost of food.

The coalition government, in the first few months after de Gaulle's resignation in January 1946, carried through a programme of economic and social reforms that were intended on the one hand to modernise the structure of French industry (particularly through the political means of nationalising the basic industries and services) and on the other hand to create better social welfare schemes. In March 1946 the coal mines were nationalised, and in April electricity, gas and most of the French banking system too. Also in April 1946, the government introduced a comprehensive social security system, giving health insurance and retirement pensions to the urban working population (the peasants—still a large proportion of the French labour force—were not yet included in these provisions).

Probably more significant, in terms of its effect on France's long-term economic prosperity, was the creation in January 1946 of the General Planning Commission, whose job was to draw up a plan for investment in the key sectors of French industry. The Commission—approved by General de Gaulle on 3 January 1946, a few days before his resignation—grew out of the ideas of a small group of brilliant economists and men of action, led by Jean Monnet, a former businessman, League of Nations official and war-time representative of de Gaulle in economic negotiations in Washington and London. Working together with a small group of colleagues—particularly the economists Robert Marjolin and Pierre Uri, and his technical adviser, the engineer Etienne Hirsch—Monnet developed a plan for modernising the backward structure of French industry by concentrating investment—public and private—in vital sectors. Thus the Planning Commission appointed eighteen subordinate commissions, each charged with producing a plan for the modernisation and development of one branch of industry, iron and steel, building materials, mines, the motor industry, merchant shipping, building and public works, and so on. Part of the success of the operation depended on Monnet's ability to coordinate employers and trade-unionists (even Communist union leaders) as members of these commissions, where the problems of an industry were discussed in realistic terms, in an atmosphere undisturbed by the political battles that were outwardly tearing the French nation apart.

A further reason for the success of Monnet's planning of France's economic future was that it was insulated from political vicissitudes in another way too: the General Planning Commission was attached directly to the Prime Minister's Office, and even though Prime Ministers came and went—twenty-six of them in the twelve years of the Fourth Republic—the Commission had only two chiefs, Monet (from 1946 to 1952) and Hirsch (from 1952 to 1958).

Out of the work of the various sub-commissions set up by Monnet and his men, long-term plans for investment were developed for six fundamental branches of French economic life: coal, electricity, steel, cement, transport and agricultural machinery. As a large part of these activities was under state control—74 per cent of the projected investments was in nationalised industries—the execution of the plan was much facilitated,

and the foundations for France's economic growth in the 1950s
(continued under de Gaulle in the 1960s) were thus laid in the
immediate post-war years.

For the moment, however, this ' economic miracle ' (in some
ways more impressive than the celebrated German one) was still
in the future. In 1946 and 1947 all that Monnet and his colleagues could do was to draw up plans which seemed wildly optimistic in the miserable immediate state of France's economy,
and to hope that the necessary funds would be forthcoming from
some source or other. With a balance of payments deficit in
1946-47 of the order of $2 million, France's only hope appeared
to be a massive American loan. Such a loan was in fact just over
the horizon, but it only became a reality with the onset of a
more acute phase of the Cold War at the beginning of 1947. As
we have seen, it was the growth of Soviet-American conflict in
the Balkans, recognised by the American President when he
proclaimed what was later called the ' Truman Doctrine ' on
12 May 1947—that led directly to the Marshall Plan in June of
the same year, and thus to the availability of the dollars needed
for France's recovery plans.

In the meantime, while Monnet, Hirsch, Uri and the others
were working out their plans in a back-room ferment of ideas,
the front of the French political stage was occupied by the battle
over the new Constitution.

The first post-war vote of the French people—the election of
the Constituent Assembly in October 1945—confirmed that the
French wanted a decisive break with the pre-war Third Republic
that had ended in humiliation and disaster. The candidates standing for a return to the Third Republic—particularly the Radicals
—suffered serious losses, and the two parties that jointly held a
clear majority in the new Assembly—the Communists and the
Socialists—stood clearly for a new constitution in which, in particular, the powers of the pre-war Senate or Upper House would
be seriously curtailed. The outcome of the election also meant
that the constitution drawn up by the new Assembly would have
to be referred back to the people for a further vote—this overruled the Communist campaign in favour of an Assembly that
would have the last word—and thus the parliamentary debates
on the new constitution quickly took the form of a wrangle
between the various parties, with the new referendum in view.

This was the moment when de Gaulle, irritated by the partisan conflicts in his coalition government, and foreseeing that the constitution produced by the new Assembly would drastically limit the powers both of the Senate and of the government, decided to resign. He did so in January 1946, being replaced by Félix Gouin, a Socialist Party leader from the south of France who was able to hold together the ruling coalition, including the Communists on the left and the Christian Democrats on the right.

On 19 April 1946, the draft constitution was adopted by the Assembly: in the final vote, the Socialist and Communist groups supported it and the MRP did not—a sign of continuing tension between the coalition parties. Shortly afterwards, on 5 May 1946, this first draft constitution was put to the people in a referendum and narrowly defeated (53 per cent of those voting were opposed and 47 per cent were in favour). This result—in which the Communist and Socialist vote combined fell by about 600,000 —was an indication that there was a limit to the swing to the left shown by the election of the previous October.

On 2 June, in a further vote—this time for the election of a new Constituent Assembly, as the work of the first had been rejected—the French electorate confirmed their verdict. The MRP, which had indicated the way public opinion was going by voting against the first draft constitution, marked an increase in its voting strength: it won 28.1 per cent of the votes and 105 seats, and the Communist strength remained steady at 26 per cent of the votes and 153 seats. The balance of parliamentary strength meant that the uneasy coalition between the three large parties had to continue, but they were now faced with strong pressure from outside Parliament to adopt a constitution more in line with the views of de Gaulle. This was the juncture chosen by the General to enter into political argument for the first time since his resignation at the beginning of the year: choosing the occasion of a speech at Bayeux on the second anniversary of his arrival there at the Liberation, the General made an elaborate speech in which he expounded the kind of constitution he thought France needed. His own ideas were familiar—France required a strong Executive, in the form of a President who would govern as de Gaulle had tried to govern immediately after the war—but what was new was that the French people, having now had further evidence of the shortcomings of coalition governments in an over-powerful Assembly, appeared to be more prepared to listen to him. In political discussions up and down the country, many Frenchmen noted with approval that a formal challenge to the quarrelling parliamentarians had at last been issued.

In the meantime, the election result had been reflected in a shift to the right of the principals in the government, as Bidault, the MRP leader who was currently Foreign Minister, replaced Gouin as Prime Minister. After long bargaining, a new draft constitution was adopted by the Assembly on 29 September: it increased the rôle of the second chamber, in comparison with its low status in the former draft, but it still left the President with much weaker powers than those possessed by the Presidents of the Third Republic.

For this reason, it was promptly and strongly condemned by de Gaulle, who made two public speeches within forty-eight hours, one on 9 October and the other on 11 October. 'This Constitution', he said, 'is a question of life or death for the country. If it is approved, you will see anarchy and disorder taking over France.' . . . 'They have deprived the President of the Republic of all power whatsoever, they have made a mere ghost of him, perhaps because they are afraid that one day it will be Charles de Gaulle who will become President of the Republic. . . .'

The lines of battle were now fairly clearly drawn. A public opinion poll conducted at this date—a few days before the referendum on the new constitution on 13 October—showed that 25 per cent of those polled regarded the referendum as a straight vote for or against General de Gaulle.

The vote on 13 October also reflected general apathy on the part of the electorate. The governing parties had argued themselves to a standstill, and the people into a degree of indifference that was reflected by the two main arguments the party leaders put forward in favour of voting 'yes'. One argument was that France could hardly go on much longer without a constitution of some sort, and the other was that this constitution—even though its makers admitted its imperfections—at least provided fairly readily for a process of revision! On the basis of such negative arguments as these, the French people went to the polls yet again, with the following results:

just over 9,000,000 (35 per cent of the electorate) voted in favour of the constitution;

just over 8,000,000 (34 per cent) voted against it;

and the remaining 8,000,000 voters (as many as 31 per cent) abstained from casting a vote at all.

The constitution of the Fourth Republic was thus approved by only a little over one-third of those eligible to vote, and it is not surprising that it later failed to command much enthusiasm or loyalty. It is also not surprising that its shaky and hardly auspicious beginnings inspired the opposition to new action: a few days after the vote, de Gaulle told a war-time follower and disciple, Colonel Rémy, that he intended to start a new organisation to fight against the régime.

Once the constitution was adopted, the next stage was yet another election, this time that of the first Parliament of the Fourth Republic on 10 November 1946. The strength of the MRP remained steady, the party's representation in the new Parliament dropping very slightly from 169 to 167 seats; the Socialists continued to decline, falling from 129 to 105 seats; and the Communist Party, showing their ability to squeeze out the Socialists as the main party of the left in France, marked up a considerable increase from 153 to 183 seats, which led them to claim that Thorez should of course be the next Prime Minister of France.

Thorez was in fact supported in his bid for the post by Guy Mollet, the new General Secretary of the French Socialist Party (he had brought about the removal of Daniel Mayer from the appointment in August, arguing that the latter—a young disciple of Blum—was too far to the right: an argument that seems paradoxical in the light of Mollet's own later evolution to extreme right-wing positions over Algeria); however, when the question came to a vote, Thorez was unable to win a parliamentary majority. The outgoing Prime Minister, Bidault, suffered the same fate—he lost the adherence of the Communists, so that the tripartite coalition appeared to be broken beyond repair—and the resulting crisis appeared to threaten worse trouble still for France. The possibility of a Fascist *coup d'état* was taken seriously and, at the very least, the politicians expected de Gaulle to try to exploit the situation by coming to power with the help of the army.

In this crisis, Léon Blum, the veteran Socialist Prime Minister of 1936, agreed to form a caretaker government, consisting only of members of his own Socialist Party, to keep things going until mid-January when the Deputies were to meet to elect the first President of the Republic and when the constitution, according to the timetable, should be fully working.

Blum's one-party government, which held office from 17 December 1946 to 16 January 1947, achieved one feat that placed it among the most popular governments of the early post-war period: it succeeded in reducing the level of retail prices by five per cent.

On 16 January 1947, the members of the French Assembly met in solemn session in the Palace of Versailles—such was the shortage of petrol that only a few Ministers were able to drive there by car, and the majority of the Deputies travelled by simple suburban train—to elect the first President of the Republic. Their choice was Vincent Auriol, a well-known Socialist leader who had been Finance Minister in Blum's pre-war Cabinet, and who had served with some distinction as President of the Constituent Assembly. Although his party, in the constitutional discussions, had made it clear that they wished the President's rôle to be a fairly restricted one, Auriol in fact made the presidency into a pretty strong element in the French political system. He was able to play quite an active part—in fact he was forced to do so—in solving one Cabinet crisis after another; he also used his position to intervene forcefully in some of the major decisions facing the Fourth Republic, notably the immense question of whether Germany should be re-armed, when this came up in the context of the European Defence Community proposed in the the early 1950s.

Once the President was elected, Blum carried out his intention of resigning, and his government was succeeded by a revived version of the tripartite coalition—Socialists, Communists and Christian Democrats—headed by another Socialist, Paul Ramadier. One feature of the Ramadier government, which received parliamentary approval on 23 January 1947, almost escaped notice: it included three Radicals among its list of Ministers. This in fact symbolised the way in which the Radical Party, thanks to dissension between the three major groups in the post-war Assembly, had been able to work itself back into the position of influence it had held under the Third Republic. It was also symbolic that the Assembly elected Edouard Herriot (as we have seen, one of the 'grand old men' of pre-war Radicalism) to be its President.

The tripartite coalition had thus been patched up under Ramadier as it had been under Gouin and Bidault, but its life was to be limited when the new government had to face basic decisions on France's international orientation.

The coalition in fact survived some difficult decisions: the beginnings of the war against the national independence movement in the far-off colony of Indo-China, which began while Blum held office at the end of 1946, was approved without difficulty, even by the Communist Ministers in the Ramadier government. On economic policy, too, there was a reasonable degree of acceptance by the Communist Ministers that their job was to keep the French working class—including the Communist trade-union leaders—hard at their task of increasing national productivity, though in fact there was growing evidence of disagreement on this front in the early months of 1947.

It was, however, the Cold War between East and West that finally forced the split with the Communists. On 4 May 1947, two months after Truman's speech denouncing the Communist peril in the Balkans and promising aid to Greece and Turkey, Ramadier manoeuvred the Communists out of his Cabinet. The immediate pretext was disagreement over wage demands, but everyone knew that the real factor underlying the crisis was that France was caught up in the Cold War.

Henceforth, the Communists were never again to become members of a French government. Their partners who survived in the Cabinet—the Socialists and Christian Democrats—had to govern in collaboration with the Radicals and other centre groups. Their position forced them to cast nervous glances both to the left—where they faced a massive Communist opposition—and to the right—where de Gaulle was now busily carrying out his intention of 'uniting the French people' in a crusade against the régime.

By April 1947, more than a year had gone by since de Gaulle's abrupt departure from the government in January 1946, and ten months since his Bayeux speech. He appears to have assumed when he left office that the parties would be unable to govern without him, and would soon call him back, and he was surprised that the régime created by the party leaders had been able to come into effective existence at all. Now, however, he realised that the ' liberation ' of France from the baneful régime imposed by the parties—which he evidently saw in terms similar to her liberation from the German occupier—could only be achieved if the French people were offered an alternative system, which would drain away the remaining support of the political parties into a new creative national movement. This was the thought behind the setting-up of the RPF, or Rally of the French People, announced by de Gaulle at Strasbourg on 7 April 1947. ' It is time ', he declared, ' for the Rally of the French People to be formed, which will act by all legal means to develop and to bring to victory—overcoming all differences of opinion—a great effort for the common good and for the profound reform of the State.'

As we have already seen, some of the parties in power in France—first and most drastically the MRP—were shortly to fall victim to the shattering blows of the new Gaullist Party. In the local elections in October 1947, the RPF was to establish itself as a threat to the Fourth Republic from the right—in some ways more serious than that already represented by the Communists on the left.

In the meantime, however, the Socialist-MRP coalition led by Ramadier struggled on, and it even tried to evolve lines of foreign policy whereby France could attempt to promote her interests in an unstable and dangerous world. So far, foreign relations had figured in French life mainly as factors of disruption impinging on French politics from the outside: the humiliations de Gaulle saw himself as suffering at the hands of his allies, the impact of the Cold War on the polarisation of French politics and the split-up of the tripartite coalition, the effect of the Indo-Chinese war in draining French resources away from other purposes, are all examples of France's position as a passive object of external political forces.

At the same time, however, France's early post-war govern-ments were making an effort to assess what her chances were of influencing the external world herself, and which objectives French foreign policy could reasonably pursue in the new situa-tion.

In the immediate post-war period, from the Liberation until the beginning of 1946, foreign policy—though nominally the responsibility of Bidault as the Minister in charge of the Quai d'Orsay—was in fact dominated by de Gaulle, the head of the Provisional government. He had two major designs in foreign policy: firstly, the practical aim of dealing with Germany, and second the more ambitious plan of reaffirming France's sovereignty and independence and her rôle as one of the big five powers in world politics.

De Gaulle's first major act in foreign policy after the Liberation—the treaty he signed when he flew to Moscow in December 1944—was a provisional answer to both problems: his initiative in signing a twenty-year treaty with the Russians, pledging France to common action against any revival of the German threat, seemed like a resuscitation of the alliance between Poincaré and the Tsar of Russia, both menaced by the Kaiser in de Gaulle's youth; the style of his visit to Moscow—a sudden move decided on without reference to de Gaulle's allies—emphasised the point that France was a protagonist on the diplomatic scene and not subject to the orders of Washington, as her very limited resources might have ordained.

When the detailed decisions had to be taken on the future of Germany, the French government of de Gaulle and Bidault stood very firmly for a policy of keeping the Reich divided into smaller units—the stock French recipe against trouble from Germany ever since the Treaty of Westphalia in 1648. Bidault pursued this policy with particular relish—he was, after all, a former history teacher who, as one writer put it, ' knew his Bainville by heart '. (Bainville was a Royalist historian, and Bidault a Republican teacher turned politician, but the German problem, he thought, remained the same.) France was not represented at the Yalta or Potsdam Conferences, but she was made a member of the Control Commission for Germany (which gave her a veto on Allied decisions), and she was also—thanks to Churchill's insistence— the occupying power in the south-western zone of Germany. She used these positions to insist on the continued decentralisation of power in Germany, and to try to carry out the separation from Germany not only of the Saar (a territory that had a special status, having been under France's economic control from 1919 to 1935), but also of the Rhineland areas that had been under French occupation from the Treaty of Versailles until 1930. De Gaulle and Bidault raised the classic French argument that the Rhine

D

was the ' natural frontier ' between France and Germany, and they attempted to put it into practice.

On other aspects of this major problem of how to deal with Germany, France was not out of line with her allies: she insisted on reparations, like the Russians, and she also took part in the Nuremburg Trials from November 1945 to October 1946, in which the leading Nazis were tried as war criminals.

The main point to be noted about French policy on the German question is that it was, on some issues, very close to the Soviet line, at least until the summer of 1946. It was France, rather than Russia, who took the lead in the Control Commission in insisting that there should be no central administrative authorities for Germany as a whole. It was France, again, who vetoed the creation of political parties extending over Germany as a whole, so that the beginnings of political life in Germany had to be planned within the frontiers of each occupation zone.

From April to July 1946, at the meetings of the Council of Foreign Ministers (a survival from the war-time coalition which failed to outlast the onset of the Cold War a year later), Molotov, on behalf of the Soviet Union, argued in favour of a centralised government to run the economic affairs of Germany, and at the same time opposed holding the levels of industrial output in Germany unnecessarily low: France led the opposition to him on both points, and continued to practise separation in Germany as well as preach it, by imposing customs barriers between the Saar and the rest of Germany.

By the end of 1946, however, France's hopes of keeping Germany administratively divided and economically weak were much more difficult to maintain. On 6 September 1946, the American Secretary of State, James Byrnes, in a speech in Stuttgart in the heart of the American zone, promised American support for the rebuilding of Germany's economy at a faster rate—essentially because the American and British taxpayers were impatient at the prospect of having to subsidise Germany any longer, but also because the lines were beginning to be drawn in the Cold War, and growing numbers of Americans saw the obvious advantage of winning Germany over to the Western side.

France was forced reluctantly to go along with this policy of rebuilding Germany as a Western ally in the Cold War. She continued to object to any measures leading towards the administrative unification of Germany—for instance, the so-called 'Bizone' Agreement of January 1947, in which the British and American zones of occupation were merged into one unit for economic policy—but France's protests were unavailing, and her objections to American policy became weaker.

By May 1947, as we have seen, the expulsion of the Communists from the French government symbolised the country's commitment to the Western cause in the Cold War, and French policy towards Germany—though some of the traditional attitudes persisted, and the acceptance of Germany as an ally was understandably slow to develop—underwent a relatively fundamental change.

One particularly difficult issue in Franco-German relations, to which a provisional solution appeared to have been found by early 1947, was the question of the Saar. This area is geographically small but economically important, and its significance in Franco-German relations for the last century has lain in the fact that its coal resources are the natural complement to the iron-ore of Lorraine. When Alsace and Lorraine were under German rule from 1871 to 1919, therefore, the iron of Lorraine and the coal of the Saar were both within Germany's frontiers; again, from 1919 to 1935, when Alsace and Lorraine had returned to France and the Saar was administered by the League of Nations, though economically part of France, the iron and the coal were again on the same side of the frontier. It was only in 1935, when the plebiscite provided for in the peace treaty led to the return of the Saar to Germany—by an overwhelming majority—that the coal and iron were separated, and even then their division lasted only five years, until Hitler reconquered Alsace-Lorraine in 1940. Five further years within the same frontiers—this time those of the Reich, from 1940 to 1945—confirmed that it made economic sense for the Saar and Lorraine to be undivided by customs barriers, and France made the most of this argument in 1945 by insisting that the Saar should come to her, as well as her own provinces of Alsace and Lorraine. By the end of 1946, as we have seen, France, as the ruler of a German zone of occupation that included the Saar, had given effect to her policy of separating this territory by establishing customs barriers between it and the rest of the French zone.

In the early months of 1947, Bidault, in part of his determined attempt to keep Germany divided, endeavoured to win the approval of France's allies for this virtual union of the Saar with France. At the decisive conference of Foreign Ministers in Moscow in March and April 1947, Bidault was forced, to his bitter disappoinment, to accept the fact that whereas the Soviet Union was not prepared to support France's claim to the Saar (despite France's approval of the corresponding annexation of parts of Germany's eastern territories by Poland and the Soviet Union), the Western Allies, represented by Marshall and Bevin, not only accepted France's economic union with the Saar, but also voted to give France a larger share of Germany's coal resources.

This situation amounted to a sharp warning to Bidault that there were strict limits to the policy of Franco-Soviet *rapprochement* sought when he and de Gaulle flew to Moscow in December 1944 (and which de Gaulle was to attempt again, with some success, twenty years later): France now had to face the need to align herself with the West in the incipient Cold War, whose existence had been clearly marked, just before the Moscow conference, in the proclamation of the 'Truman Doctrine' on 12 March.

One reason for France's lack of influence in Europe, as the new balance between the super-powers developed, was her obvious economic and military weakness: Russia could detach territory from the east of Germany because she had an army of 150 divisions, but France—with an army of only nine divisions— could not do so in the West. A further reason was that even such limited military power as France did possess was increasingly drained away in attempts to safeguard her standing and her possessions in other parts of the world.

A first example of this—fortunately brief and not too costly for France except as a blow to her prestige—was the question of Syria and the Lebanon. These two states had been part of the Ottoman Empire until they were placed under French mandate by the League of Nations: they were in fact one state, until the French authorities divided them in 1926. France's position had been critically weakened by the Second World War—in 1941, Syria was the scene of fighting between rival French forces, Vichyite and Gaullist—and the rise of Arab nationalism, encouraged by the formation of the Arab League under British patronage at the end of the war, meant that France had little chance of regaining her former foothold. In 1945, de Gaulle made an attempt to do so, but this was condemned to failure by the combined opposition of Britain and the United States, so that— instead of being handed back to France as trusteeship territories of the United Nations Organisation—Syria and the Lebanon became fully independent.

This inability to re-establish France's power in the Levant was one of the reasons why the next challenge from a colonial nationalist movement—in Indo-China—provoked determined resistance in Paris, in which all political parties—from the Communists to the right wing—were united. The story of France's colonial war in Indo-China can be sketched only briefly here, but as the war lasted from 1946 until 1954, and was the cause of a massive drain of French military and economic resources away from European affairs (which in turn profoundly affected the way French governments saw the problems of European defence and organisation), it forms an important part of our subject.

The nationalist movements in the French colonies of Indo-China, encouraged by the Japanese during their occupation in the Second World War (which, as in the British and Dutch colonies in the Far East, made a major contribution to undermining colonial rule) began their post-war activity along quite moderate lines, and even accepted the return of the French Army early in 1946, and a political compromise signed at Fontainebleau in the summer of the same year. However, in December, a political demonstration in favour of independence in the city of Hanoi in the north of Indo-China provoked a strong reaction from the local French commander, Admiral Thierry d'Argenlieu, who ordered the French Navy to attack the port of Haiphong, when several thousands of Vietnamese were killed.

This action was accepted even by the left-wing parties in France—Blum endorsed it as Prime Minister in December 1946, and not even the Communists opposed it—as a necessary step towards the re-establishment of order, after which a new political settlement for Indo-China was expected to be worked out. In fact, however, the bombardment of Haiphong marked the beginning of an eight-year struggle that was to become increasingly onerous for France, and which was only to end—after profoundly damaging consequences both to France's political life and to her policy in Europe—with her bloody defeat at Dien Bien Phu in May 1954.

The impact of the Cold War, 1947-50

As we have seen, the expulsion of the Communists from the government in May 1947 coincided with the general sharpening of the Cold War. For the next few years, the dividing-line between domestic and international politics was to be a very hard one to draw. The massive Communist-led strikes in 1947 and 1948, the split between the Communist and non-Communist trade-union movements, and the increasing polarisation of French political life, form part of the history of the Cold War, as well as of the history of the Fourth Republic. Conversely, external events such as the founding of the Cominform, Stalin's conflict with Tito and seizure of Czechoslovakia, and the deepening East-West dispute over Germany, had a direct effect on the course of politics in France.

There was a second sense in which French political life came to possess an external dimension with a direct bearing on internal events. Although in the 1940s France's colonial war in Indo-China did not reach the heights of military and political drama of the early 1950s, it was already beginning to drain economic and human resources away, and led to sharp divisions of opinion within the country. As the national liberation movement led by Ho Chi Minh was more clearly seen to be Communist-inspired, and as the American government in consequence gave increased military and economic aid to France, the Indo-Chinese War turned into another channel whereby the conflicts of the Cold War were fed into French politics.

The period 1947-50 was thus marked by acute political dissension. The Communist Party, which was France's largest, representing about one voter in four, no longer held a share of ministerial office, and therefore embarked on a campaign of violent propaganda against its former colleagues, winning widespread support as a result of the continuing economic hardships France was suffering. Despite the gradual recovery of industry and agriculture from the disastrous situation of 1944-45, prices were still high—and rising—while earnings trailed behind. The vast strike movements of 1947 and 1948 could certainly not be blamed on Communist agitation alone: they arose from the physical deprivation of large sections of the French working class.

One result of the Communist Party's strength was the practical exclusion, when it left the government, of one-quarter of the French from political life: since no other party would enter a coalition with the Communists, their five million voters were virtually disenfranchised, and their personal opposition to the Fourth Republic was correspondingly heightened. Another result of the Communist Party's large size was that the balance of power in French politics was disproportionately shifted in favour of the right. The Socialists and MRP, who had been the allies of the Communists in 1944-47 in carrying out a number of social and industrial reforms, were now forced to make coalitions with parties of the centre or right, and the paradox arose of a country with a largely left-wing electorate pursing policies of a generally conservative complexion.

Though they presented a serious threat to the Fourth Republic in these years, the Communists alone hardly appeared able to overthrow it. They did seem to have some chance of this, however, when their attacks were reinforced by those of the rapidly growing movement led by General de Gaulle. The RPF (Rally of the French People), as we have seen, was created by the General in April 1947, and his untiring campaign of speeches, in which he violently denounced both the Communist danger and the deficiencies of the Fourth Republic, quickly won him a massive following. His heroic leadership during the Second World War was of course not forgotten; and this lent credence to the slogans with which he assailed the parliamentary system and its leaders, repeating the well-known message of the Bayeux speech that France needed a strong régime led by a strong President. The first formal test of de Gaulle's popularity came with the municipal elections on 20 October 1947. Ever since the General had left office in January 1946, the monthly opinion polls had shown 30-35 per cent in favour of his return. It came as a shock, however, when the RPF won as many as 40 per cent of the votes in the municipal elections, taking control of—among other places —the thirteen biggest cities in France, including Paris. As the Communist Party also did well, winning 30 per cent of the votes, this left only 30 per cent of the voters faithful to the parties upholding the Republic. It is true that the Communists almost certainly had no real intention of trying a revolution against the régime: they merely wanted to cause the maximum disruption. It should also be noted that many of the local political figures elected to town councils in 1947 and to departmental councils in 1949 under the Gaullist label had formerly been leading lights of the Radical Party, and soon abandoned Gaullist intransigence for the opportunistic habits for which the Radicals had long been famous.

The Republic did, however, face a crisis, which was underlined by a poignant scene in the Assembly in November 1947. The Ramadier Cabinet—France's seventh since 1944—had been defeated, and the President of the Assembly, Edouard Herriot, called on Léon Blum, the 75-year-old Socialist leader, to form a government. The handshake which Blum gave Herriot before starting his speech—the Socialist Prime Minister of 1936 saluting his Radical predecessor of 1924—symbolised the irony of how the brand-new Fourth Republic was already forced to rely for its very existence on the leaders of its despised predecessor. Blum failed to get a majority—his criticism of de Gaulle, significantly, went too far for some Radical members—and the new government was formed by Robert Schuman, a politician who might well have been a Radical, but was in fact a member of the Catholic Party (MRP). Schuman came from Lorraine: he was a 63-year-old lawyer who spoke fluent German and had served in the German army in the First World War. During his period as Prime Minister (from November 1947 to July 1948), Schuman formed the view that France's problems and Germany's could not be solved separately, and that only a merging of their respective economic and political resources could save them.

When Schuman was in turn voted out of office, he was replaced successively by two Radicals: André Marie, whose government lasted only a few weeks, and Henri Queuille, whose thirteen-month Cabinet (September 1948 to October 1949) set up a record of at least outward continuity. Queuille achieved this partly because he *was* a flexible Radical of the old school: a country doctor, he had been in parliament since 1914, and had held minor posts in more than 20 Cabinets between the two wars. With Schuman and Queuille, the concept of the Third Force was born: this meant a coalition of all the ' reasonable ' (i.e. non-Communist and non-Gaullist) parties, from the Socialists to the

Independents, a coalition which—in varying forms—was to rule France until the Gaullists won more influence in the early 1950s.

Under the benign and fatherly figure of Queuille—not to mention the reassuring and influential President of the Republic, Vincent Auriol—France's fortunes began slowly to mend. Investment in industry began to approach pre-war levels again. True, it took the country some time to recover from the massive and costly waves of Communist-led strikes of 1947—indeed, in November 1947, the trade union movement split firmly into its Communist (CGT) and non-Communist (FO) components on the question of the strikes, and has never been reunited. However, with the start of American aid under the Marshall Plan in 1948-49, and excellent harvests, the lot of the French people began to improve.

One feature of French politics during this period was a considerable degree of continuity, even when the Prime Minister changed. Not only did the Civil Service provide a powerful administrative backbone to the government, but several key Ministries hardly changed hands for several years. For instance, Bidault remained Foreign Minister practically without interruption from 1944 to 1948, and Robert Schuman, his successor, held the post until 1953. Again, the Ministry of the Interior—a critically important one in this period of civil disorder—was held by the Socialist Jules Moch from 1947 to 1950: he became a byword of abuse to the Communists by organising strong resistance to their strike actions, including setting up a special force of riot police (CRS) in 1947.

Foreign affairs, as we have noted, impinged heavily on France during this time. The Communist take-over in Prague in February 1948 helped to solidify the Western alliance known as the Western European Union, in which France—modifying her earlier hopes of East-West mediation—played a leading part. France also helped to develop the work of OEEC (see Chapter 5 below), which administered Marshall Aid and became in some ways a kind of Western counterpart of the Cominform.

It was the evolution of the German problem, however, which forced the French government to seek a fundamentally new approach to the political and economic organisation of Europe. France was now getting little support for her original post-war policy of keeping Germany totally divided and very weak.

Indeed, by 1949, after the Berlin blockade (see Chapter 3), France joined the other Western powers in establishing the German Federal Republic, including all three Western zones of occupation.

This formal revival of a German state, as well as the American policy of encouraging Germany's economic strength, was one of the motives leading Robert Schuman, now Foreign Minister in a government led by Bidault, to make his famous proposal of June 1950 for a High Authority to control the coal and steel industries of all Western Europe. A concern for France's international interests—the attempt to check German independence by giving up some of France's too—pointed in the same direction as that for France's economic well-being. Despite the combination of American aid, prudent financial management by Queuille's and later governments, and the pioneering work of Jean Monnet and his colleagues in the Planning Commission, French hopes of a higher standard of living were being disappointed. It was in fact Monnet, as we shall see (Chapter 5), who played a leading part in the work that preceded Schuman's historic offer of June 1950.

The pressures of the outside world had for several years made France's internal problems more acute: she was now to attempt to solve them by a bold international initiative of her own.

3 Germany 1945-50

The end of the Third Reich

In 1918, Germany had not been invaded: her people had not known the full horrors of war, and after her defeat, her armies had marched home from the battlefields abroad, almost as if they had been the victors. In 1945 it was different: Hitler's policy of fighting to the last, combined with the Allies' policy of Unconditional Surrender, ensured that the invading armies took over a country whose urban areas were mostly ruins and rubble. Almost every German city had by now suffered from Allied bombing, though not always on a scale like that inflicted by the Luftwaffe on Coventry, Rotterdam or Warsaw. Berlin—where the Russian and Western armies met—was in a state of utter chaos. A reporter of the *New York Herald Tribune* who got there on 3 May 1945 wrote:

> Nothing is left in Berlin. There are no homes, no transportation, no government buildings. Only a few walls . . . are the heritage bequeathed by the Nazis to the people of Berlin. . . . Berlin can now be regarded only as a geographical location heaped with mountainous mounds of débris.

The complete breakdown of public services and of food supplies caused untold suffering among the civilian population: as late as the end of 1946 a hundred thousand people were dying of hunger in the city of Hamburg alone, and in Cologne an Allied medical mission found that only 12 per cent of the children were of normal weight.

The four Allies thus took control of a Germany whose government had ceased to exist and whose population was suffering grievous hardship. It was also a Germany whose very position on the map of Europe was shifting and whose size was abruptly reduced. On 5 June 1945 the Allies, in announcing the arrangements for their four zones of occupation and the four-power control of Berlin, declared that the frontiers of Germany would henceforth be those of 1937, i.e. after the acquisition of the Saar through the plebiscite of 1935 but before Hitler's eastern conquests. However, one of the occupying powers had already gone beyond these provisions: by a unilateral decision of 21 April 1945 the Soviet Union had handed over the territories to the east of the Oder and Neisse rivers (the so-called Oder-Neisse Line) to Poland, keeping for herself the part of East Prussia around the port of Königsberg (re-named Kaliningrad). The Western Allies, who had resisted the transfer of German territory to Poland at the Conference of Tehran in 1943, had reluctantly accepted it at Yalta in February 1945 as the price for Soviet participation—in the event unnecessary—in the war against Japan. The Potsdam Agreement signed by the four victors in the Prussian garrison town near Berlin on 2 August 1945—at the end of the further conference—confirmed the West's agreement to the Soviet occupation of Königsberg and to the establishment of Polish control over the territories east of the Oder-Neisse Line. With this in mind, the agreement ran, the territories in question 'shall not be considered as part of the Soviet zone of occupation in Germany'. These Polish and Soviet acquisitions removed one-fifth of Germany's pre-war territory from the area to be occupied by the four powers, and added to the already acute shortages in western Germany by starting a vast migration of people across the country. It was not only the Poles and Russians who occupied German lands to the east: the Czechs also expelled the Germans from the former Sudetenland, and altogether about ten million German refugees flooded westwards. Many of them, of course, were not strictly 'expelled' but they all left under pressure. The Potsdam Agreement laid down the rule that the transfer of German population westwards should take place in 'an orderly and humane manner'; but in the chaotic conditions of 1945, and with the memory of ghastly Nazi atrocities still fresh in the minds of the Red Army and the Polish population, it was almost inevitable that a good deal of cruelty and suffering should come about as the Germans were ejected. Several thousands of elderly people, women and children died on their appalling journey. Germans, particularly those from East Prussia and elsewhere who survived the migration, were naturally more vividly aware of the horrors of their own expulsion than of the horrors of the Nazi concentration camps. Even though many of them realised that the one was in a sense retribution for the other, the presence of a substantial group of embittered refugees was to be an important factor in rendering west Germany so markedly anti-Communist.

The war-time agreement about zones of occupation was respected by the Allies as they advanced into Germany: the American troops who had occupied Saxony and Thuringia—part of the Soviet Zone—duly evacuated the areas in favour of the Red Army, and the Red Army in turn handed over the three western sectors of Berlin. The situation of Berlin was in fact very anomalous; although the city was to be administered by all four Allies, the western boundary of the Soviet Zone, which completely surrounded the city, lay a hundred miles to the west. This position arose partly from the fact that the Soviet Union, by ceding Germany's territory in the east to Poland, needed to move farther west in compensation; and partly from the war-time assumption that the four Allies would continue to agree on the general lines of their policies in Germany, and thus no problems would arise from the curious position of Berlin. In reality, dissension between the Allies would very soon divide Berlin in two, and render its western part a pawn in the Cold War.

The Potsdam Agreement ordained that during the period of military occupation, Germany 'would be treated as a single economic entity', and that the German population would be accorded uniform treatment throughout the country. The Control Commission for Germany, however, was unable to work effectively as a united agency, partly because of the Soviet government's unilateral actions in the Russian Zone and also because France deliberately obstructed the functioning of what she saw as the embryo of a future reunited German Reich. The four occupation zones thus developed as separate entities, and each of the four occupying powers applied in its own way the general principles of denazification, demilitarisation and democratisation agreed at Potsdam.

The start of economic and political reconstruction 1945-46
The first two of these objectives were of a negative nature: the attempt to purge German public life of the noxious elements that had been responsible for the atrocities of the Nazi régime and the Second World War. The four Allied powers agreed on the first step to be taken: a trial of the surviving leaders of the Third Reich, which took place in Nuremberg—formerly the scene of

Hitler's spectacular party congresses—from November 1945 to October 1946. Göring, Speer, Ribbentrop and the other defendants were accused of crimes against peace, war crimes, and crimes against humanity, and the court condemned twelve of them to death. This judgment, and indeed the legal validity of the trial, aroused some opposition among the Germans—the impartiality of a court where only the victors were the judges was of course open to question—but many of them recognised the responsibility of the Nazi leaders for the heinous crimes of the Third Reich. A more difficult question was that of 'denazification' at lower levels of society. The four Allies were committed to removing all ex-Nazis from positions of authority and influence in the civil service, the legal system, and the schools and universities of Germany. They applied these principles with varying degrees of severity: one of the problems was the difficulty of proving that a given individual had in fact been an active member of or sympathiser with the Nazi Party, since many Germans—particularly officials—had been forced to become nominal party members in order to keep their jobs. As the occupying powers soon discovered, it was necessary to overlook the Nazi party membership of many officials who were needed to get a system of public administration working again; as the Cold War developed and the Western powers and Soviet Union realised they needed German help in building up their respective parts of Germany, several fairly highly-placed servants of the Third Reich again found themselves in important official posts. Lesser Nazi party members—teachers and local government officials—were often not so lucky, and many suffered undeserved hardship. However, when it came to tracking down the real criminals of the Third Reich—those responsible for massacring millions of victims in the concentration camps—an intensive and widespread detective operation was carried out by the occupying powers and later by the new German authorities themselves.

The Allies met with varying degrees of success in their attempts to 'demilitarise' and 're-educate' German society. The abolition of the German armed forces was relatively easy—and, as we shall see, the attempt to convert the Germans to peaceful habits of thought led some of them to resist rearmament strongly when the Allies pressed for it in the 1950s. 'Re-education' was interpreted differently by each of the four occupying powers: the Russians

acted on the view that the capitalist system had been responsible for Nazism, and hence that nationalisation of the means of
production was the first step towards a democratic Germany;
the French tended to believe that all Germans were capable of
reverting to nationalism if the country were allowed to unite,
and therefore obstructed any attempt at the creation of central
inter-zonal authorities; the British and Americans tended to
act as if Nazism had been a horrible but temporary aber-
ration in German life, and that the Germans could be
re-educated in democratic ways by lectures on British or American methods of running local government or parent-teacher
associations.

Political life in post-war Germany was slow to develop, but the
main lines of later events were quite quickly laid down. In the
Soviet Zone, the Russians made a determined attempt to create
a pro-Soviet régime under Communist leadership: Walter
Ulbricht, one of the German Communist leaders of the 1920s
who had evaded the Third Reich's concentration camps by flee-
ing to Moscow in 1933 (and who had also, unlike many of his
colleagues, escaped being murdered by Stalin), was flown back to
Berlin in May 1945, and set about organising the new system.
The Communist Party itself was small, but there was a strong
feeling among some Social Democrats that the division between
the two left-wing parties before 1933 had helped Hitler to take
power, and Ulbricht was able to exploit this feeling for his own
ends. In May 1946, after considerable manoeuvring by Ulbricht
and his Soviet masters, the Communist and Social Democratic
Parties in the Soviet Zone were merged into the Socialist Unity
Party (SED) in which the Communists Ulbricht and Wilhelm
Pieck had the whip-hand over the former Social Democrats under
Otto Grotewohl.

The detailed history of how the Soviet Zone of occupation
evolved by 1949, under Russian and SED leadership, into the
German Democratic Republic, belongs to the history of the Soviet
bloc rather than to that of Western Europe. It was, however,
influential in determining two features of West Germany's own
political life: the deep-rooted anti-Communism of the Christian
Democratic Union (CDU) led by Konrad Adenauer, and the equally
deep-seated wish of the Social Democratic Party of Germany
(SPD) under Kurt Schumacher to bring about reunification and

the liberation of their East German fellow-Socialists from Communist domination.

Christian Democrats and Social Democrats were to dominate the political life of the emergent West German state. In fact both of them in turn were to form coalition governments with the third main (though smaller) party, the Free Democrats (FDP), and the scene was also to be somewhat complicated by the presence of other minor parties, but the parties of Adenauer and Schumacher were by far the major political forces.

The Christian Democratic Union, established soon after the war under Adenauer (a Roman-Catholic Rhinelander who had been Mayor of Cologne from the First World War to 1933, and nearly became Chancellor in 1926) was an enlarged successor of the Centre Party of pre-Hitler days. It was enlarged in the sense that it now included Protestants as well as Roman Catholics, and also in the sense that, whereas the old Centre had been a somewhat right-wing party, the CDU made a deliberate attempt to bring left-wing and trade-union elements into its leadership. Adenauer's early colleagues included Karl Arnold, a Roman Catholic trade unionist who for several years held the post of Minister-President of the important federal *Land* ('state') of North Rhine-Westphalia; Jakob Kaiser, who gave up the attempt to keep Christian Democracy alive in East Germany and became Adenauer's Minister for all-German Affairs; and Gustav Heinemann, a Protestant pastor who was Minister of the Interior until he resigned in September 1950 in protest against West German rearmament and Adenauer's authoritarian methods of government. (Heinemann was later to join the SPD and in 1969 to become President of the Federal Republic.)

Under the influence of these men, the Christian Democratic Party began with a notably progressive approach to social and economic issues, though under the influence of the Cold War and the revival of German industry it soon moved towards the more capitalist economic policies of Ludwig Erhard, the minister who presided over Germany's 'economic miracle' in the 1950s.

The Social Democratic Party also evolved in the post-war years from a left-wing to a more right-wing posture. Kurt Schumacher and some of his colleagues in the revived SPD of 1945-46 were strongly influenced by the party's traditional Marxism, and the party's full acceptance of a modified form of capitalist economics only came, after long debates, at the end of the 1950s. Schumacher, as will be seen, was also fundamentally opposed to all those policies of Adenauer which had the result of strengthening the West German state as such: the SPD longed for reunification with East Germany—where Schumacher and many of its other leaders had originally lived, and where the majority of voters would be Socialist—and condemned Audenauer's policy of integrating *West* Germany into *Western* Europe because it appeared to preclude this reunification completely.

The impact of the Cold War 1946-47

The growth of a West German political authority, which was to develop by 1949 into the Federal Republic, was precipitated by the rising tension between the Soviet Union and the Western Powers. In part, as we have seen, this originated in areas remote from Germany—Greece, Turkey and Iran—but differing views about policy towards Germany were a major source of conflict too.

The first issue at stake was that of reparations. The wartime agreements had specified that each occupying power might take industrial equipment and food from its zone of occupation to make good losses inflicted by the Germans, but that all such reparations deliveries should be accounted for to the Allied Control Commission. By early 1946 this body was scarcely functioning—partly, as has been noted, because of French opposition to any unitary authority—and the Russians were continuing to take industrial equipment out of their zone without giving any account of the value involved (which should have been set against the final total due to each recipient). The Western powers were also dismantling Germany's industrial capacity—partly to use it to repair the damage done to them, and partly to keep Germany's output down to the levels agreed during the war—but Britain and the United States (if not France at this stage) were now developing doubts about whether this policy was wise. As the British and American Zones were largely industrial regions which had depended on eastern Germany for their food supplies, the Allies were forced to provide resources of their own to replace those being taken out by the Russians, and to keep the German population alive. In these circumstances it was natural that the Western Allies should develop hostility towards the Soviet refusal

E

to account for reparations deliveries, and that they should begin to relax the restrictions on Germany's capacity to earn her own living. The levels of permitted industrial output were gradually raised, and in September 1946 the American Secretary of State, James Byrnes, in an important speech in Stuttgart, promised American support for the economic and political rebuilding of a Germany which would henceforward be regarded as a partner of the West.

This decision had rapid results both on West Germany's political evolution and for her relations with the rest of Europe: in fact, this phase of German politics can hardly be disentangled from the politics of Europe in the Marshall Plan era. In May 1947 the British and American Zones were merged for purposes of economic policy into the so-called 'bi-zone'. France was still reticent about joining in—Bidault, her Foreign Minister, still rigidly applied the principle of keeeping Germany divided, and hoped to avert the threatening Cold War by East-West mediation —but events were to force her towards the Anglo-American position by the end of the year. In July, a month after Marshall's Harvard speech promising economic aid to Europe, the 16 West European countries accepting this aid declared in their conference in Paris that 'the German economy should be integrated into the economy of Europe'. This commitment implied that Germany would become a member of the Organisation for European Economic Cooperation, set up to administer Marshall Aid— though at first she was to be represented in this by the three occupying powers; it also, by using the key word 'integration', indicated the lines of Germany's future participation in a united Western Europe in which Konrad Adenauer would collaborate closely with Robert Schuman.

Adenauer, as early as January 1948 (i.e. well over a year before the Federal Republic was established) was making his presence felt in the European Christian Democratic movement: a conference of the Christian Democratic 'Nouvelles Equipes Internationales' held in Luxembourg in that month, included among its participants 'Dr Adenauer, former Mayor of Cologne'.

At the same time as these links were being forged between west Germany and the remainder of Western Europe, a further severance of links between the two parts of Germany occurred. December 1947—the end of the year which had seen the Cold

War develop, with the Truman Doctrine, the Marshall Plan, and the setting-up of the Cominform—saw the consolidation of Communist power in east Germany by the first ' Congress of the German People ', in which the ruling Socialist Unity Party took a further step towards establishing the German Democratic Republic.

The Berlin Blockade 1948-49

The decisive steps towards the division of Germany into two rival republics came during the Soviet blockade of west Berlin, which lasted from June 1948 to May 1949.

The background to this crisis was a series of further developments relating to West Germany's economic recovery. On 9 February 1948 the Western Allies published the so-called ' charter of Frankfurt ' which set up an Economic Advisory Council for the Anglo-American Bi-zone—in effect, a German government for economic affairs, with an executive branch and a parliamentary assembly with advisory powers. (As an apparent counter-measure, the Soviet authorities handed over more powers to the Economic Committee of their own zone on 10 March.)

On 19 March the Allied Control Commission in Berlin held its last meeting, which the Soviet member Marshal Sokolovsky left after a spectacular clash over the irreconcilable policies of East and West, in particular west Germany's realignment with the Western Powers. The West now went ahead with its plans for Germany's economic and political rehabilitation. On 4 June, after a conference in London between the British, French and Benelux governments, the setting up of an international authority to supervise the industrial development of the Ruhr was announced. So was a plan for the calling of a Constituent Assembly to prepare a constitution for a state comprising the three Western zones— France having now accepted the need for Western unity. This Assembly was to be brought into existence by the military governments of the three Western zones, acting in conjunction with the local authorities which they had already set up as a first testing-ground of German democracy.

Two weeks later, on 18 June, a currency reform was announced. The Western powers, acting together with the German Economic Advisory Council, regarded this as a vital next step in Germany's economic development, since the war-time currency still in circulation had inflated dangerously in value. The introduction of the new money in west Germany led to an escalation of the conflict with the East, where a new currency was in turn brought into use on 23 June.

The Western powers wished to introduce their new currency in west Berlin, whereas the Russians claimed that their new east German money should be valid for Berlin as a whole. The deadlock on this point led to a breakdown of the East-West Military Government (*Kommandatura*) for Berlin, and an attempt by the Soviet Union to force the Western Allies out of the former capital by cutting off all roads, railways and canals leading to the city, so that no food, industrial raw materials, or supplies of any sort could reach Berlin, by land or water transport.

West Berlin's population of about four millions was, however, kept going by the so-called ' air-lift ' run by the air forces of the Western Allies. For nearly a year west Berlin was supplied by aircraft carrying, in the early days, about 4,000 tons a day of food, raw materials, coal and other supplies, a figure which was later stepped up to a daily total of 12,000 tons. This firm Western response showed the Soviet Union that there was no chance of forcing the West to abandon Berlin: on 5 May 1949 after hard negotiations, Stalin called off the blockade and Berlin's links with west Germany were re-opened.

In the meantime, the consolidation of the Cold War blocs, each including a German component, had inevitably gone a stage further. In the east, the split in the Allied *Kommandatura* led to the establishment of a separate east Berlin city government in November 1948. In the west, the close understanding between west Berlin's mayor, Ernst Reuter (SPD), with Konrad Adenauer on the one hand, and the Allied authorities on the other, paved the way for the establishment of a west German state.

Early in April, before the ending of the blockade, a series of agreements signed in Washington brought about the full merger of the French Zone with the Anglo-American Bi-zone, as well as the decision to replace the Allied Military Government with a tripartite High Commission, which was to supervise the potential west German government.

On 8 May, three days after the lifting of the blockade (and on the fourth anniversary of Germany's surrender), the German Constituent Assembly adopted the ' Basic Law ' or Constitution of the future German Federal Republic. (An important division of opinion between the German parliamentarians and the Western Allies arose on the subject of West Berlin: the Germans wished this to be fully included as a province or *Land* of the Federal Republic, whereas the Allies, preoccupied by their own responsibility for Berlin's military defence, refused to accept this part of the draft constitution. The Germans were to accept the Allies' view on this point only in 1971.)

On 15 May—following the now customary ritual of mirror-image developments in West and East—the Russians held elections in their Zone for a further People's Congress which approved, two weeks later, the constitution that was to change the Zone into the ' German Democratic Republic '. On 16 August 1949 West Germany held her first general election—the first free German election, in fact, since November 1932—which gave Konrad Adenauer's Christian Democratic Union a small majority. By September, the new Federal Republic was functioning, and it was duly followed a month later by the German Democratic Republic.

The Federal Republic and Europe 1949-50
The founders of the Federal Republic made a determined effort to avoid some of the errors which had made the 1919 constitution of the Weimar Republic practically unworkable. In particular, they adopted an electoral system which, while it contained an element of proportional representation, also included rules designed to eliminate the proliferation of small parties which the Weimar system had encouraged. The new provision—that no party should hold any seats in parliament unless it got at least five per cent of the total vote—worked to good effect: the political system of the Bonn Republic (the sleepy little Rhineland town of Bonn became the provisional capital rather than Frankfurt, partly thanks to Adenauer's personal preference) functioned well and stably, essentially as a three-party system, in marked contrast to the chronic instability of Weimar.

Dr Adenauer became Chancellor, elected by a parliamentary majority of one vote—his own—and the post of Federal President went to Theodor Heuss, a highly respected elder statesman of the Liberal or Free Democratic Party. Adenauer, the most powerful figure in German politics (since the constitution, again in the hope of avoiding the abuses of the past, deliberately restricted the President's powers) was in fact to hold the post of Chancellor for fourteen years—longer than the entire lifespan of the Weimar Republic.

The main tasks of the new government were in economic policy. Germany had begun to make a good recovery from the catastrophic situation of 1945—partly through successive relaxations by the Allies of the limits on her industrial output—but there were still terrifying shortages of housing, food, and the other necessities of life. Adenauer used his considerable diplomatic skill to get further concessions from the Allies—both with regard to the ending of industrial dismantling and to the flow of American aid—and also developed the policy of the 'socially-conscious market economy' in collaboration with his Minister for Economic Affairs, Ludwig Erhard. Erhard's policy, based on free enterprise with a low rate of tax on profits, encouraged a rapid rate of growth (Germany's so-called 'economic miracle'), though it did so at the price of considerable inequality of incomes, which was later to lead to more militant action by the trade unions, as the supply of surplus labour from the East dried up and their bargaining strength increased. In the short run, the unions cooperated actively with Erhard's policies, concentrating their own efforts on the claim for workers' control ('co-determination') in industry.

In a sense, the new West German state had no foreign policy: it had no Ministry of Foreign Affairs, and there was no question of Adenauer's government undertaking any diplomatic negotiations except with or through the three occupying powers. In a deeper sense, however, the very decision to create the Federal Republic in collaboration with the West was a foreign policy decision of the first magnitude. As Adenauer's critics saw it— notably Kurt Schumacher, the SPD leader—it precluded any chance of the reunification of the two parts of Germany. Schumacher—an East Prussian by origin, and a patriot who was determined not to let the SPD be tarred with the brush of 'national treason' as in the 1920s—bitterly castigated Adenauer's 'capitulation' to the West, calling him, in one violent parliamentary clash, 'the Chancellor of the Allies'. Adenauer defended his choice of a Western orientation for Bonn by saying that the way to reunification lay through 'negotiation from strength' with the Soviet Union. It seems clear, however, that he regarded reunification as out of the question in the shorter run, and was in fact concentrating on good relations with the West for the sake of the Federal Republic as it stood—or rather grew.

The Cold War gave Adenauer a remarkable chance to build up the independence of the West German state, and he made the most of it. He won the support of the American Secretary of State Dean Acheson—as later of his successor, John Foster Dulles—and made West Germany a leading partner of the United States in Europe.

Adenauer also saw to it that Germany played an active part in the construction of the new institutions of Western Europe. As we have seen, Germany's position as a prominent recipient of Marshall Aid brought her into OEEC, and she also joined the Council of Europe (see Chapter 5). From Adenauer's point of view, the Coal and Steel Community proposed by the French Foreign Minister Robert Schuman in June 1950 offered a way of liberating Germany from some of the restrictions still placed on her by the Ruhr Authority, and giving her equality of status with France in this respect; from the French point of view, the Community offered a way of controlling Germany's strength, which would inevitably rise, with American support, whatever France and the Benelux countries did.

The Schuman Plan thus offered the logical next step forward in solving 'the German problem', both from Germany's point of view and from Europe's. Konrad Adenauer therefore responded with active and convinced approval when Robert Schuman put the plan forward.

4 Italy and the Benelux Countries 1945-50

The background to post-war Italy

The Italian dictator Mussolini—the man who brought the word 'fascist' into the political vocabulary of Europe—was deposed and executed by left-wing partisans in April 1945. The last King of Italy, Umberto II, abdicated when a majority of the Italian people voted to establish a republic in June 1946. With these two changes—particularly the first—Italy prepared to make a completely new political start in the post-war world. However, just as French political life came to be dominated, within a few years after the Liberation, by the parties and some of the leaders of the 1930s, so Italian government was powerfully influenced by survivals from the past. For a start, most of Italy's post-war political leaders were quite literally elder statesmen, whose political careers had begun in the early 1920s before Mussolini's fascist régime cut them short: Alcide De Gasperi, the chief figure in Italian politics from 1946 until his death in 1954, had become leader of the Catholic Popular Party as early as 1923 (Mussolini forced him to resign in 1925); De Gasperi's colleague Count Sforza, Minister of Foreign Affairs from 1947 to 1951, had already held the post in 1920; Togliatti and Nenni, the leaders of the Italian Communist Party and of the non-Communist left, both had political experience going back to pre-fascist days; and among the statesmen who contended for power after Mussolini's fall were the vintage Liberals Nitti and Orlando, the latter of whom had represented Italy at the Paris Peace Conference of 1919.

It was not only Italy's pre-fascist past that lived on in the new Republic: many politicians, and even more officials and judges, had served the fascist régime, and many traces of Mussolini's administrative structure—for instance, the extreme centralisation of political life, and the failure to establish effective regional government for twenty years after the war—meant that the republic of 1946 marked something less than a completely new departure. (To keep the influence of fascism in post-war Italy in perspective, it should be remembered that many of the officials and others who had held their jobs during Mussolini's reign had been very far from convinced supporters of totalitarianism: there were many Italians like the eminent surgeon in Florence, whose bookshelves in the 1950s still contained the *Complete Writings and Speeches of Benito Mussolini* in a dozen beautiful leather-bound volumes—every page of which was immaculate and uncut. In any case, the fascist régime of Mussolini was incomparably less virulent than the Nazi régime of Hitler: the virtual absence of anti-semitism and of concentration camps was only the most obvious evidence of this.)

As well as the political legacy of the previous quarter of a century, Italy in 1945 was also dominated by the economic heritage of a much longer period of under-development and stagnation. Even without the destruction of 20 per cent of the country's industrial capacity in the savage fighting that raged over central Italy for the last two years of the war (in the worst damaged areas, Campania and Tuscany, the output of the iron and steel industry was reduced by as much as 90 per cent), there was a long history of economic backwardness, particularly in the South. Although Italy had been united into a single kingdom in 1871 (the same year that Bismarck created the German Empire), the process of unification had in some ways amounted to a conquest of the under-developed South by the more industrialised North, and the whole of southern Italy, particularly Sicily, had continued to be exploited as if a conquered territory. Sicily, even after 1945, could in some ways hardly be counted as part of Europe at all: a source of cheap unskilled labour for the North, with a standard of living only half that of Northern Italy, and an illiteracy rate which in the early 1960s was still as high as 20 per cent (the overall figure for Italy in 1961—eight per cent—was already bad enough), Sicily—separated by less than a hundred miles from the coast of Africa—symbolised in an extreme form the economic backwardness of Southern Italy. At the beginning of the Second World War, agriculture had contributed more than industry to Italy's national income (36 as compared with 34 per cent), and as much as 48 per cent of the population had been employed in agriculture. By 1952, the proportion of the population employed on the land was still as large as 42.4 per cent, strikingly higher even than the corresponding French figure of

31.8 per cent. Against this background of economic backwardness and the domination of a traditional type of peasant agriculture, the survival of pre-industrial social attitudes was quite
natural. In particular, a marked characteristic of Italian life was
a sense of solidarity with family and friends, rather than with
more remote bodies such as political parties. The power of the
Mafia in Sicily (based largely on family connections, and for
long defying any imposition of law and order by the state) was
only an extreme example of the prevalence of loyalties and attitudes inhibiting the growth of a modern political party system.
The Christian Democratic Party that dominated Italian politics
after the war, acting in close concert with the Vatican, on the
whole constituted a conservative political force, reflecting the
chief interests of the rural Centre and South; whereas the parties
of the left, more strongly implanted in the northern industrial
cities, were reduced until the 1960s to a rôle of almost constant
opposition, on the whole ineffective.

The political life of post-war Italy followed a period of fairly
complete confusion and dispersion during the latter part of the
war: in 1943-45, Italy was not only a battlefield for the opposing armies, but was also divided between three political authorities
—the government of King Victor Emmanuel supported by the
British and American forces in the South; the Allied Military
Government which these powers established as they moved north-
wards through central Italy; and Mussolini's régime, the so-called
Fascist Republican government, under the control of the German
occupying power in the North. There was also, of course, dissension within each of these areas: in the South, the British and
American governments disagreed on which factions to back, with
Churchill backing King Victor Emmanuel and Marshal Badoglio,
while President Roosevelt favoured a group of Italian leaders
slightly to the left (Bonomi and Sforza); in the central part of
Italy, political life was beginning to revive under the influence
of Christian Democrats but also of other opponents of fascism;
and in the North, the fascist régime of Mussolini (now completely
under German domination, since his rescue from captivity by
German troops) was the target for violent resistance, largely under
Communist leadership. This division of Italy between rival factions, coming on top of eighty years of tension between North and
South, was to provide a difficult legacy for the post-war Republic.

Another aspect of Italy's predicament with which her post-war régime had to come to terms was her international position. Italy had never been fully accepted as one of the great powers, even after her achievement of unity in 1871. One of her African colonial adventures—the invasion of Abyssinia in 1896—had ended in humiliating disaster at the Battle of Adowa; she had played a very inglorious part as a minor ally of Germany and Austro-Hungary before 1914, only to remain neutral when the First World War started and then to come in on the side of Britain and France against her late allies; and Mussolini's bombastic attempts to revive the glories of the Roman Empire, by a policy of generally stirring up international trouble during the 1920s, invading Abyssinia in 1935 and then intervening in the Spanish Civil War and World War II had led to resounding and convincing disaster by 1945. Thereafter it was clear to the Italians, as it was to the Germans, that their proper international rôle must henceforth be a much more modest one: in the event, this realisation was to lead Italy—under the Christian Democratic leadership of De Gasperi and Sforza—into active partnership with her European neighbours in the movement towards the integration of the western part of the European continent.

The new political system
Italy's first national election after the war—the vote for the Constituent Assembly on 2 June 1946, the same day as the Referendum on the future of the monarchy—indicated the balance of forces that would dominate the country's future. Three-quarters of the seats in the new Assembly were held by three large parties—the Christian Democrats with roughly 35 per cent of the vote, the Socialists with almost 21 per cent, and the Communists with almost 19 per cent—and the political life of the new Republic was to be guided by the interactions between these three forces, including to a striking degree their differences of opinion on foreign policy.

The Christian Democratic Party, which held 207 seats out of 556 in the 1946 Assembly, was formally established in 1943 by Catholics opposed to the fascist régime, but the political philosophy of Christian Democracy had a history going back beyond the First World War, and was represented in the Popular Party led by Don Luigi Sturzo between the First War and Mussolini's establishment of the Fascist State. De Gasperi, the Christian Democratic leader who was Prime Minister continuously from December 1945 almost until his death in 1954, had succeeded Don Sturzo in 1923. Any party which won as high a share as 35 per cent of the Italian vote—and this share was to go up to 53 per cent in 1948—was inevitably a coalition between several interests: Roman Catholic religious belief provided a powerful cement holding the party together—it was always actively supported by the Vatican and by the priesthood at election times—but on the practical details of policy there was inevitably a constant need for compromises to be made between the views of the many social and economic groups represented in the party. Peasants, industrialists, trade unionists and shopkeepers clearly had somewhat divergent economic interests, and part of the success of De Gasperi as party leader was due to his skill in acting as a broker between them: after his death, his successor Amintore Fanfani proved less successful in keeping the various factions together, and was in turn succeeded in 1959 by Aldo Moro, who shifted the centre of gravity of the party to the left, taking it into a coalition with the Socialists. During the ten years of De Gasperi's leadership, however, the main lines of Christian Democratic policy were distinctly right-wing: the encouragement of private industry with American help; a relatively passive policy in economic aid to Italy's under-developed regions; and a clear alignment on the side of America in the emergent Cold War that became a very important factor in Italian domestic politics. At the time of the elections of June 1946, De Gasperi had already been Prime Minister for several months—he had replaced the first post-war Prime Minister, Feruccio Parri, the leader of the small Action Party, in December 1945—and the right-wing course of his policy was confirmed not only by his action on the general issues just mentioned but also by his reinstatement in the early part of 1946 of civil servants, judges and others who had served Mussolini.

In view of the conservative orientation of the Christian Democrats, it is remarkable that De Gasperi succeeded in holding together the coalition government with the two left-wing parties—the Socialists under Pietro Nenni and the Communists under Palmiro Togliatti—which lasted until May 1947. The main reason for his success was that the two left-wing parties were prepared to adopt a moderate line on the major problems confronting Italy—including the question of the form of the new Constitution—in the interests of national reconstruction.

In the Constituent Assembly elected in June 1946, the Italian Socialist Party, with 20.7 per cent of the votes, held 115 seats, and the Italian Communist Party, with 19 per cent of the votes, held 104 seats. Both parties could trace their origins back to the influence of Marxism in Italy before the First World War, and both were in theory revolutionary parties in their programmes; but the Bolshevik Revolution of 1917, by splitting off the Communists from the bulk of the Socialist movement, as in other western European countries, had caused a bitter feud between them. The rift had occurred in 1921, as a result of the 21 Conditions imposed by the Soviet-dominated Communist International, and both Nenni and Togliatti were well aware that the resulting division of the left had been one of the reasons for Mussolini's success in coming to power. This helps to account for the moderation displayed by both party leaders towards each other in the period after 1945, and also for their readiness to put their revolutionary aims into the background and to collaborate with the right-wing Christian Democratic Party. Of the two, the Communist Party was internally the stronger and better disciplined: Togliatti was able to maintain a unity in the well-ordered Communist Party that Nenni could not achieve with the Socialists. The Socialist Party was in fact to cleave in two, in January 1947, with about a quarter of its Deputies following Giuseppe Saragat into a new Social Democratic Party of Italy: this party aligned itself firmly with the Christian Democrats— Saragat was a member of a series of centre coalitions before becoming President of the Republic in 1964—while the majority of the Socialist Party under Nenni remained in opposition, and drifted into a close alliance with the Communist Party which was to last until the 1960s. Among the reasons for the continuing strength of the Communist Party, and its success in attracting the Nenni Socialists towards the left, should be mentioned the party's hold over the main Italian trades union organisation, the Confederation of Labour.

As well as the three big parties—Christian Democrats, Socialists and Communists—the 1964 Constituent Assembly contained representatives of a number of less important political forces. As already mentioned, the Action Party, a small left-wing group created during the resistance, actually produced Italy's first post-war Prime Minister, Feruccio Parri, but his base of public support was limited to the Milan region, and he was manoeuvred out of office in December 1945, even before the weakness of his party had been confirmed by its failure to win more than a handful of votes in the June 1946 election. Among parties with rather more substance were the Liberal Party (6.8 per cent of the votes and 41 seats in the 1946 Assembly), which was led by the eminent philosopher Benedetto Croce, and claimed to continue the tradition of Italian liberalism going back to the nineteenth-century stateman Cavour; the Republican Party (4.4 per cent of the votes and 23 seats), representing the slightly more left-wing version of liberalism originally associated with Mazzini, and led after 1945 by Count Sforza, Foreign Minister from 1947-51; the right-wing neo-fascist party *Uomo Qualunque* ('Man in the Street'), which obtained 5.3 per cent of the votes and 30 seats; and the Monarchist Party (2.8 per cent of the votes and 16 seats), which kept up a noisy but ineffective opposition to the Republic for some years.

Italian politics 1945-50
After the confusion of the later years of the war, with rival governments controlling different parts of the country, the whole of Italy came under the control of a government in Rome in the early summer of 1945. This government was a coalition of six parties, under the leadership of Parri, the head of the Action Party and a hero of the anti-fascist resistance. His main task, apart from ensuring the maximum amount of financial and material help from the Allies (much of this came through the United Nations Relief and Rehabilitation Agency) was to prepare for the Referendum in which the Italian people would decide on their future constitution. King Victor Emmanuel III, who had reigned since 1922, had gravely compromised the monarchy by his support of Mussolini, and had been persuaded to nominate his son Umberto as Lieutenant-General, pending the outcome of the Referendum. Parri, despite his personal appeal, had, as we have seen, a limited political power-base as Prime Minister and, when he tried to force the pace of developments and get a Constituent Assembly elected and the constitutional issue settled very

soon after the war, his coalition broke up, and De Gasperi, leader of the Christian Democratic Party—the strongest political force in Italy, and heavily backed by the Vatican—was able to take over as Prime Minister in December 1945.

De Gasperi's Cabinet, like Parri's, was a coalition of all six of the main parties, but its general orientation was much more right-wing, and it was under the auspices of De Gasperi himself—with, it must be said, active support from Togliatti, the Communist Minister of Justice—that a large number of former fascist officials, suspended from their posts at the Liberation, were reinstated. (Many of them, in fact, joined the Communist Party, which was happy to use their talents in establishing its control over local government in some of the main cities of Italy.)

The rehabilitation of former fascists did not, however, signify a revival of support for the monarchy—at least not for King Victor Emmanuel. When the local election results of early 1946, combined with public opinon polls, showed how unpopular the King was, the Monarchist Party, in desperation, persuaded him to abdicate in favour of his son, who became King Umberto II on 10 May. This was less than a month before the critical Referendum, and even the final dismissal of Victor Emmanuel, and the active support of the Vatican, were unable to hold back the anti-monarchist tide of popular feeling. Despite an eloquent appeal by Pope Pius XII on 1 June, the day before the Referendum—he exhorted the voters to choose between materialism and Christianity, between the supporters and the enemies of Christian civilisation (a barely-disguised message that Catholics should vote for the monarchy and also for the Christian Democratic Party in the election held simultaneously)—the Republic won a clear majority of 54 per cent of the votes against 46 per cent in favour of the monarchy. King Umberto accepted this verdict—the pressure of the Allied Commission of Occupation gave him no choice—and Italy was formally declared a republic.

With the 'Institutional Question' out of the way, the new Constituent Assembly—whose political composition has already been described—proceeded to work out a constitution for the new Republic. The constitution itself, which came into force at the beginning of 1948, reflected the mixture of Roman Catholic, Marxist and Liberal doctrines represented in the Assembly. The influence of the Christian Democrats, for instance, could be

seen in Article 7 of the constitution, which reaffirmed the
Lateran Pact concluded between the Vatican and Mussolini in
1929, giving the Catholic Church a preponderant say in the state
education system and other aspects of public life, commensurate
with the fact that 90 per cent of Italians were Catholics; the
ideas of Marxist Socialism were reflected in the Constitution's
emphasis on the principle of political control over economic life,
but at the same time economic liberalism was given its due with
a formal guarantee of the rights of private property. Many provisions of the constitution remained pious aspirations only: for
instance, the section providing for democratically elected regional
assemblies was only to be put into operation in 1970.

The constitution did, however, provide a framework for the
democratic evolution of Italian political life, its basic principle
being that the government should be formed by the largest
party, or the dominant coalition of parties, in a parliament elected
by popular vote. Almost as soon as the Constituent Assembly
had begun its work in June 1946, in fact, the atmosphere of electioneering was renewed, since the first parliamentary election was
due in 1948, and the parties—at the same time as agreeing on
the essentials of the constitution—were being driven into discord on other issues. The impact of world politics—which at this
stage meant the widening split between Russia and America
as the Cold War developed—was decisive. De Gasperi realised
that Italy's economic recovery depended very largely on support from America, and it was at the moment when he was in the
United States negotiating a large loan—in January 1947—that
his coalition went through its first major crisis. The majority of
the Socialist Party, under Pietro Nenni, refused to follow De
Gasperi, who was left with only the support of a minority of the
Socialists, led by Giuseppe Saragat. A deep breach in the Socialist Party followed, with the adherents of Nenni reverting to the
historic name of Italian Socialist Party, while Saragat and the
minority—who were to remain in De Gasperi's Cabinet—took
the name of Italian Social Democratic Party. The formal dropping of the Communists and Socialists from the government
was delayed until May 1947, but it was rumoured that the
American government had made their dismissal a condition for
the loan negotiated by De Gasperi as early as January.

It is certain that American support was forthcoming for the

anti-Communist side in the bitter struggle that now followed in the Italian trade union movement and which resulted, by the end of 1947, in the creation of separate Communist and Catholic-Socialist trade union organisations (the Catholics and Socialists in turn separated in 1949). The Communist unions, as in France, sponsored massive strike actions in 1947-48 against the Marshall Plan, and the first general election under the new constitution held in April 1948 took place in an extremely tense atmosphere. The impact of the Cold War was absolutely plain after the Communist *coup* in Czechoslovakia in February, and it was emphasised by the American government's announcement that economic aid would be cut off if the Communist-Socialist alliance were returned to office.

The United States also attempted to help De Gasperi back into power by persuading the British and French governments to join the USA in recommending the return to Italy of the entire Free Territory of Trieste, currently disputed between Italy and Yugoslavia. (In the final compromise, Italy was to receive the urban zone of Trieste itself, and Yugoslavia the rural hinterland of the Istrian Peninsula.) American citizens of Italian origin were also urged to bombard their relatives at home with anti-Communist admonishments by letter, and the Church in Italy continued to intervene actively in favour of the Christian Democratic Party.

In the subsequent election, this party achieved the remarkable score of 48.5 per cent of the votes (against 35.2 per cent in 1946), and held 305 seats out of 574 in the new parliament. The Communist-Socialist block obtained 183 seats, the Social Democrats 33, and no other group more than 20: the Neo-Fascist, Monarchist and Liberal Parties, which were to play a part in a later stage of Italian history, were hardly represented in the 1948 parliament.

De Gasperi continued, predictably, to pursue a rigidly pro-American course in foreign policy, and his economic and social policies reflected the tensions within his government. This was again a coalition, the dominant Christian Democratic Party being joined by the Social Democrats, the Liberals and the Republicans. The Social Democrats, under Saragat, pressed for land reform and improvements in Italy's social services, but these were opposed by the Liberal Party and the right wing of the

F

Christian Democrats, and progress was slow. In particular, the grave differences between the North and the South persisted.

In 1949, Italy went through an acrimonious argument about whether to join the North Atlantic Treaty Organisation, as the United States was pressing her to do. De Gasperi, convinced by the arguments of his Foreign Minister Sforza, wished Italy to do so: the Prime Minister put the case for this largely in terms of her need for economic aid and close links with America rather than of the need for defence against the Soviet Union; but they were at first opposed by a section of the Christian Democratic Party, who argued that Italy, as the centre of the Roman Catholic Church, ought to remain neutral in the East-West conflict. This opposition was overcome when De Gasperi and Sforza prevailed upon Pope Pius XII to speak out in favour of Italian membership of NATO.

Just as Sforza had had to talk De Gasperi into joining NATO, he had to work quite hard to persuade him that European unity would help Italy to overcome her problems of economic stagnation. Sforza had been a believer in European unity for many years, and his first major initiative as Foreign Minister was to try, in 1948, to conclude a full customs union with France. This was in fact opposed both by Italian and by French industrial interests, and the treaty was never ratified: the attempt did, however, pave the way for Italy's acceptance of the Schuman Plan in 1950. Again, the economic interests affected took fright: both the coal and steel producers of Italy feared the effects of German competition on their small and backward industries, and Italy was allowed a transition period of five years before the full removal of tariff barriers. With the help of this special concession, Italy's coal and steel industries were to show themselves well able to stand up to European rivalry, and in the meantime De Gasperi's government gained international goodwill—including that of America by taking part in the West European integration process launched by Robert Schuman.

The Benelux countries 1945-50

The first major question to be faced after the war by Belgium—a small country with a population of about four million French-speaking Walloons and six million Flemings speaking a form of

Dutch—was the future of the monarchy. King Leopold III, who had come to the throne in 1934, had brought the royal family into some discredit by his decision to surrender to Germany in May 1940: this decision was made without consultation with the government, who disavowed the King by continuing the struggle as a government-in-exile in London. A further aspect of the King's behaviour that increased his general unpopularity was his attitude during the German Occupation, when he discouraged the Belgians from making any contact with the government-in-exile and—even though he did not publicly support the Germans—failed to give his people any patriotic lead.

The issue of whether Leopold be allowed to return to the throne after Belgium was liberated was linked with the other main problem of Belgian politics—the dispute between Walloons and Flemings. In the French-speaking regions—Brussels and the South—the majority was for abdication, but the Catholic and more conservative Flemish-speaking regions supported the King. When the referendum on his future was held in October 1949, he received 72 per cent of the votes in Flanders; despite this, and notwithstanding the fact that he obtained nearly 58 per cent of the votes in the country as a whole, the opposition continued a campaign of strikes and demonstrations. Leopold concluded that he did not command a sufficient degree of popular support: he abdicated in August 1950 in favour of his son, Prince Baudouin.

The other hotly-contested issue in Belgian politics—the linguistic dispute between Walloons and Flemings—was less acute in the early post-war years than it was later to become. In theory, all Belgian citizens had to learn both languages at school, but in practice the Flemings—the majority—felt oppressed by the French-speaking minority. In the period immediately after 1945 this issue was, however, kept in the background by the question of the monarchy and the urgent need for economic recovery. A series of coalition governments—ten of them in the period 1944-50—tried to deal with these problems. The composition of the governments varied—the Socialist Prime Ministers van Acker and Spaak presided before 1947 over coalitions including the Communists and, after 1947, over coalitions between the Socialists and the Christian Social Party—but their general economic policy was the same. The country depended heavily on

American aid under the Marshall Plan, and also continued and developed a pre-war experiment in economic integration. Belgium and her neighbour Luxembourg had been partners in an Economic Union since 1922, and this was expanded in negotiations between the Belgian, Netherlands and Luxembourg governments in exile in London into the Benelux Customs Union, signed in 1944. The Customs Union came into effect in January 1948, with the abolition of all tariffs between the three members and their adoption of a single tariff on imports from outside. At the same time Belgium was an active participant in the work of OEEC (see Chapter 5); she also welcomed—with some fears for her backward coal industries—the Schuman Plan of 1950.

The Netherlands suffered severe damage during the war. The low-lying position of the country, after the destruction of many of the dykes, led to serious flooding by the time the Germans were driven out, after bitter fighting by the Allies and an active resistance movement. Politically the country presented the paradox of combining a multiplicity of small parties—many of them based on religious differences—with a basic underlying stability and unity stemming from a strong national tradition and the phlegmatic temperament of the people. In contrast to France and Italy, the Dutch Communist Party reached a maximum strength of just over 10 per cent of the votes in the post-war election of 1946, after which it decisively declined: this was partly due to the effective policies of the Dutch Labour Party, whose leader, Willem Drees, was Prime Minister of four coalition governments between 1948 and 1958.

A pressing problem in the early post-war years was the nationalist revolt of the Dutch East Indies against colonial rule. Japanese occupation had destroyed the control of the Netherlands over this colony, and after an attempt at its re-establishment, the Dutch granted independence to Indonesia in 1949.

Once this question was out of the way, the government in The Hague was free to concentrate on social reforms at home. Advanced programmes for social welfare and housing were implemented, and a policy of state-controlled wage negotiations kept inflation at bay. The Netherlands also benefited from membership of the Benelux Customs Union from January 1948, and—as a nation with an active commercial tradition—joined wholeheartedly in the movement for West European integration begun by the Coal and Steel Community proposed by Schuman in 1950.

If Belgium and the Netherlands—two of the smaller states of Western Europe—found they were not large enough to solve the problems of post-war reconstruction in isolation, the same applied *a fortiori* to Luxembourg. The Grand Duchy, with a population of only one-third of a million, had attempted a policy of permanent neutrality from 1867 onwards, but after being overrun by Germany in both world wars, she amended her constitution in 1948 to allow membership of international organisations, including military alliances. Luxembourg had in fact been economically linked with Belgium since 1922 by the Belgo-Luxembourg Economic Union, and this was developed into the Benelux Union by 1948. The largest of Luxembourg's three political parties, the Christian Socialists, held office continuously after 1945, in varying coalitions, either with the Socialists or the Liberals or with both. The parties all agreed on the main lines of foreign policy, including membership of the Western European Union, NATO, OEEC and the European Coal and Steel Community.

When Luxembourg became the headquarters of the Coal and Steel Community in the early 1950s, her citizens were able to rejoice in recovering a European vocation. She had been an integral part of European politics since the early Middle Ages— four of her Grand Dukes had occupied the throne of the Holy Roman Empire—and her rôle as the centre of a new experiment in European unity was seen as a worthy continuation of this long tradition.

5 The Organisation of Europe 1945-50

Reconstruction: national or international?
As we have seen, every one of the states of Continental Western Europe suffered a drastic break in the continuity of its political life as a result of the Second World War. In France, the collapse of the Third Republic in 1940 led to a division of pronounced bitterness between the Vichy régime and the Gaullist Free French movement, which joined with the Resistance to reconstruct French politics after the Liberation. In Germany and Italy the dictatorship which had lasted since 1933 and 1922 respectively were swept away by 1945. In Belgium, the Netherlands and Luxembourg, where the pre-war governments had gone into exile and where no equivalent to the French Vichy régime had existed, the years of Nazi occupation, and the social and political ideals developed by the Resistance, had led to the same determination to make a 'new start' as existed in the other countries.

The fundamental question about the new political structure of Europe was whether it should be based essentially on the traditional framework of nation-states, or on something radically new. As we have seen, each of the European countries began its post-war reconstruction by trying to pour the new wine of anti-fascist idealism into the old bottles of the pre-war nation-state, or something very like it. But even in a case—like that of France—where the new constitution was framed with the explicit intention of avoiding the mistakes of the old, the familiar political and social forces soon re-emerged with enough vigour to make the Fourth Republic almost a replica of the Third.

There were many reasons why European political life should resume essential aspects of its traditional forms: even the catastrophes of 1939-45 could hardly sweep away every trace of a tradition like that of the nation-state, which had been the basic European political organisation for several centuries. The simple revival of the nation-state system did, however, come under a powerful challenge from a rival conception—that of a federated United States of Europe.

This conception was of course not new. The idea of merging national sovereignties was almost as old as the European state-system itself, since political thinkers from the sixteenth century onwards (including the French minister Sully and the English Quaker William Penn) had put forward schemes for more or less federal European authorities.

In the aftermath of the First World War, the idea of a United States of Europe had been taken up not only by crusading idealists such as the Austrian Count Coudenhouve-Kalergi, the leader of the 'Pan-Europa' movement, but also by leading statesmen. Both Aristide Briand, the French foreign minister from 1925 to 1932, and Gustav Stresemann, his German counterpart from 1923 to 1929, spoke out in favour of a United States of Europe as the way to prevent future catastrophic wars. However, a major obstacle to closer European unity, in the situation of the 1920s, lay in the fact that the interests of France and Germany were in many ways irreconcilable. Briand, at heart, wanted a United Europe which would preserve the political settlement imposed on Germany by the Versailles Treaty—or at the most, allow very gradual relaxations of the Treaty in Germany's favour—whereas Stresemann saw a United Europe as a framework within which Germany could achieve rapid and substantial concessions, which he needed in order to hold at bay the mounting pressures of German nationalism. In the words of a biographer of Stresemann, 'their two Europes mutually excluded each other'. In the event, the political forces unleashed by the Great Depression after 1929 swept away any chance of a democratic United States of Europe—in which even the conflicting interests of Germany and France might gradually have been resolved. By an appalling paradox, Europe was politically united, between 1940 and 1945, not by the free will of the European peoples, but by the force and terror of the Nazi régime.

Hitler's 'New European Order', however, provoked a reaction which impelled men towards a Europe of another sort. In the resistance groups throughout occupied Europe, and even in the concentration camps of the Third Reich, anti-Nazi political leaders, trade unionists and others were discussing plans for a united Europe which would make anything like a repetition of

Nazi Germany's domination of Europe impossible. As early as 1944, several international meetings of Resistance leaders, including Danish, French, Italian, Norwegian, Polish, Czech and Yugoslav representatives, took place in Geneva, in neutral Switzerland. From these meetings emerged, in July 1944, a 'Draft Declaration of the European Resistance', which condemned the system of sovereign states as the cause of Europe's catastrophic wars, and concluded that 'This anarchy can be solved only by the creation of a Federal Union among the European peoples'.

The first European Federalist Congress, which launched the movement for an integrated Europe, took place in liberated Paris in March 1945—a month before Hitler's defeat and suicide. The participants, who included the great French novelist and journalist Albert Camus, the British author George Orwell, and the Labour MP John Hynd (later Minister responsible for Germany in the Attlee government), launched a campaign for 'the federal organisation of the European peoples', which turned into a formal movement, the European Union of Federalists, at a further conference in Montreux in August 1947. One of the leaders of the movement, the Italian Resistance leader Altiero Spinelli, was to have a chance of applying his ideas within a European institution when he became a member of the European Community's Commission in 1970—continuing a career of more than a quarter of a century of vigorous campaigning for the European cause.

The federalist approach to European unity—implying the radical transfer of political sovereignty to a new central authority—was of course not the only one. There was also the 'functionalist' approach represented by Jean Monnet, a remarkable French businessman and thinker, who was, as we have seen, the first head of the French Economic Planning Commission after the war. Monnet had had long experience in international affairs: he had been Deputy Secretary-General of the League of Nations, had been instrumental in the attempt to bring about an Anglo-French Union in 1940, and had worked as de Gaulle's agent for economic procurement in Washington during the war. From these experiences he had drawn the conclusion that a new international order could be built not by a frontal attack on the sovereignty of states, but by the establishment of specialised agencies with real power to carry out certain functions, which, by operating successfully, would attract political authority away from national governments.

In the years after 1945, the European governments themselves—taking their cue from the speeches of leading statesmen (notably Winston Churchill's Zürich speech of September 1946, calling for 'a sort of United States of Europe')—came to realise that their economic and political problems could not be solved within a purely national framework, and that some form of international cooperation was the best way to go forward.

The first European organisations 1947-48
The form of these structures—of which the earliest was the Organisation for European Economic Cooperation, established in May 1948—was determined by the interplay of a number of political forces. The federalist movement was taking the lead in a series of unofficial congresses which mobilised European opinion in favour of unity; the functionalists, notably Monnet, were winning support within national political systems for their view that the problems of post-war reconstruction were insoluble within the existing framework; and by 1947 a new and powerful impetus towards European unity came from the United States, with the Truman Doctrine proclaimed on 12 March and the Marshall Plan announced on 5 June.

As has been observed, the war-time harmony between the Soviet Union and the Western Powers deteriorated rapidly during 1945 and 1946, the main issues at stake being the future of Germany, the unwillingness of the Soviet Union to evacuate northern Iran, and her persistent pressure on Greece and Turkey. By February 1947, after a period in which the American administration had been slower to appreciate the possible dangers of this situation than the British governments of Churchill and Attlee, a critical turning-point was reached. The British government, after a winter of chronic economic difficulties—particularly shortages of fuel, combined with the worst blizzard since 1894—took the drastic step of telling Washington that Britain could only continue her military and economic aid to Greece and Turkey for a maximum of three weeks.

The American government was forced to make a positive response to this virtual ultimatum, which was of course only part of a generally alarming world situation. Not only was Britain giving up her traditional balancing rôle in the Eastern Mediterranean (including her mandate over Palestine) and her control of India, farther eastwards round the Soviet Union's perimeter; in Western Europe as a whole, the economic situation was as desperate as it was in Britain. America had of course been supplying Europe with coal ever since the war, but the disastrous winter of 1946-47 increased Europe's needs. In west Germany, although coal production had reached two-thirds of the pre-war level, steel output was only one-quarter.

In this situation of deprivation and despair throughout Western Europe, the American response was inevitably influenced by the strength and potential appeal of Europe's very large Communist Parties—especially in France and Italy—and the apprehension of a real risk of all Western Europe falling under Soviet influence.

As we have seen, the first American response was the Truman Doctrine proclaimed by the President on 12 March 1947, which promised military and economic support not only to Greece and Turkey, but also by implication to any other European country threatened by Soviet pressure. More directly related to the growth of European cooperation was the Marshall Plan announced by Secretary of State George Marshall in a speech at Harvard on 5 June. Warning his audience that the world confronted 'the dislocation of the entire fabric of European economy', Marshall proceeded to put forward an American offer of massive economic aid—which was to take the form of aid for Europe as a whole, and to be administered according to a plan which the European governments themselves must collaborate in working out.

The West Europeans lost no time in responding to this signal: the British and French foreign ministers, Bevin and Bidault, took the lead in convening meetings between European governments, the first of which was held in Paris three weeks after Marshall's speech. These conferences led to a systematic assessment of Europe's requirements and the way to meet them, and by April 1948 had established the Organisation for European Economic Cooperation (OEEC) to administer the American aid programme.

It is important to note that Marshall's offer of American

assistance was made to Europe as a whole, including the Soviet Union. Stalin's Foreign Minister Molotov in fact participated in the Paris consultations of the summer of 1947, but the USSR soon withdrew from the whole enterprise, dragging with her the Czechs and Poles who had originally accepted the Marshall Plan with enthusiasm.

Probably the American government had always expected the Soviet response to be negative—especially as the Marshall Plan came after the Truman Doctrine, which amounted to a public declaration that the Cold War existed—though Bidault at least was full of regret that the structures arising from the Marshall Plan were limited to *Western* Europe alone.

OEEC in fact took the form of an organisation of 16 West European countries, collaborating closely with the United States—in other words, forming part of the ' Western bloc ' in the developing Cold War. It succeeded remarkably well in its three principal tasks—cooperating in the distribution of Marshall Aid, freeing trade between its members from tariffs and other barriers, and creating a multilateral clearing system for monetary transfers, the European Payments Union established in 1950.

OEEC remained, however, quite firmly an *inter-governmental* organisation, with no supra-national powers of decision at the centre. This was in line with the wishes of the British government and some others (notably the Scandinavians, who also still believed in the capacity of national institutions to solve their problems). It thus failed to satisfy either the demands of the European federalist movement—which had by now taken the lead in organising a massive conference at The Hague in May 1948, with many eminent European statesmen, including Churchill—or the views of Jean Monnet, still working on the prospects of extending the functional principles of French economic planning to the European level.

Within less than two years after OEEC was set up, the inadequacy of its inter-governmental method was fully accepted by six at least of its members—the six who moved on to adopt the Schuman Plan of May 1950 for the establishment of the European Coal and Steel Community. Their path to this decision had been prepared partly by their experience of the limitations of inter-governmental European organisations, and partly by the

successful experiment in integration already undertaken by three
of them—Belgium, the Netherlands and Luxembourg—at the
beginning of 1948.

As early as September 1944, the governments of these three
small countries had signed the Benelux Convention, which laid
the foundations for an economic union providing for the abolition of internal tariffs (put into effect in January 1948) and the
harmonisation of the member states' economic policies. The
Benelux union faced difficulties in its early years, but it was to
provide a model for the broader development of integration
among the Six.

NATO *and the Council of Europe 1949*

The two most important Western organisations to be set up in
1949 were formally established within a few weeks of each other:
the North Atlantic Treaty was signed on 4 April and the treaty
instituting the Council of Europe on 5 May. Both these institutions, like the OEEC, were inter-governmental rather than supra-
national in character. The North Atlantic Treaty merely committed each of its members—a group of Continental European
States plus the United States, Canada, the United Kingdom and
Iceland—to consult together on the means of planning their
common defence, and to 'take such action as it deems necessary'
in case of attack; the members of the Council of Europe—ten,
later 15 European states—set up an elaborate system for inter-
governmental consultation and joint action in certain fields but,
as we shall see, they stopped short (in particular, British hesita-
tions stopped them short) of anything amounting to a hand-over
of executive authority to a central body.

The international background to the setting-up of NATO was
the further worsening of the Cold War. As we have seen, the
Marshall Plan and Truman Doctrine had led to a consolidation
of the countries of Western Europe (Greece and Turkey being
included as 'Western' for purposes of the balance of power),
in the face of what was perceived as a Russian threat; during the
same period, the Soviet Union had drawn her East European
satellites, and the Communist Parties of Western Europe too,
into a new organisation of her own. This was the Communist
Information Bureau or Cominform, established in September
1947 as a centre of anti-Western propaganda. This amounted

to a Soviet equivalent of the Truman Doctrine: while Stalin's abolition of the old Communist International (Comintern) in 1943 had symbolised the peak of Soviet-Western collaboration in the war against Hilter, the creation of the Cominform four years later marked the renewal of organised Soviet hostility towards the capitalist West.

The Western European countries had in fact begun to establish a system of defensive military alliances before this 'escalation' of the Cold War in 1947, though in fact in the early stages a future revival of Germany was seen as the possible threat, rather than pressure from the Soviet Union. Both the Franco-British Treaty of Dunkirk—signed in March 1947, partly as a British gesture of atonement for Britain's failure, along with America, to give France the guarantee she had sought in 1919—and also the Treaty of Brussels, signed by Britain, France, Belgium, the Netherlands and Luxembourg in March 1948, were conceived partly as safeguards against a revived German threat. Only partly, however, since—at least during the year that separated the signing of these two treaties—Western Europe had come increasingly to see the Soviet Union as the potential aggressor.

The establishment of the Cominform in 1947, and its outpourings of anti-Western propaganda, were followed in February 1948 by the *coup d'état* of Prague, in which the Czech Communist Party, strongly supported by the Soviet Union, overthrew the parliamentary régime of Edvard Benes, and established a one-party dictatorship. This could of course have been interpreted as a defensive move by the Soviet Union—the ' pre-emptive ' capture of a neutral state which the Western powers might have tried to drag over into their own now-hardening bloc—but this was not how the forcible addition of a Western-type democracy to the group of People's Democracies appeared to the West at the time.

Coming close to President Tito's revolt against Stalin, and the expulsion of Yugoslavia from the Cominform (June 1948), it appeared to give Soviet Russia increasingly the appearance of a new threat not unlike Nazi Germany.

The crisis that led the Western countries to expand the Brussels Treaty Organisation into NATO—implying the fundamental new step of an American commitment to contribute to the defence of Western Europe—was the Berlin blockade of June 1948-May 1949. As we have seen, the development of the Cold War, and the economic burdens facing the Allies in supporting the western zones of Germany, had led during 1947 to the fusion of the British and American zones, and in June 1948 the process was continued by the carrying-out of a reform of the Germany currency, which laid the foundations for her so-called ' economic miracle '. As the Western Allies proposed to introduce the new currency in their sectors of Berlin, the Soviet government responded by a blockade to cut off west Berlin completely from the western zones. As we have seen, the blockade failed in its objective, and one of its results was to accelerate the foundation of the West German Federal Republic. Another was to rouse the American administration to the need for a commitment to Europe going beyond the Truman doctrine of 1947: on 11 June 1948 the United States Senate voted in favour of Senator Vandenberg's resolution authorising the Administration to join the Brussels Treaty powers in an enlarged defence pact (a radical breach with isolationalism, promoted by a man who had held strongly isolationist views before Pearl Harbor), and on 4 April 1949 the resulting North Atlantic Treaty was signed. This alliance, and the organisation structure to which it gave rise, were to provide a secure framework for the political development of Western Europe, including such important new steps as the rearmament of West Germany (which became a member of NATO and also of the Brussels Treaty Organisation—broadened into Western European Union—in 1955). NATO was, however, as we shall see, to be criticised in the 1950s by the German left as a barrier to the reunification of Germany, and in the 1960s by the French right—notably de Gaulle—as an instrument of American domination over Europe.

In the meantime, May 1949 had seen the birth of another European organisation, modelled closely on OEEC in having an inter-governmental basis, but differing in the sense that its terms of reference were much broader. This was the Council of Europe, whose origins can be traced directly to the Congress of the European Movement at The Hague in May 1948. The political leaders assembled at that Congress—of whom the most eminent was the British Opposition leader, Winston Churchill—passed a resolution demanding the establishment of a Council of

Europe as a framework for consultation and cooperation between the governments of Europe.

The governments took this recommendation seriously, and the structure and functions of the Council of Europe were very quickly agreed. The Council would provide for international consultation both at the level of governments—in the Committee of Ministers—and at the parliamentary level—in the Consultative Assembly, consisting of members of national parliaments. It is true that in the course of the negotiations— particularly between July 1948 and January 1949—a sharp distinction emerged between the position of the British and Scandinavian governments, who wanted the powers of the Assembly to be strictly limited, and that of the French and Belgians, who wanted a more autonomous Assembly capable of giving authoritative direction to the work of the Council of Ministers. In the end, the Anglo-Scandinavian view prevailed: not only did the powers of the Assembly remain strictly consultative, but the Committee of Ministers itself was restricted to a forum for the voluntary co-ordination of the policies of national governments, without any question of their being bound to execute majority decisions. Despite this clear limitation of the Council of Europe to a consultative rôle, however, its meetings in Strasbourg helped to bring about closer cooperation between governments—for instance, on transport and cultural matters— and to provide a campus for the mutual education of European parliamentarians. The Council's Commission on Human Rights has also carried out most valuable and important work.

The first step to integration: the Schuman Plan
The Anglo-French disagreements about the shape of the Council of Europe did a good deal to make it clear in Paris that the British government was not willing to hand over real power to any international authority: even the weakened form which the new Council finally took is said to have inspired Ernest Bevin to make the gloomy prediction 'when you open that Pandora's Box, you'll find it's full of Trojan horses'. Another field of Anglo-French dealings which brought fresh evidence of differing views was a series of discussions of economic policy which arose out of the Dunkirk Treaty of 1947. At the end of a number of meetings during 1948 and 1949, the French government

—and in particular, Jean Monnet, the head of its Commission for Economic Planning—came to the conclusion that the Labour government in London was unwilling to commit itself to the degree of joint economic planning which Monnet, with his long experience of international cooperation, regarded as necessary. This conclusion was confirmed by the British government's refusal to take part in the negotiations for a European Coal and Steel Community proposed by the French Foreign Minister, Robert Schuman, on 9 May 1950.

Part of the background to this proposal was the series of talks Monnet—the main author of Schuman's proposal—had held with the British, in the hope of including Britain in the plan. Another important factor was the development of relations between France and West Germany. As has been seen, West German industrial production had been allowed to rise steadily since 1947, and Germany also benefited from the Marshall Aid funds distributed through OEEC from 1948 onwards. This rise in Germany's economic strength provoked some concern in France: the re-establishment of a West German government in 1949, even though France accepted it and joined with the other occupying powers in supervising its activities, added to these fears. French political leaders naturally wanted to ensure that Germany's renascent economic and political strength could never again dominate Europe. In particular, France was concerned to maintain some control over the industrial Ruhr area—which she did through the International Ruhr Authority established in April 1949, even though the Germans pressed hard, with American support, for a relaxation of Allied controls. She also wished to keep control of the Saarland, a German-speaking area with rich coal reserves, which had been formally attached to France in 1947. Even though the French government conceded political autonomy to the Saar in 1949, she kept up the area's economic union with France, and this created difficulties with the new German government, which maintained that the Saar government installed in power by the French was no more than a pawn in French hands.

To Monnet and many other Frenchmen—as indeed to Adenauer and other German leaders, including Karl Arnold, the Prime Minister of North Rhine-Westphalia—the revival of Franco-German discord over the Ruhr and the Saar was an ominous reminder of the conflicts of the 1920s and 1930s. For the simple political motive of removing a potential cause of serious trouble, the best solution appeared to be the placing of the coal and steel industries of both France and Germany (and of any other countries willing to join) under a common European authority. This political objective, as well as the economic argument that the pooling of resources was more rational, was made quite clear in the declaration which the French Foreign Minister read at his press conference at the Quai d'Orsay on 9 May 1950: 'The pooling of coal and steel production will immediately provide for the establishment of common bases for economic development *as a first step in the federation of Europe*, and will change the destinies of those regions which have long been devoted to the manufacture of munitions of war, of which they have been the most constant victims.' (Author's italics.)

This language made a direct appeal to the generation of European political leaders who had known two catastrophic wars and the disaster-laden period between them. Robert Schuman, the French Foreign Minister who had been brought up in German Alsace-Lorraine; Konrad Adenauer, the Roman Catholic Rhinelander who sometimes seemed to turn more readily to Paris than to Berlin; and Alcide De Gasperi, the Italian Prime Minister who had grown up as a citizen of the multi-national Austro-Hungarian Empire, all felt the need to attempt a bold experiment in constructing a future for Europe different from her past. They were all ready to accept Monnet's view that the institutions of the new Coal and Steel Community should be fundamentally different from those of OEEC or the Council of Europe. As the Schuman Plan put it, 'the common High Authority entrusted with the working of the whole system will be composed of independent persons designated by governments on a basis of parity . . . Its decisions will have the force of law in France, in Germany, and in the other member countries . . .'

This language, however, went too far for the British government—particularly the Labour government of 1950, which had recently carried out its long-cherished aim of nationalising the coal mines (incidentally, mines which produced as much as all those of Western Europe put together—another reason for British aloofness) and was about to nationalise the steel industry too. After three weeks of hectic discussions and exchanges of

G

diplomatic correspondence, the British government and those of the Six in effect announced at the beginning of June that they would go their separate ways: Britain would not accept the commitment to a supra-national European authority as a basis for negotiations, while the Six were determined that this was the essential principle on which their new construction would be based.

After June 1950, the political institutions of Europe took two separate paths, which were not to cross again for more than twenty years. On the one hand, OEEC and the Council of Europe continued to function as inter-governmental organisations, with Britain playing a leading part in each of them. In contrast, the six countries which accepted the Schuman Plan and established the Coal and Steel Community (which was formally set up by a treaty signed in April 1951) took the path of supra-nationalism —the nine-man High Authority of the Community had real power to enforce its decisions on member states, even though its functions were limited to control of the coal and steel industries. This principle was to be applied to broader fields in the European Economic Community and European Atomic Energy treaties of 1957.

There was of course a strong element of national interest in the negotiations that produced the Coal and Steel Community. We might even say that just as Briand and Stresemann had meant somewhat different things by a ' United States of Europe ' in the 1920s—one wanting essentially a static Europe, the other a Europe with changes in favour of Germany—so Schuman and Adenauer in 1950 had somewhat different motives. Schuman indeed saw the Coal and Steel Community in part as a way of channelling and checking the growing power of Germany (especially as world politics—including the outbreak of the Korean War—were inducing the United States to move ever faster in restoring Germany's strength). Adenauer, again, like Stresemann before him (it should not be forgotten that Adenauer—Chancellor from 1949 until 1963—was actually born before Stresemann, whose political career ended with his death in 1929!) saw European unity in part as a way of rehabilitating Germany and giving her greater status and freedom of manoeuvre. These Franco-German differences in perspective should not, however, be allowed to dominate the picture: the essential feature of the

Schuman Plan was that six European governments were prepared to accept voluntary limitations on their national sovereignty in respect of a vital part of their economic life, with the avowedly political aim of surmounting their centuries-old conflicts and going forward together towards a united federal Europe.

6 France in the Fifties

Introduction: the Third Force and the European Defence Community

The first six years of French politics after the Liberation had been marked by idealistically high hopes placed in a new régime, which had been revealed as illusory: from 1944 to 1950, 13 governments had succeeded one another, finishing by resembling those of the Third Republic not only in their rapid death-rate, but even in their very personnel. The remaining eight years of the Fourth Republic were to be equally unsatisfactory: from July 1950 until the Republic was overthrown by the army's revolt of May 1958, a further 13 governments held office, and proved increasingly unable to solve the acute problems of France.

These problems were of many kinds: France could even be said to have faced simultaneously the intractable legacies of time and the irresistible pressure of space. The legacies of time included the residue of problems bequeathed by several centuries of history. The political divisions of the country represented at the same time the Church-State conflict of the eighteenth century; the unresolved problems of an incomplete industrial revolution, which left a large and often backward peasant population confronting the modern society of the cities; the capitalist/socialist or left/right split of nineteenth-century industrialisation; and, even within the left, the Socialist/Communist split created in the French Socialist movement by the Bolshevik Revolution.

The pressures of space were represented in French politics by the ever-growing demands made by the Cold War in Europe (which the strength of the Communist Party reproduced within France herself); by the rebirth of German power which the Cold War facilitated and which included Germany's projected re-armament within the European Defence Community; by the anti-colonial revolt in Indo-China, which developed into a sanguinary and damaging war; and by the subsequent revolt of France's North African territories—Morocco, Tunisia and Algeria—the last of which was to lead to the crisis that brought the end of the Fourth Republic.

The multiplicity of these problems helps to explain the fragmented character of French political parties, and the kaleidoscopic changes in the coalition governments they formed. A coalition which agreed on matters of economic policy would fall apart when it had to turn to the problems of church schools or colonial revolt. Coalitions of the so-called ' Third Force '—all the parties between the Gaullists and Communists—remained feasible until the election of 1951 but, as we shall see, the triumphant entry of over a hundred Gaullists into the new Assembly now made this formula almost unworkable. A brave attempt at decisive action—cutting through several tangled knots even at the price of great unpopularity—was to be made by Pierre Mendès-France: his seven-month government from June 1954 to January 1955 provided one of the more inspiring episodes of the Fourth Republic. After his realistic granting of independence to Morocco and Indo-China, and his controversial burial of the European Defence Community, the remaining governments of the Republic failed to show equal comprehension of the nature of the Algerian problem, a revolt within a territory which constitutionally formed part of France. The increasingly bloody war which raged in Algeria from 1954 onwards was to stir up the ferments of dissolution which brought the Republic to an end.

This, however, is to anticipate the story of events.

The 1950s began with France's imaginative gesture in putting forward the Schuman Plan, which was to lead within two years to a successful common market for the coal and steel industries of the Six. France's next proposal for an experiment in European integration—the European Defence Community —was to end abortively, with the acrimony it aroused not merely poisoning French political life, but nearly jeopardising the existence of the Coal and Steel Community.

The immediate cause of the European Defence Community proposal was the Korean War. When North Korea attacked southwards in June 1950, the American Administration feared this might be a prelude to further offensives, particularly in the other country divided into a Communist and a non-Communist state, Germany. The rearmament of West Germany, which had already been considered by the United States military authorities, now became a matter of urgent priority for Washington, and in

September 1950 this policy was formally pressed by Secretary of State Acheson on his British and French colleagues, Bevin and Bidault. The French government, whose Prime Minister from July 1950 to March 1951 was René Pleven, responded with pre-dictable alarm to the suggestion of a new West German army. Germany's industrial power had already been substantially built up with American aid and guidance, at a time when France, despite the Marshall Plan, was relatively stagnant: the prospect of this industrial power supporting German armed forces—even though these were to defend France as well as her allies against a threat from the Soviet Union—was very hard for Frenchmen to accept a mere five years after the war's end. Pleven and his col-leagues, faced with irresistible American pressure to let Germany contribute to the West's military strength, devised an ingenious compromise: in October, Pleven proposed a European Defence Community, along the lines of the Coal and Steel Community, in which German units would be integrated with those of France and the other member states: thus Germany would have no General Staff of her own, and could never use her army inde-pendently. This proposal—which meant, according to one critic, that Germany would produce armed forces strong enough to help deter the Red Army, but not strong enough to outweigh the much smaller French Army!—was to collapse four years later, partly because Britain refused the French invitation to join, and partly because French political opinion itself turned against it. In 1950, however, the plan seemed to provide a posi-tive solution to the problem of getting West Germany rearmed without frightening her allies, and it was discussed in detail by the whole Western alliance.

The domination of French political life in 1950-51 by this issue of external relations was symptomatic. It illustrated the ex-tent to which French governments, at the same time as battling with their domestic problems of monetary inflation, industrial backwardness or educational reform, felt their country exposed to humiliating pressures from the outside world. The increasingly costly war in Indo-China, which by 1951 was beginning to swallow up the best units of the French army, was another example of the same phenomenon. It was also—in that it tied up so much of France's military strength on the other side of the globe and left her weak in the European balance—a further

reason why French opinion was unwilling to accept the rebuilding of Germany's armed forces, even in the form of the EDC.

The 1951 elections: the ungovernable parliament

In this atmosphere of domestic stagnation and looming international pressures, the French people went to the polls to elect
their second post-war parliament on June 1951. The resulting
assembly was composed in such a way as to guarantee permanent
instability: the 627 members were divided into six blocks of
roughly equal size, each of whom disagreed with the others on
several important aspects of policy.

The basic issues in French politics at this time could be outlined as follows. Firstly, should the policy of nationalisation of
industry, begun by the Communist-Socialist-MRP coalition after
the war, be continued? Secondly, should Catholic schools outside the state educational system be subsidised from public
funds (this hoary issue, going back to the early years of the Third
Republic, was now revived, partly as a device by the Gaullists
to split the Catholic MRP from the 'lay' Socialist Party)?
Thirdly, should France pursue a 'European' foreign policy,
including not only the Western alliance with America, but also
economic and military integration with Germany? Fourthly,
should the war to keep Indo-China within the French colonial
domain continue? And lastly—a fundamental issue which under-
lay all the more immediate ones—should the Fourth Republic
which barely a third of the voters had approved in 1946, continue, or should it be revolutionised along either Communist
or Gaullist lines?

On each of these issues the line-up between the six blocks in
the new Assembly was different. To start from the left, the Communists (103 seats: leaders Duclos and Thorez) fundamentally
opposed the Republican régime as such, argued in favour of the
nationalisation of private industry, opposed state aid for church
schools and opposed both European integration and the war in
Indo-China.

The group to their right, the 107-strong Socialist Party led
by Guy Mollet, agreed with the Communists in standing for
nationalisation and opposing church schools and the Indo-
Chinese war (at least in principle), but it had divided views on
European integration, and differed sharply from the Communists

in that it supported the institutions of the Fourth Republic.

The next party rightwards, the Catholic MRP of Schuman and Bidault (86 seats), naturally supported church schools and was also actively pro-European and committed to colonial rule in Indo-China. It still agreed with the Communists and the Socialists in supporting a socialist-inspired economic policy (at least in principle) but it was with the Socialists and *against* the Communists in supporting Republican institutions.

The Radical Party and its allies, who had now gained a parliamentary strength of 94 (their leaders included René Mayer and Pierre Mendès-France) also supported the Republic and the war in Indo-China, as well as siding with the Socialists and Communists on the church school issue, but they believed firmly in economic free enterprise, and contained a broad span of views on European integration.

The Republican Independent Party (Conservatives or ' classical right ') led by Antoine Pinay and Joseph Laniel and numbering 96, supported the Fourth Republic and capitalist economics, as well as a ' European ' foreign policy and the war in Indo-China; on the school issue they sided with the MRP, whose views on some of the other issues were of course different.

The sixth group, on the right of the Assembly, was the Gaullist RPF (121 members) led by Jacques Soustelle and Senator Michel Debré, which in fact insisted that it was *not* a right-wing party but a spokesman of social progress, and was thus given seats behind the Independents rather than to their right. The RPF of course, followed de Gaulle in preaching all-out opposition to the Fourth Republic as such and also differed from the Independents in opposing European integration, which Debré described as entailing ' the dissolution of France '. (On these two fundamental issues the RPF was thus aligned, paradoxically, with the Communists.) On the economic, educational and colonial issues, however, the RPF sided with the Independents against the more left-wing parties.

This very confused situation could be represented in tabular, form, as follows:

Party	Seats	Support for the régime	Socialist Economic Policy	Opposition to RC Schools	Support for 'European' Foreign Policy	Support for War in Indo-China
Communists	103		x	x		
Socialists (SFIO)	107	x	x	x	x	
Christian Democrats (MRP)	86	x	x		x	x
Radicals & allies	94	x		x		x
Independents ('Classical right')	96	x			x	x
Gaullists (RFP)	121					x

(A cross indicates support for the policy indicated at the top of each column)

It will be seen that a stable coalition, agreeing on how to deal with a range of separate issues simultaneously, or even one after another, was out of the question. Any coalition for a start, had to include at least three of the six groups, plus if possible a few deserters from one or more of the others. The opposition of the Gaullists and Communists to the entire régime ruled them out as partners in any coalition, so that a government had to be based on a combination of three of the remaining four groups: however, the differences between these groups, according to which issue was dominant, made durable coalitions impossible.

For instance, a government based on the Socialists, MRP and Independents might have agreed (though with some difficulty) in pursuing a 'European' foreign policy, but when the Catholic school issue arose the MRP and Independents would at once find themselves on one side, and the Socialists on the other—sharing now the views of the Radicals and Communists.

On this issue, Socialists and Radicals might have agreed on a policy—at least the negative one of blocking state aid to church schools—but as the Communists were ineligible for governmental office because of their opposition to the régime, no workable coalition was possible. Again, the Radicals, MRP and Independents might agree on supporting the war in Indo-China, but would split apart on the issues of Europe, economics or education.

This very schematic representation, of course, is somewhat removed from the way the system actually functioned. The parties did not in fact adhere rigidly to the programmes they had presented to the electors: for instance, the SFIO and MRP, in practice, forswore their commitment to socialist economics when they joined coalitions to their right, and the MRP in fact became a distinctly right-wing party in the course of the 1951 parliament. Again, the Socialists accepted a compromise on the church school issue, which allowed a centre-right coalition to continue in office with their support. A further factor mitigating the apparent clash between six homogeneous blocks was that each of them was in fact severely divided internally: the Socialist party split almost exactly in half on the question of German rearmament; the Radicals tended to split their votes on almost any major issue; and even in the ranks of the Gaullist group party discipline turned out to be scarcely stronger than in the more traditional parties, and within two years of the election some of them had betrayed their nominal principles by going so far as to accept ministerial office—to the disgust of the RPF's outraged founder, General de Gaulle.

René Pleven, the author of the ill-fated plan for a European army, continued as Prime Minister (with a brief interlude when he was replaced by Henri Queuille) until January 1952. France was then governed—after a short-lived coalition led by another Radical, Edgar Faure, whose political career (as we shall see) was to be brilliant and fascinatingly varied—by a series of cabinets of markedly right-wing orientation.

Antoine Pinay, Prime Minister from March 1952 to January 1953, was a traditional conservative: the head of a small family tanning business, he was a provincial bourgeois whose ultra-orthodox views on financial policy reassured the French middle class that the post-war era of socialistic experiments was over, and helped to stimulate the flow of private investment.

René Mayer (January to June 1953) belonged to a rich Jewish family, and symbolised a different kind of commercial interest from Pinay's: the large banking and heavy industrial activities of a more modern French *bourgeoisie*. Although the Radical Party, to which Mayer belonged, was on the whole sceptical of European integration—on the grounds that German competition would be too much for the more backward industrial structure of France—Mayer's own experience in the more modern sector of the French economy, together with his political connections, allowed him to accept the presidency of the Coal and Steel Community's High Authority after he left office as Prime Minister.

When Mayer's government fell—the specific pretext which the Assembly found to overthrow one government after another need not detain us—he was replaced by Joseph Laniel, another rich industrialist with an unshakeable belief in the divine right of capitalist enterprise, who remained in power for exactly a year, until June 1954. It was in fact during the formation of the Laniel government that several Gaullist parliamentarians broke their vows of all-out opposition to the Fourth Republic, and became members of the cabinet. One consequence of this was that the Laniel government was much more lukewarm in its support of European integration—notably the EDC proposal—than those of Pleven and Pinay; this confirmed a trend already indicated in January 1953 by Mayer, who had dropped the ardent 'European', Robert Schuman, as Foreign Minister, bringing back to the Quai d'Orsay Georges Bidault, a man much less committed to European integration than to the Atlantic Alliance, and even influenced by the lingering hope of an understanding with the Soviet Union.

The right-wing governments of 1951 to 1954—on the whole tolerated by the Socialists, who thus earned savage attacks from the Communists—gave France a certain degree of stability and the promise of a slow but sure increase in prosperity. There were, however, occasions when the working class, disappointed at the way the social revolution anticipated at the Liberation had run into the sands, exploded in strike movements reminiscent of those of 1947-48. The largest of these explosions occurred in the summer of 1953, when four million workers in industry and in the transport and postal services went on strike for nearly six weeks and the entire life of the country was paralysed.

The Laniel government, forced to make concessions to appease the strikers, was placed in a weaker position to deal with the international pressures which showed no signs of relenting. The treaty establishing the European Defence Community had been signed, under considerable American pressure, in May 1952, but the various governments of France had hesitated to seek parliamentary ratification for it: the Assembly of 1951, with its large Communist and Gaullist contingents, was not at all certain to approve the Treaty, and the Laniel-Bidault government attempted to sweeten the pill by getting their allies to accept a settlement of the Saar issue in France's favour as the price of French agreement to the EDC Treaty which she had originally proposed. Germany and the other allies were naturally not very well-disposed to this line of argument, and France was isolated and weak in dealing with her European partners.

In relation to Indo-China, her situation was if anything weaker. The Vietminh nationalist forces under Ho Chi Minh were winning, and the war was sucking in and destroying the cream of the French army: the equivalent of a whole year's graduating class from St Cyr (the French Sandhurst or West Point) was being killed each year, and large amounts of American aid and equipment were also being used up. This in itself increased America's leverage in pressing France to accept German re-armament, the more so as the Indo-Chinese war was increasingly unpopular in France itself: the Laniel cabinet went through agonising debates about whether to reinforce the French army by sending conscripts to Indo-China, before deciding that this would be politically disastrous *vis-à-vis* the French public, who were profoundly unenthusiastic about the war their army was fighting on the other side of the world.

When the French army suffered its crushing defeat at the siege of a fort called Dien Bien Phu—ironically, this occurred just before 8 May 1954, when the streets of Paris were decked with tricolour flags to celebrate the victory of 1945—the public mood combined humiliation and relief at the realisation that the war must now be regarded as virtually over. The Laniel government shook and fell, and France turned to a political leader who had been an outsider since his resignation in 1945, Pierre Mendès-France.

Mendès-France and the defeat of EDC: 1954
Pierre Mendès-France, who became Prime Minister on 18 June 1954, was a Radical politician who had been a junior minister

in Blum's government in 1936 and had had a distinguished record in the Second World War. He had resigned from de Gaulle's government in 1945 because he regarded the policy of the General's Finance Minister—who was, incidentally, René Pleven—as insufficiently rigorous to help France's economic recovery. Since 1945, Mendès-France had been a political outsider—in a way, like General de Gaulle himself—though he had remained in parliament, and had even come near to forming a government in 1953. A year later, with a desperate situation in Indo-China—Dien Bien Phu had fallen and the United States refused to save the situation by using atomic bombs against the Vietminh as Georges Bidault requested—the country turned to Mendès-France to salvage what he could. In an austere speech outlining his programme to a hushed National Assembly, Mendès-France promised to conclude the Indo-China peace negotiations —already in progress in Geneva—within a month. The agreement was in fact signed by 21 July: it provided for a partition of Vietnam (described as temporary, though reunification had still not occurred by the early 1970s) and for the independence of the other Indo-Chinese states of Laos and Cambodia. Mendès-France was inevitably accused of betraying France's national interests, but he had included a number of Gaullists in his government—among them such impeccable patriots as General Koenig, the Minister of Defence—and they were able to confirm that the settlement was the best France could now hope for.

Mendès-France also incurred the wrath of the French right for giving independence to the protectorate of Morocco (as well as some ridicule for his policy of encouraging the French to drink more milk and less alcohol), but the most controversial act of his Prime Ministership was the way he disposed of the European Defence Community.

He found a state of affairs in which France's allies were pressing insistently for ratification of the treaty; the French parliament was almost certain to reject it (for this reason the previous governments had failed to submit the treaty for ratification); and he had only been able to form a government capable of dealing with the desperate problem of Indo-China by including Gaullists who were anti-EDC as well as other politicians who favoured it. After a series of attempts to modify the treaty so that the French army would no longer be subject to supra-national authority, and a final bid to get the British government to change its mind and join the EDC (these efforts were energetically pursued during August, and both were unsuccessful), Mendès-France submitted the treaty to Parliament on 30 August 1954. The whole cabinet, by agreement, abstained from voting, and the treaty was defeated by 319 votes to 264, to the accompaniment of jubilant singing of the *Marseillaise* by the Communist left and the Gaullist right. Mendès-France was violently criticised—especially by the MRP and the 'European' wing of the Socialists —for refusing to take a stand for or against ratification. The fact was, however, that his cabinet itself was divided, and if it was to stay in office and tackle its heavy agenda of urgent problems—including the demand for independence from Tunisia—the course of abstention was the only one open to it. There were several precedents for a French cabinet abstaining in a parliamentary vote—the 1951 law providing state aid for church schools was one of them—and Mendès-France could also argue that he had at least brought the EDC issue to Parliament for a decision, unlike his predecessors.

One incidental result of the defeat of EDC was that the related project for a European Political Community was also destroyed (see Chapter 9 below). The immediate issue of how West Germany was to be rearmed was, however, resolved by a burst of diplomatic energy in September, when Mendès-France, Eden and Dulles between them devised a scheme for Germany's membership of NATO, including her participation in a strengthened Western European Union. Mendès-France won parliamentary approval for this agreement in December 1954—the opposition to EDC had been only partly to German rearmament, and rather more to the loss of French sovereignty implied by EDC—and a profound source of rancour had been removed from French political life.

The manner in which Mendès-France had dealt with a number of issues had, however, won him numerous enemies and his government was overthrown in February 1955. His successor was Edgar Faure, another Radical who was a long-standing personal friend of Mendès-France (the latter had even accompanied Faure and his bride on their honeymoon trip to the USSR in 1932!), but whose capacity for political manoeuvring lived up to the worst traditions of the Radical Party. In 1952, Faure, at 43, had made history by becoming France's youngest Prime Minister since 1881, and although his government had fallen after 40 days, his political career had continued to flourish. Equally at home as Finance Minister in a government of the right (Laniel) or of the left (Mendès-France), Faure now stepped into his friend's place as Prime Minister, and remained in office until the end of 1955.

Faure presided over the granting of independence to Tunisia, and was then faced with the mounting tide of nationalism in Algeria, where armed revolt had started in November 1954. At the United Nations Assembly in the autumn of 1955 Pinay, Faure's Foreign Minister, took the unprecedented step of walking out of the hall in protest against the UN Assembly's discussion of the problem since, legally, Algeria was part of French territory and therefore still a purely domestic problem: within a few years, France would have to face the fact that Algeria was a nation with the same claim to independence as Indo-China, Morocco and Tunisia.

The 1956 election: Mollet and Algeria

A parliamentary defeat of Faure's government in late 1955 provided the occasion for a general election, which was held on 2 January 1956. The resulting Assembly looked ominously unwieldy, though in a somewhat different way from its predecessor. The Communist strength had grown from 98 (at the end of the previous Assembly) to 150; the centre parties all showed a slight decline (the Socialists from 104 to 96, the MRP from 87 to 73, the Radicals and their allies from 99 to 91); the conservative Independents and Gaullists—both now split into several groups—lost heavily; and a strange new party, holding 52 seats, made its appearance on the far right. These were the Poujadistes, named after their leader Pierre Poujade, a village shopkeeper who represented a protest movement of the dying class of artisans and small tradesmen of France's underdeveloped regions against the encroachments of modern commerce and industrialisation. This 'revolt in the desert' (as the brilliant Swiss observer Herbert Luethy described it) was short-lived as a political movement, but its electoral success in 1956, combined with the 50 per cent increase in the protest vote given to the Communists (now 150 strong) helped to condemn the new Assembly to the same degree of futility as the old.

The new government was a centre-left coalition under Guy Mollet, a former schoolmaster and General Secretary of the Socialist Party, which had emerged from the elections as the largest party except the Communists. Mollet had the support of the Radicals and the MRP as well as of his own party, and his government, unexpectedly, was the longest-lived of the Fourth Republic, surviving until June 1957. Mendès-France joined the cabinet as Vice-Premier, but resigned after four months in opposition to Mollet's policy of repressing the Algerian nationalist movement. Algeria, as we shall see, was eventually to bring about the death of the Fourth Republic. The passions involved in this problem were made clear to Mollet when he visited Algiers shortly after taking office, and was greeted with a hail of tomatoes and other missiles from the white minority of the population. He rightly took this as a warning not to proceed with the plan for Algerian independence at which he had hinted during the election campaign: instead, he intensified military repression in Algeria and increased the strength of the French army there. The slogan of ' Algérie française ', which Mollet and the French left had repudiated in opposition, became their own once they were in power.

The Mollet government carried out some necessary reforms in France—including an increase in social security benefits and in the annual paid holiday for industrial workers from two weeks to three—and it also took a vital step forward in European integration by negotiating the Treaty of Rome, which it signed in March 1957. The Coal and Steel Community had by now succeeded in uniting Western Europe's markets for coal and steel into one, and the movement towards more comprehensive European integration had been given fresh impetus by the Messina Conference of June 1955 (see Chapter 9 below).

France, like the other members of the Six, continued to be aware of the difficulty of achieving economic progress within a purely national framework, and Guy Mollet—who had always been a convinced members of the ' European ' wing of the Socialist Party—contributed actively to carrying the recommendations of the Messina Conference forward to the signing of the Rome Treaty.

Mollet's government was defeated shortly afterwards, and in June 1957 he was replaced by Maurice Bourgès-Maunoury, a

Radical leader who held office for only four months. He in turn
gave way to another Radical, Félix Gaillard, but the intervening crises became longer and more ominous. Between Mollet's
fall in May 1957, and the revolt in Algiers twelve months later,
France was without a government for a total of 86 days. The
root of the trouble—apart from the difficulty of constructing a
majority in the Assembly as it stood—was the Algerian war.
Bourgès-Maunoury was thrown out of office in September 1957
because he had put forward a 'framework-law' envisaging Algerian autonomy; in February 1958 Gaillard was forced to condone
the French Air Force's bombing of the Tunisian village of
Sakhiet, in retaliation for Tunisia's support for the Algerian
nationalists; and on 13 May, when it seemed that Algerian independence was again being considered in Paris, the French army
in Algeria revolted against the Gaillard government, and the final
crisis of the Fourth Republic was unleashed.

De Gaulle's return: the end of the Fourth Republic
The crisis of May 1958 was not like the earlier ones: as well as
the parliamentary tumult in the Palais Bourbon—where the
MRP leader Pierre Pflimlin was hastily voted into office to replace
Gaillard—there were noises of military insubordination from
across the Mediterranean. The army command in Algiers made
it clear that they would not obey the orders of any Paris government which undermined the four-year effort of the army in
Algeria by granting independence to the nationalist movement.
When Pflimlin persisted in affirming his intention of considering this step, army units occupied Corsica, which looked like
the prelude to an invasion of metropolitan France. There appeared to be little doubt that any serious resistance by the Paris
government would lead to civil war. In this tense situation eyes
began to turn to the village of Colombey-les-deux-Eglises, where
General de Gaulle had retired after his resignation in 1946. The
General, of course, had by no means contented himself with
passively waiting for the Fourth Republic to collapse from its
internal contradictions. The period of militant RPF propaganda
from 1947 onwards had, it is true, been followed by an abrupt
disavowal of the movement when some of its leaders sullied
themselves by joining the government in 1953; but even then,
the General had regularly visited his office in Paris, maintaining

H

contact with political circles, and keeping the way open for a return to power at the right moment.

In May 1958 the moment had come: after some days of hectic consultations between the General, René Coty (Auriol's successor as President of the Republic) and other political and military leaders, de Gaulle appeared before the National Assembly on 1 June, and was invested as Prime Minister by 329 votes to 224. He thus became the last Prime Minister of the Fourth Republic, but was clearly empowered to replace it by a Fifth. It was evident that he had the backing of very broad sections of French opinion: as well as having the support of the army and the European population in Algeria—whose revolt against Paris had brought him to power—he was flanked in his new government not only by Gaullist politicians like Debré but also by men from the non-Gaullist parties—Pflimlin and Pinay among them.

The Fourth Republic had represented a brave attempt at a new start for France in the post-war world. Its attempt to superimpose a new and socially progressive system on to an essentially conservative country appeared, by 1958, to have failed: the legacy of the past, and the external pressures which no other contemporary European state had had to face, appeared to have been too heavy. In retrospect, however, it became clear that the discredited Fourth Republic had laid the foundations for a more modern France—for instance, by its planning of industrial investment—and that its ' opening-up ' of France to Europe through the Schuman Plan and the Treaty of Rome had provided the right answers to many of the country's problems. In 1958 it remained to be seen whether a Fifth Republic, based on the now-familiar principles of Gaullism, could do any better.

7 Adenauer's Germany

'Bonn is not Weimar': the political system
The Federal Republic, whose capital was established in the provincial town of Bonn in 1949, was very different from the Republic whose constitution had been drawn up in Weimar 30 years earlier. As we have seen, the political stability of Bonn was in marked contrast to the turbulence of Weimar: this was symbolised by the simple fact that the first Chancellor of the Federal Republic, Konrad Adenauer, stayed in office continuously from 1949 to 1963—longer than the entire life-span of the Weimar Republic which had seen more than 20 cabinets come and go.

This striking contrast was certainly due in some degree to the personal prestige of Adenauer, who exercised a remarkable ascendancy over his political colleagues and rivals. He was, however, helped by a constitutional system deliberately designed to limit political instability. Whereas the Weimar constitution had provided for an elaborate system of mathematically exact proportional representation, which resulted in a proliferation of as many as 37 political parties, the Bonn constitution took careful steps to avoid this. Not only did a party have to win five per cent of the votes to get any seats in the Bundestag at all; the system of proportional representation was also modified by an electoral law combining a proportional element with single-member constituencies. The result was that German voters concentrated their support on a small number of large and well-organised parties: the political spectrum of Bonn developed in a much more orderly way than that of either Weimar or the Third or Fourth Republics of France.

At the first Federal election of 1949 the proportion of votes going to the two major parties—Christian Democrats and Social Democrats—was just over 60 per cent; in the following elections of 1953, 1957 and 1961 their joint share of the vote rose respectively to 74, 81 and 81.6 per cent. The only other party of any substance, the Free Democratic Party, normally gained between seven and 13 per cent of the votes, so that the Federal Republic was virtually a three-party system. It is true that a scattering of smaller parties obtained a total of 22 per cent of the votes in the 1949 election, and the Refugee Party of Germans expelled from the East got six per cent of the votes in 1953, but no party except the three leading ones was represented in the Bundestag after 1961.

The Christian Democratic Union and its Bavarian ally, the Christian Social Union, held 139 seats out of 402 in the 1949 parliament. The party led by Adenauer, as we have seen (Chapter 4), originally represented a broad span of social and economic viewpoints, including a Catholic trade union wing of some militancy, but it soon became associated with industrial interests, and its prevailing policy was well to the right. After the excessive political party battles of the Weimar Republic and the catastrophic extremism of the Third Reich, most Germans were content to concentrate on rebuilding the material fortunes of their shattered country, and gave their support to the reassuring father-figure of Dr Adenauer, rather than to the politicians of the left who called for new experiments in socialism.

It is true that in some ways the Germans *were* prepared to experiment once their new Republic was established: for instance, the principle of co-determination in industry, whereby the workers could elect representatives to the boards of their firms, was widely developed under one of the first laws passed by the new parliament. (This, like so much of German political practice at the time, represented an attempt to avoid the errors of the past: part of the case for co-determination was that certain industrialists had helped Hitler into power by supporting him financially, and it was argued that the new system would prevent any similar misuse of private wealth in future.)

In general, the Germans did not allow themselves to be distracted by political issues from the enormous task of economic reconstruction, which was to make Germany the dominant industrial power of Western Europe by the end of the 1950s. Under the free-enterprise economics of Ludwig Erhard their standard of living rose rapidly.

This material prosperity made life difficult politically for the opposition Social Democratic Party since Adenauer could always, at election times, win support with the simple slogan of 'no experiments'. The SPD in the early post-war period was still strongly dominated by its Marxist past and took a number of years to evolve towards a more flexible view on economic policy.

There could hardly have been a greater contrast than that between the two party leaders who confronted each other in the first Federal Parliament. Konrad Adenauer was a Roman Catholic Rhinelander with a deep distaste for everything connected with Berlin, Prussia and the east (the Rhineland had been governed as part of Prussia during his political career before 1933): this meant that he was hostile towards both Socialism and Communism, and was more favourably inclined towards France and Western European integration. His manner was dry and authoritarian, and he was clearly exasperated by the vociferous and even demagogic style of the Opposition leader, Kurt Schumacher. Schumacher, who had a Protestant background and came originally from East Prussia, was a man of lively temperament and burning political passion, made all the more bitter by his personal experiences. After losing an arm as an officer in the First World War, he had begun a political career as one of the younger Social Democratic members of the Reichstag in the 1920s. He had in fact crossed swords with Goebbels and other Nazis in a number of tumultuous debates—he once denounced Nazism as 'an appeal to the inner beast (*Schweinehund*) in mankind '—and was imprisoned by the Nazis as soon as they came to power. He spent the twelve years of Nazi rule in a concentration camp, from which he emerged in such poor health that one leg had to be amputated. Schumacher was passionately convinced that Adenauer's policy of leading West Germany into intimate alliance with the West was blocking any hope of the country's reunification, and was determined that the left should not be charged, as it had been in the 1920s, with betraying Germany's national interests. On the contrary, he vehemently opposed any sign that Adenauer was abandoning these interests—whether by allowing France to occupy the Saar or by accepting Soviet occupation of the eastern territories—and in an explosion against Adenauer in the Bundestag denounced him as ' the Chancellor of the Allies '. (For this attack Schumacher was punished by several days' suspension from attending parliament, and his action hardly helped the public standing of his party.)

Schumacher died in 1952, and the SPD under his successor—the worthy but uninspiring party official Erich Ollenhauer—stood very little chance against Adenauer and the CDU. At the 1953 election, the CDU increased its share of the votes from 31 to 45.2

per cent, and the SPD's share fell from just over 29 per cent to just under that figure.

Adenauer's position was greatly strengthened (in 1957 he was to do even better, winning 50.2 per cent of the votes, so that the CDU was able to govern without forming a coalition with the Free Democrats) and the demoralised SPD Opposition, though it obtained 31.8 per cent of the votes—just over the 'magic hurdle' of 30 per cent—went through a considerable shake-up. They were helped in developing a new programme and a new leadership by the fact that West Germany was organised as a federal state, with real powers remaining in the hands of a dozen provincial (or *Land*) governments. This meant that, although the SPD under Schumacher and Ollenhauer at the Federal level appeared condemned to doctrinaire and sterile opposition, the party also contained a group of able political leaders who were gaining valuable experience by exercising power locally. Even though Schumacher and Ollenhauer never became Ministers, their attitude was counterbalanced by the so-called 'Lord Mayors' wing' of the party: men like Ernst Reuter, Wilhelm Kaisen, and Heinrich Braüer, the Lord Mayors of Berlin, Bremen and Hamburg respectively. These were all men of considerable stature, who administered their cities successfully for several years—in the case of Kaisen, for two decades. They were backed by a group of younger politicians—Willy Brandt and Karl Schiller in Berlin, Helmut Schmidt in Hamburg, and others—who joined them in pressing the SPD to adopt a more moderate attitude.

Under these influences, the SPD was, as we shall see, to change its leadership and policies very considerably by the later 1950s.

In the meantime, there were stormy battles over Adenauer's policy of strengthening the Federal Republic's ties with the West. While the Federal government put up stone or brick buildings of a more and more solid kind in Bonn—giving the town the air of a permanent capital—the SPD firmly kept its headquarters in a wooden hut on the edge of the town, symbolising a refusal to regard Bonn as anything but a preliminary staging-post on the road to a reunited Germany centred once more on Berlin.

The SPD's hopes of reunification—certainly shared by quite large sections of the German public—were kept alive by the action of the Russians in making tempting offers of reunification (at least, offers which seemed tempting), notably in 1952 and 1955.

The 'German problem' 1950-55: the 'missed opportunities'
As we have seen, Konrad Adenauer's early moves in foreign policy were directed entirely towards the West: the very creation of the Federal Republic was accomplished by agreement with the Western Powers in defiance of Soviet hostility, and the new state took her place in the organisations of Western Europe, OEEC and the Council of Europe. The next stage was the Coal and Steel Community resulting from the Schuman Plan: Germany was very pleased to accept the new arrangement under which France, Italy and Benelux were subject to the same degree of supra-national control as she was, and Adenauer became an active apostle of Germany's commitment to the West. His attitude revealed a mixture of national and 'European' interests. On the one hand, there was no doubt that European integration offered Germany a way back towards equality of status and the recognition of her national claims; on the other hand, Adenauer was convinced that the aberrations of German policy between the wars—the Rapallo Treaty of 1922 with Russia, and the scarcely believable atrocities of Hitler—had been due to Germany's isolated position in the middle of an unstable and divided European power system, and he wished to protect the Germans against any temptation to repeat these excesses by replacing the Europe of nation-states by an integrated super-state in which West Germany would be firmly anchored. When the Opposition under Schumacher objected that this was the short-sighted action of a Catholic Rhinelander, putting the interests of a West German 'part-state' before those of the German nation as a whole, Adenauer retorted that reunification as preached by Schumacher could only be had on Soviet terms. These would imply either Germany's subjection to the Soviet Union or her neutralisation between East and West: either of these situations opened up risks that were anathema to Adenauer, and he proceeded unremittingly with his aim of embedding West Germany in the Western world—in the meantime warding off criticism by the neutral (and perhaps sincerely-meant) argument that 'negotiation from strength' offered the only hope of persuading the Russians to allow German reunification on acceptable terms.

West Germany thus became a leading member of the European Coal and Steel Community; the American demand for German rearmament, which followed the outbreak of the Korean War in June 1950, provided the next occasion for her status in the Western world to be brought level with that of her allies.

Although Allied ' re-education ' of Germany after the war had tried hard to remove all thoughts of militarism from the Germans, and any thought of rearmament was far from the minds of those who established the Federal Republic, the onset of the Cold War from 1947 onwards made the United States army command look eagerly towards the possibility of recruiting German military manpower by the end of 1949. At the same time—a mere three months after taking office as Chancellor—Dr Adenauer indicated the lines of the future political controversy by saying, in an interview with an American newspaper, that he would only consider the incorporation of Germany in the West's military strength on the basis of equality with her future allies.

In December 1949 such talk was purely hypothetical, like the American army's views on the desirability of recruiting expert German manpower. The Korean War created a totally new situation, in which the planners setting up the North Atlantic Treaty Organisation (the Treaty itself had been signed in April 1949) began to reckon with an imminent Soviet attack driving them back to the Atlantic coast in a matter of days. The Administration in Washington rapidly decided that a West German contribution to NATO's strength was essential, and it was in September 1950 that Dean Acheson, the Secretary of State, pressed this view on Bevin and Bidault. As we have seen, France responded in October by proposing the Pleven Plan, a military counterpart to the Schuman Plan, providing for an integrated European Defence Community or European army.

Germany's response was very mixed. Predictably, a large section of opinion opposed rearmament in any form, for a variety of reasons: pacifists were opposed on principle; many democrats feared that any re-introduction of Germany military forces would endanger the new Bonn Republic as the Reichswehr had helped to undermine Weimar; business circles saw that a diversion of economic resources to military production might endanger the industrial recovery of the country; and the Social Democratic

Opposition under Schumacher argued violently that the Federal Republic's rearmament as part of the Western alliance would destroy any hope of reunification for ever. Faced with these complementary and powerful forces of opposition, Adenauer still stuck to his policy: in face of the Russian threat, he argued (and who could deny that the Russians had menaced West Berlin in 1948-49, after annexing Czechoslovakia and bullying Yugoslavia?), Germany's only hope of security—and one day, perhaps, of reunification—lay in negotiating from a position of Western strength to which she must now contribute. In his dealings with his American and other allies, however, Adenauer was able to point to the strength of German opposition to rearmament as a reason for arguing that Germany could only accept rearmament on terms which did not discriminate too obviously as between herself and other members of the alliance.

The treaties providing for a European Defence Community, within whose framework West Germany was to become a member of NATO, did in fact preclude any notion of an independent German General Staff: unlike France and the other states who signed the EDC treaty, West Germany was to place her forces—when these were raised—one hundred per cent under the integrated command structure. The EDC treaty was signed in May 1952 in Paris by the same six governments who were already linked in the Coal and Steel Community; Britain, while signing a complementary agreement providing for the Federal Republic to become a sovereign state, refused to join the EDC on the grounds of her responsibilities outside Europe. (This attempt to place herself in the category of the United States rather than alongside her European allies was perhaps understandable at the time, but represented an attitude which later British governments were to abandon.) Before signing the Paris Agreement in May 1952, the Western governments had to give their attention to an unexpected Soviet proposal on the future of Germany—the draft treaty put forward on 10 March. This treaty, together with an explanatory note sent a month later, urged the signing of a peace treaty with Germany as soon as possible, and even accepted in principle the Western demand that the government of a reunited Germany should be based on free elections. (It should be recalled that the war-time Council of Foreign Ministers had not met since 1947, when the Soviet and Western sides failed to agree on Germany; and that the Western position had ever since then demanded free elections as a first stage towards German reunification.) If this plan had been accepted there might have been some difficulties over who was to supervise the free elections—the Soviet Union refused to allow a United Nations commission to enter East Germany—but the main obstacle to agreement was the further Soviet condition that the reunited German state should be forbidden to join any pact or alliance. This would have created just the powerful German weight, neutral between East and West, which Adenauer and his Western allies agreed in regarding as intolerably risky for the future balance of power in Europe. They therefore rejected the Soviet proposal, arguing that its aim was the propagandist one of obstructing West Germany's rearmament and her recovery of partial sovereignty, and pressed ahead with the scheme for the European Defence Community. In September 1953, Adenauer's victory in the second West German election appeared to give him a clear mandate for this proposal. Three months earlier, on 17 June 1953, a mass uprising of the East German people—a rising which was crushed by Soviet tanks—had shown the unpopularity of the German Democratic Republic and the difficulty of reaching any agreement between the two German states. (It also incidentally showed that John Foster Dulles, Secretary of State in the newly-elected Eisenhower Administration, was not going to implement his pre-electoral threats of 'rolling back' Communism and 'liberating' Eastern Europe—Washington remained inactive—so that the West Germans had no real choice but to strengthen their own direct links with the United States.)

The Soviet proposals of 1952 were at least thoroughly discussed, and a conference between Foreign Minister Molotov and his Western counterparts was held in Berlin in early 1954. This resumption of East-West contacts at Foreign Minister level, after a break of seven years, symbolised a certain relaxation in the Cold War (the Korean armistice had been signed in mid-1953, and France's war in Indo-China was almost over), but the two sides were far from agreeing on Germany: the Western governments stuck to their intention of rearming West Germany, and the Soviet side maintained its view that Germany might be reunified, but must remain neutral between East and West.

Even the agreement between the same powers in May 1955 to

evacuate and neutralise Austria (which, like Germany, had been under four-power occupation for ten years) did not inspire the Western allies with any confidence that a similar solution for Germany—again suggested by the Russians—would be feasible: a neutralised Austria would hardly upset the East-West balance in Europe by moving to one side or the other, but a neutralised Germany would be a different mattter.

The French rejection of the European Defence Community in August 1954 was a setback to the plans of Adenauer and his allies, but a new set of agreements, bringing a rearmed West Germany into NATO and the Western European Union, was negotiated by the end of the year. This episode underlined the very close working partnership which had by now developed between Adenauer and Dulles.

In May 1955, ten years after the end of the war, West Germany was formally granted sovereign status by the Western allies (except for West Berlin, where they still kept their occupation rights and responsibilities), and became a member of NATO. Adenauer's policy had succeeded in its aim of giving Germany equal status with her allies—who also committed themselves to continuing to strive for German reunification on Western terms, i.e. the improbable combination of free elections leading to a reunified Germany free to remain within the Western alliance. The Soviet Union, recognising that the policy of neutralising Germany had failed, reacted by setting up the Warsaw Pact, in which East Germany was included, to counterbalance NATO.

The SPD changes course: the Bad Godesberg programme
Adenauer's success in using the circumstances of the Cold War to enhance West Germany's position (she also participated as an equal in the next stage of European integration, the Messina Conference of 1955, leading to the Treaty of Rome in March 1957) was rewarded by a further resounding electoral victory in September 1957: this time, as we have noted, the Christian Democrats won an absolute majority of seats in the Bundestag (with 50.2 per cent of the votes they held 270 out of 497 seats), and Adenauer was able to form a government without his troublesome allies, the Free Democratic Party. (The Free Democrats' vigorous leader, Thomas Dehler, had in fact embarrassed

Adenauer by calling for a more flexible policy towards the Soviet bloc, in a way foreshadowing the line of policy his successor Walter Scheel was to follow as Foreign Minister 15 years later.) Adenauer's domestic policy was clearly a vote-winner too—the 'economic miracle' connected with his Economics Minister Ludwig Erhard was making the Germans remarkably prosperous—and the opposition Social Democratic Party (despite a small increase in its own vote to 31.8 per cent) was forced to take serious note of its position. As we have seen, the party was divided between the national leadership, now represented by the doctrinaire and somewhat discredited Erich Ollenhauer, and the 'Lord Mayors' Wing' of men who had acquired a solid reputation as rulers of Germany's large cities and other *Länder*—and who, incidentally, had been much more favourable towards Adenauer's European policy than Schumacher and Ollenhauer. Within a short time of the 1957 defeat this more pragmatic wing of the SPD had taken control.

This was made clear by the new party programme, adopted after long debates at the Party Congress in Bad Godesberg in 1959. It threw out much of the radical Marxist phraseology of the earlier programme, replacing it with a clear commitment to a moderate policy of support for private enterprise, for precise but limited social reform proposals, and for the Christian Church (an important point in a country where religious and philosophical *Weltanschauungen* have often inflamed political arguments). This fairly drastic shift in the SPD's social and economic policy was followed in 1960 by a clear statement (from the party's spokesman Herbert Wehner) that in foreign policy as well the SPD would move nearer to the line already taken by the Adenauer government, in abandoning the hope of early reunification and accepting NATO and European integration.

In terms of personalities, the SPD went into the 1961 election with a new 'Chancellor candidate', the popular and dynamic Mayor of West Berlin, Willy Brandt, backed by an impressive Shadow Cabinet, including Fritz Erler, the spokesman on foreign policy (whose death in 1967 was to be a tragic setback at the time of his party's greatest success), the defence expert Helmut Schmidt (formerly Minister of the Interior of the State of Hamburg), Professor Karl Schiller, the Economics Minister of West Berlin, and several others who had made their names by successful administration of the large towns and states of the Federal Republic.

In electoral terms, as we shall see, this change of programme and leadership was to bring large rewards in the 1960s.

Adenauer and the West: the Hallstein Doctrine

In the meantime, Chancellor Adenauer successfully continued his policy of cementing Germany's links with the West. He did make certain gestures towards the East, partly with the aim of silencing critics who accused him of neglecting possibilities of negotiation with the Soviet Union. In September 1955, for instance, he went so far as to visit Moscow. The general East-West climate now seemed more relaxed, after the Geneva summit conference of that summer; in the more limited German context, Adenauer had now achieved his immediate aim of bringing West Germany securely into NATO. The visit had some real benefits for Germany (as well as allowing the Chancellor to argue that he was neglecting no opportunity to talk with the Soviet leadership); it led to the repatriation of several thousand German prisoners-of-war who had remained in captivity in the Soviet Union ever since the war. It also—by establishing diplomatic relations between Bonn and Moscow—led to the curious anomaly that West Germany exchanged ambassadors with a state which recognised East Germany—a practice incompatible, in theory, with a fundamental principle of Adenauer's foreign policy. Bonn naturally refused to recognise the East German régime—a state based on Soviet military force rather than democratic consent—and any state which recognised the East German régime had normally to pay the price of forgoing diplomatic relations with Bonn. This principle—known as the 'Hallstein Doctrine' after the Permanent Under-Secretary of the West German Foreign Ministry at the time—was evolved in 1956-57 with reference to the case of Yugoslavia. West Germany had recognised Yugoslavia in 1955, partly at the insistence of the Free Democrats (one of whose leaders, Karl-Heinz Pfleiderer, became Ambassador in Belgrade), but as Marshal Tito's relations with the Soviet Union improved his country re-established relations with Moscow's allies, including East Germany. This faced Bonn with the possible problem of apparently continuing to deal with a government which recognised the two German states as equals: the West

German answer, under the terms of the Hallstein Doctrine, was to break off diplomatic relations with Yugoslavia. This refusal by Bonn to engage in an active diplomatic dialogue with her Eastern neighbours—Adenauer's exception in favour of the Soviet Union was justified on the sensible grounds of the country's importance in German affairs—was very much criticised in Germany and abroad as evidence of a dogmatic unwillingness to look beyond the Cold War to a more relaxed system of East-West relations.

Adenauer's foreign policy certainly concentrated on the West—on Germany's rearmament in NATO and the further development of European integration through the Treaty of Rome—and he showed great hostility towards a number of suggestions made at this time for the reduction of armed forces by NATO and the Warsaw Pact. To every one of these suggestions—whether it was hinted at by the British Prime Minister, Sir Anthony Eden, or put forward by the Polish Foreign Secretary Adam Rapacki, the British Opposition leader Hugh Gaitskell or the American ex-diplomat George Kennan—Adenauer responded with the blunt view that *real détente* in Europe was only possible after German reunification. He argued that agreements on arms limitation *before* reunification would only strengthen the Soviet position and perpetuate a European situation which West Germany found unacceptable if not intolerable.

The Berlin crisis from Khrushchev's ultimatum to the building of the Wall 1958-61

The intransigent attitude of Adenauer towards East-West negotiations which tacitly or explicitly accepted the territorial *status quo* (Germany's division) was seriously shaken by the Berlin crisis which began in 1958 with an ultimatum from the Soviet leader Nikita Khrushchev. His speech of 10 November 1958, followed by further Soviet statements, made in essence three demands. Firstly, the Potsdam Agreement of 1945, giving the Western allies the right to keep troops in West Berlin, should now be regarded as obsolete and the Soviet Union would no longer accept the presence of these forces. Secondly, the future status of West Berlin, and German affairs in general, should be discussed no longer between the former occupying powers but between the two German governments of East Berlin and Bonn.

Thirdly, if the Western allies failed to reply to these demands within six months the Soviet Union would unilaterally sign a peace treaty with East Germany (though both the Soviet Union and the Western powers had made agreements with their respective German allies, no formal peace treaty had yet been signed), which would, among other things, hand over control of access to West Berlin to the East German government. All these demands were judged unacceptable by Bonn and her Western allies. The same applied to a series of further Soviet demands and proposals—including the notion that West Berlin should become a ' free city ' totally severed from the Federal Republic—and the tension between West and East rose seriously.

The situation in 1958 was in many ways different from that of 1948-49, when the first Berlin crisis had rapidly created a solid Western front and expedited the creation of the Federal Republic as a Western ally. In 1958 the threat of all-out war was taken more seriously by the United States and Britain—the Soviet Union had demonstrated by sending the Sputnik rocket into orbit in 1957 that she was in some ways equal to the United States in missile technology—and Washington and London were correspondingly cautious in their handling of the crisis. They were in fact quite firm in their basic refusal to negotiate under the pressure of Mr Khrushchev's six-month ultimatum—which was first prolonged, then forgotten—but their apparent readiness to consider some of the Soviet proposals at all led to serious concern on the part of Bonn. Even Dulles, the erstwhile close partner and confidant of Adenauer, earned the latter's horrified disapproval by a couple of injudicious remarks at press conferences: first in November 1958, when his immediate reaction to Khrushchev's demand was to agree that East Germany might after all be given a share of control in the access to West Berlin; and again in January 1959, when he said that German reunification did not necessarily require free elections as a first step, but might—at least in theory—develop from a confederation between the two German states. These heretical utterances caused a mistrust between Adenauer and Dulles that the latter had to work quite hard to remove, but which was obliterated in February 1959, when the ailing Secretary of State paid a final visit to Bonn before his resignation and death. Adenauer's distrust of his British ally was somewhat harder to allay, since her Prime

Minister, Harold Macmillan, made a special point, during the
1959 election campaign, of flying to Moscow to discuss East-
West affairs in a way which reminded some Germans of Neville
Chamberlain's flight to Munich in 1938.

Unfortunately for the United States, Britain, and the cohesion
of the Western alliance, Adenauer thought he had formed a true
friend and protector in General de Gaulle, newly installed as
President of France after the events of May 1958 (see Chapter 6).
De Gaulle was in fact paying his first official visit to Adenauer,
at the small spa of Bad Kreuzbach, when the news arrived of
Dulles' alarming statement about an East German share in controlling access to West Berlin. The French President immediately
reassured the German Chancellor that France, at least, would
never desert her commitment to defend West Germany's interests
in such a way; France did, in fact, win considerable credit in
Germany for her outwardly very firm attitude during the ensuing crisis, and the basis for the Franco-German treaty of friendship of January 1963 was laid at this stage.

The reasons for Khrushchev's *démarche* of November 1958
remain obscure. It is possible that he simply wished to exploit
the growing strength of the Soviet Union in missile technology,
or at least to see whether it could be used to make political
capital in the sense of enforcing a more favourable situation in
Berlin. A better explanation is probably that Khrushchev's hand
was forced by a combination of East German pressure (West
Berlin had always formed a serious threat to the prestige of the
East German régime, if not to its very stability) and the rising
power of China. Relations between Moscow and Peking, the
two main Communist powers, had deteriorated gravely since their
treaties of friendship and cooperation of the early 1950s, and it
is quite possible that Khrushchev, faced with a growing threat
from the East, was determined to stabilise his Western front by
clearing up a potential source of trouble there, in the shape of
West Berlin.

At all events, the Western powers were not willing to yield
to Soviet pressure. A conference of Foreign Ministers in Geneva
in the summer of 1959 confirmed that Washington and London
(despite the signs of softness which had alarmed Adenauer) were
not willing to abandon their basic support for the West German
position: West Berlin—even though they would not accept that

it was fully part of the Federal Republic—could not be the subject of negotiations with the East German government (which they refused to recognise), and the Soviet ultimatum was unacceptable. Khrushchev had by this time removed the time-limit from his demands, and the subject of Berlin was due to be discussed again at a summit conference convened in Paris for the month of May 1960. This conference was, from one point of view, to symbolise the growing importance of Paris, in President de Gaulle's eyes, as a centre of diplomatic activity. As we shall see, the French President, while remaining very firm in his support of the German position, was beginning at the same time to embark on a policy of increasing France's standing in the alliance and in the world (see Chapter 10 below).

In the event, the summit conference of May 1960 failed to occur: at the last moment, after arriving in Paris to attend it, Khrushchev revealed that Soviet anti-aircraft defences had shot down a high-flying American espionage aircraft (of the type known as 'U2'), whose pilot was now a prisoner in Russia. Khrushchev's insistence on an American apology, and Eisenhower's refusal to make one, caused the summit meeting to end in a fiasco, with no formal sessions being held before the delegates returned home. The reason for Khrushchev's decision to use the spy-plane incident to wreck the conference in this way is probably that he saw he had very little chance of softening the Western allies' positions on Berlin, Germany, or European affairs in general, and therefore preferred an apparent prestige victory to a diplomatic defeat.

The humiliation brought on the United States by the shooting down of the U2—and by Eisenhower's original inept lying about the missions these planes carried out—certainly helped Khrushchev to cover up the fact that his bid to remove the West German and Allied presence from West Berlin was a total failure. At the end of 1960, two years after his six-month ultimatum, the situation of West Berlin was unchanged, and an increasingly prosperous West Germany was making additional efforts to induce industrialists to invest in Berlin to help the economy of the former capital. The Federal Parliament was still holding occasional meetings in Berlin instead of Bonn, to symbolise the West German hope of reunification, and—most serious of all—the border between the Eastern and Western sectors of Berlin was still open. This last

I

fact was particularly serious for East Germany since, in the 12 years from 1949 to mid-1961, the East German state lost two million of its 18 million inhabitants who—to use Lenin's phrase—'voted with their feet' by emigrating to West Germany via West Berlin. The frontier between the two German states—except in Berlin—being by this time protected by dense barbed-wire barriers and minefields installed by the East Germans, Berlin was the only escape-route: East Germans would travel to East Berlin, carrying what they could of their belongings, and then move across the open border into West Berlin, whence air transport would take them to the Federal Republic. The two million DDR citizens who had taken this escape-route since 1949 included—unfortunately for East Germany—many who had been trained as doctors and engineers by the East German state (which had a better system of scholarships for workers' children than West Germany), and who rightly judged that their potential earning capacity would be higher in the West. There were also, of course, a number of refugees who had little material motive for flight, but simply preferred Western society, with its relative freedom of information, thought and political activity, to the enforced conformity of Communist East Germany. (It should also be said that there were a few refugees who crossed the Berlin border from West to East, but not many.)

It was this 'brain-drain', rather than the official pretext that West Berlin was a centre of spying and sabotage, that explained the East German and Soviet action in separating East from West Berlin by a physical barrier on the night of 13 August 1961. The Berlin Wall was probably necessary to prevent the life-blood of East Germany from being drained away. It also marked a striking setback for the 'reunification' policy of Adenauer, whose allies (including the recently-elected President Kennedy) made it quite clear that they would do nothing to make the Russians take the Wall away.

Instead of being able to regard West Berlin as the nucleus of a future reunited Germany, the Germans now had to face the fact that an important element of Adenauer's policy (at least his declared policy) had been a failure, and that their country was likely to remain divided for a long time. This disillusion with the situation to which Adenauer's dozen years in office had brought Germany was to play an important part in the 1961

West German general election: the Wall and this election were to mark the beginning of the end for Adenauer (though he remained in office until 1963), and the start of a new phase in German politics.

8 Italy and Benelux in the Fifties

Italy enters the 1950s: economic growth and the 1953 election
The early 1950s was a period of relative calm in Italian politics, in contrast to the turbulence of the early post-war years and the instability and political fragmentation which were to come. The massive electoral victory of the Christian Democrats in 1948 kept De Gasperi in power effortlessly until the 1953 election, although rising pressures on both the left and right began to challenge him.

These were the years when serious efforts were begun to overcome the economic backwardness of the Italian South. The national income rose fairly rapidly—thanks to American Marshall Aid funds—increasing by 5.9 per cent in 1951, 2.9 per cent in 1952 and 7.3 per cent in 1953.

What was new was the deliberate effort of De Gasperi's government to channel some of this growth into the backward South. The land reform of May 1950, redistributing land to the peasants in a particularly disturbed part of Calabria, was followed by a wider measure in October of the same year, which went some way at least towards meeting peasant demands in the Southern areas and Sardinia. Ironically, the Christian Democratic Party failed to win the political rewards it expected for these reforms: the peasants, even with their former masters' land in their possession, continued to vote Communist, and the dispossessed landowners gave their votes to the Monarchists or to the resurgent neo-fascist party (now called Italian Social Movement or MSI as the *Uomo Qualunque* movement had disintegrated).

As well as land reform – which of course applied to all Italy, not just to the South—the government tried to bring industry to under-developed southern regions by a variety of planning measures. The best-known and most successful of these was the *Cassa per il Mezzogiorno* (or Fund for Southern Italy), established in 1950 with an original ten-year budget of 1,200 billion lire, later expanded. Half of the original sum came from Marshall Aid funds, and the aim of the scheme—to reduce inequalities between Northern and Southern Italy, thus increasing political stability—was strongly supported by the United States. The aim of keeping Communism at bay was not wholly successful, as we shall see.

The Fund operated in two main ways: it provided for direct investment from public funds in the infrastructure of the Southern economy—roads, aqueducts, irrigation; and it also provided low-cost loans and tax reductions to help private industry to invest in the development areas.

The Fund made some progress in its aim of bringing new industry to the South, but it was also criticised for bureaucratic inefficiency, and for the fact that much of the heavy earth-shifting machinery and other equipment used in the South was manufactured in the North, so that the aim of redirecting industrial activity was, ironically, only partly achieved. There is no doubt, however, that the South benefited more from the Fund than from the policies of any previous Italian government.

On the broader front of national economic policy, the De Gasperi government regrouped a number of industries which had been nationalised by Mussolini during the Depression: his Institute for Industrial Reconstruction (IRI) was given new authority over the range of industries and services which it controlled, varying from coal-mines and railways to insurance. A new agency, the National Hydrocarbons Trust (ENI) was established in 1952 under the dynamic management of Enrico Mattei (a leading figure of the Christian Democratic left), to take charge of developing the petrol industry and Italy's newly-discovered reserves of natural gas.

On the political front, De Gasperi and his allies had little difficulty in holding the parliamentary majority they had won in 1948: there were strains on the coalition—notably between the predominantly right-wing Christian Democrats and the Social Democrats led by Saragat—but the government held together.

A test of its popularity—and a warning of harder times ahead —came with the municipal elections of 1951 and 1952. Here the Christian Democrats lost over 4 million of the votes they had won in the 1948 elections—their share fell from 48.5 to 31.1 per cent—in many cases to the Monarchists and neo-fascist parties, which tripled their vote. This threat from the right, together with growing Communist strength on the left, limited De Gasperi's freedom of action: in Rome, for instance, where the Vatican pressed him to make a local alliance with the extreme right, he had to fight hard for his view that the new local administration should be a coalition between the Christian Democrats, Social Democrats and the other centre parties represented in the national cabinet.

In these local elections of 1951 and 1952 the governing parties limited the damage to their position by a series of tamperings with the electoral laws, designed to give a comfortable working majority to any party or coalition that won a bare majority of the votes. These measures—obnoxious in terms of pure democratic theory, but perhaps necessary in a country where powerful, extremist parties threatened the whole structure of the republic— were similar to those adopted in France in 1950-51 against the Communists and Gaullists.

In preparation for the 1953 general election, De Gasperi and his coalition partners passed a law which provided that any coalition of parties winning more than one-half of the people's votes would be granted two-thirds of the parliamentary seats. This stipulation—which went further than the contemporary French measures and was ominously like a law passed by Mussolini in 1923—was bitterly criticised during the election campaign and in the event De Gasperi's coalition failed by a small margin to get the 50 per cent they needed. The four centre parties – Christian Democrats, Republicans, Liberals and Social Democrats – in fact won 49.85 per cent of the votes, gaining respectively 261, 5, 14 and 19 seats. On the left, the Communists won 143 seats and the Socialist Party 75; on the right, Monarchists and Fascists held respectively 40 and 29.

In this new Assembly, coalition government as practised by De Gasperi was much more difficult. His attempt to rebuild a four-party coalition failed significantly; this was because Saragat's Social Democrats were now beginning to look leftwards towards unity with Nenni's Socialists—and after a further failure to get parliamentary approval for a one-party government De Gasperi retired from politics. He died the following year, remembered as the man who gave Italy a new start in political freedom and economic prosperity after 1945, and who led her into closer union with the other countries of Western Europe.

De Gasperi's successors: tensions in Christian Democracy
The years between the parliamentary elections of 1953 and 1958
—the immediate post-De Gasperi period—were unsettled. In
particular, the ruling Christian Democratic Party experienced
considerable tensions between its right and left wings, oscillating
between alliance with the frankly reactionary forces to the right
and the 'opening to the left' which was to become the party's
orientation in later years. Major issues, such as legal reforms and
the introduction of elected regional assemblies (provided for in
the 1946 constitution) were postponed by a series of weak
coalition governments, in which the Christian Democrats depended on the votes of right-wing allies who blocked any progress.

De Gasperi's successor as Prime Minister was Giuseppe Pella,
whose government—although he belonged to the right wing of the
Christian Democratic party—was regarded as an 'administrative'
cabinet, and contained a number of civil service 'technicians' as
well as politicians. His main attention had to go to foreign affairs,
since Italy's conflict with Yugoslavia over the Free Territory of
Trieste once more became acute. In the 1948 election the United
States, Britain and France, in an attempt to help the Christian
Democrats, had publicly called for the award of both the urban
Zone A and the rural Zone B to Italy, even though only the
former now had a mainly Italian population. Shortly afterwards,
however, when Tito had dramatically broken away from the
Soviet Union, the Western Allies—not wishing to antagonise
Yugoslavia—stopped pressing for a pro-Italian solution and left
their occupation forces in position. This naturally led to Italian
resistance, and rioting against the Allies occurred both in Trieste
and more generally in other parts of Italy. In the 1953 election
campaign the United States again adopted a pro-Italian line in
order to help De Gasperi, offering this time an award of at least
part of the area, though no longer all of it, to Italy. The administration in Washington promised to press Marshal Tito to accept
this solution, but De Gasperi – fearing that Italian acceptance
would look like capitulation – rejected anything short of the 1948
promise of the whole territory.

After the election, De Gasperi's successor Pella felt obliged to
adopt an equally intransigent position, since he depended on the
support of right-wing political elements who would otherwise
accuse him of lack of patriotism. In a belligerent speech in

September 1953, he demanded a plebiscite throughout the Trieste territory (this would have given an Italian majority) and warned the United States that Italian agreement to the European Defence Community would depend on a satisfactory solution of the Trieste issue. (It should be noticed that Italy's policy here was very similar to that of France, who made a satisfactory outcome of the Saar dispute a condition for ratifying EDC.)

The American and British governments reacted by suggesting that Italy should replace them in administering the largely urban and essentially Italian Zone A of the Trieste territory. This appeased Italian opinion and strengthened Pella's position, but Tito refused to allow Italy to occupy any part of Trieste, and the Allies therefore withdrew their offer. Rioting ensued in Trieste in which six Italians were killed by occupying forces, and both Italy and Yugoslavia moved army units towards the border. The two governments were in fact bluffing—their forces were soon withdrawn—but the problem continued to simmer until October 1954, when a compromise was reached; Italy was awarded the occupation of Trieste itself (technically, replacing the Allies as administrators, but in reality annexing the city), and Yugoslavia declared herself content with the remainder of the Istrian peninsula. Italian honour had been to some extent preserved, but the solution was less to her advantage than the one demanded so vehemently by De Gasperi and Pella. Italy's position had in fact been somewhat weakened by the rejection of EDC in April 1954, which removed the Italian threat of non-ratification as a bargaining counter.

In the meantime, there had been more than one change of government in Italy. Pella's cabinet was replaced in January 1954 by that of Mario Scelba, after an abortive attempt at the formation of a government under Amintore Fanfani. The latter was the spokesman of the left-wing current now gaining influence in the Christian Democratic Party: he was not strictly a socialist, but in his view Christian principles demanded a much greater degree of public control of private industry, and a less unequal distribution of wealth. Although his views were popular with some sections of the Christian Democratic leadership, and he was to become the General Secretary of the Party a few months later, his attempt to form a government in January 1954 failed because the majority view was still decidedly right-wing.

Scelba, a representative of this right-wing majority (he was well known as a strong anti-Communist, and as Minister of the Interior had organised anti-riot squads which had deeply antagonised the left), presided over the government which accepted the compromise solution of the Trieste issue late in 1954. This paved the way both for growing trade with Yugoslavia and for Italy's participation in the European Economic Community based on the Treaty of Rome. Italy was brought into an even more active role in international affairs when she became a member of the United Nations—the earlier Soviet objection now being dropped—in 1955.

Scelba's government also attempted to continue the industrial development of the post-war years, though a coherent policy was made difficult by the divisions within the Christian Democratic Party. Despite these divisions, the Christian Democrats increased their vote at the 1958 election, raising their share of the poll from 40.1 to 42.2 per cent of the total and their number of seats from 261 to 273. The shifts in the positions of the other parties were superficially slight—except for serious losses by the Monarchists —but the real significance of the 1958 election lay in the rising influence of the left *within* the Christian Democratic Party. This, together with the evolution of the Socialist Party under Nenni, towards a more conciliatory view, made collaboration between Christian Democrats and Socialists – the 'opening to the left' – seem by the end of the 1950s to be at least a possibility.

The late 1950s: the 'opening to the left'
The Italian Socialist Party, as we have seen, had split in 1947 into the pro-Communist majority led by Pietro Nenni and the Social Democratic wing under Giuseppe Saragat, which participated in the government. Nenni was a leader of very great prestige (comparable with Léon Blum as a Socialist leader whose portrait still hung in many working-class dwellings after the mass of the French and Italian workers had abandoned Socialism for Communism) and it was only through this prestige that he was able to carry the Italian Socialist Party through its considerable changes of attitude during the 1950s.

In the years after 1947, when the Cold War was developing and the right-wing Social Democrats under Saragat shared power in a series of increasingly right-wing Christian Democrat-led coalitions, Nenni's party leaned heavily towards the Communists under Togliatti. (This alignment was so pronounced that in the 1948 election, when Nenni and Togliatti entered a close coalition, the British Labour Party, under Clement Attlee, expelled a small number of Labour MPs who had signed the celebrated ' Nenni telegram ' wishing the Italian Socialists success.) By temperament and in reaction to the ' rightward ' evolution of Italian politics under Pella and Scelba, Nenni continued the alliance with the Communists until the mid-1950s.

The turning-point came with the Soviet repression of the Hungarian revolt in 1956. This repelled not only the Nenni Socialists, but also, to a considerable degree, the Italian Communist Party itself. The Italian Communist Party had always contained a higher proportion of independent-minded intellectuals than the Communist Party in France. One reason for this was that the Fascist régime in Italy had prevented the growth of a mass Communist Party like the German party of the 1920s or the French one of the 1930s: Moscow had therefore not seen the · need to impose on the Italians the ' obedient servant ' party leader of the type of Ernst Thälmann or Maurice Thorez, and the leaders of Italian Communism were men like Antonio Gramsci (a brilliant intellectual imprisoned and murdered by the Fascists) or Togliatti himself. Even though Togliatti was a man of action—he fought with distinction in the Spanish Civil War—he was also an intellectual with great powers of independent judgement, and criticised Soviet policy on several occasions.

The developments in the entire Communist world in the crucial year 1956—notably Khrushchev's speech condemning Stalin in February, and the invasion of Hungary in the autumn—accentuated Togliatti's tendency to criticise Soviet actions, and this was the period when he coined the term ' polycentrism ' to describe the need for the world's Communist Parties and Communist states to gain more independence from Moscow. This declaration of (at least modified) independence set the tone for the Italian Communist Party's attitude after 1956. There was, of course, a very long distance to be travelled before there could be any question of Communists and Christian Democrats joining forces politically—indeed, this was still to appear very difficult in the early 1970s—but at least a dialogue of a kind now developed between Christianity and Marxism.

If the Communist Party could not yet ally itself with the parties of the centre, the position of Italy's other Marxist party, the Nenni Socialists, was of course more flexible. The years after 1956—when Nenni's reaction to Soviet developments was naturally even stronger than Togliatti's—saw a growing *rapprochement* between the two parts of the Italian non-Communist left which had separated in 1947. As we shall see, the union of Nenni's Socialist Party and Saragat's Social Democrats was to occur only in the 1960s, and even then was to be short-lived: unity of tactical action between the two parties, however, was to develop as a reality by the end of the 1950s. (For instance, the acrimony between the two parties was much less marked in the 1958 election—when both of them somewhat increased their vote—than in those of 1948 and 1953.)

The further development—the 'opening to the left' in which even the Christian Democrats would form a liaison with the Nenni Socialists—was also to wait until the 1960s, but again the dialogue between Nenni and the more left-wing Christian Democrats such as Fanfani was under way by the end of the 1950s.

Italy by 1960 thus presented a picture in many ways different from that of 1950: in foreign policy, the basically pro-Western and 'European' orientation of De Gasperi was sustained; economically, the country was considerably more affluent, and even the desperate poverty of the South had begun to be alleviated; and the alignment of political forces already showed some of the signs of the 'opening to the left' that was to transform the balance of Italian politics in the 1960s.

The Benelux countries in the 1950s

As we have seen, Belgian politics, dominated by the question of the monarchy until King Leopold's abdication in 1950, also reflected the serious problem of racial tension between the French-speaking and Dutch-speaking populations. This conflict showed itself during the 1950s in the growing differences within the political parties. Basically the Belgian party-structure was much simpler than that of France. There were three major forces: the Christian Democrats (normally gaining about 45 per cent of the vote at elections), the Socialist Party (whose normal share was about 35 per cent) and the Liberal Party (about 15 per cent). By the end of the 1950s, however, the pattern had become more complex, with a split in the Socialist Party between French- and Flemish-speaking groups, and a sizeable growth in the Communist Party on the far left.

Belgium was naturally, because of its small size, one of the West European countries to realise most readily that the nation-state was no longer viable as the basic unit of political life. (The conflict between the country's two communities also did a good deal to make Belgians wish to merge their country into a larger grouping, in which the tensions between French- and Flemish-speaking might appear less acute.)

Belgium was the country which produced one of the leading pioneers of the European integration movement in the 1950s, the Socialist Party leader Paul-Henri Spaak. Born in 1899, Spaak was active on the left wing of Belgian politics in the 1930s, when he was Foreign Minister and briefly Prime Minister shortly before the collapse of 1940. He spent the war years in London, when he helped to develop the Benelux economic union, and returned to Belgium to play a leading political role, joining passionately in the campaign for the abdication of King Leopold.

In 1948 Spaak became the first president of the ministerial committee set up by the 16 recipients of Marshall Aid to plan the spending of the American funds through the OEEC. His diplomatic talent and Churchillian tenacity—he had in fact a marked physical resemblance to Churchill—earned him the nickname of 'Mr Europe' and had made him a natural choice for the presidency of the Consultative Assembly of the Council of Europe, established in 1949.

Spaak was out of office when the next dramatic step in European integration was taken, with the Schuman Plan of 1950; but by 1955 he was once again Foreign Minister, and helped to press ahead the plan for a European Common Market which emerged from the Messina Conference of June 1955.

After his substantial work on the preparation and signature of the Treaty of Rome in 1957 (see Chapter 9), Spaak became Secretary-General of NATO at the end of the 1950s. Through him, Belgium had made a decisive contribution to the integration of Western Europe.

Dutch politics in the 1950s continued to be confused—superficially, at least—by the religious animosities which had produced a proliferation of political parties after the Liberation. The economic recovery of the country continued at an impressive rate with the help of Marshall Aid, and no fundamental political conflicts interrupted either economic or foreign policy. Although the Netherlands at this stage produced no statesman of the European stature of Paul-Henri Spaak, there were occasions when her political leaders took important initiatives in European affairs. For instance, after the collapse of EDC in 1954—which appeared to set back the entire cause of European integration very drastically—it was the Netherlands Foreign Minister, J. W. Beyen, who took the crucial step of pressing for the Messina Conference of June 1955, which marked the next step forward on Europe's path to integration.

Luxembourg, in the meantime, had quietly continued to play her part as a junior partner in the Benelux union, combined now with a more important function as the seat of the Coal and Steel Community, the first working model of European integration. The political life of the Grand Duchy remained very simple, untroubled by anything comparable to the communal tensions that plagued her neighbour Belgium. The three political parties— Christian Social, Socialist and Liberal—continued to share power in coalitions in which the dominant Christian Social Party always took the lead, but the slight changes in the government's coalition never affected the continuity of Luxembourg's foreign policy. Under her long-standing Foreign Minister, Joseph Bech, this remained firmly committed to European unity.

9 European Institutions: ECSC to the Treaty of Rome

The ECSC: integration in action

By the summer of 1950, the six states forming the hard core of Western Europe had come to realise that their next steps forward must be taken together. Most significantly, France and Germany —the two powers whose rivalries had disrupted the peace of Europe for generations—were both now prepared to submit to a more powerful European authority than OEEC or the Council of Europe. Even though they had arrived at this state of mind by calculations of national interest—including the negative reason for accepting ' Europe ', that the nation-state had been tried and found wanting—their readiness to go forward together was all the more real for this.

The governments were backed by the great majority of politically-conscious Europeans. It is hard to recapture, in the more complacent Western Europe of the 1970s, the passionate excitement with which the peoples of Europe responded to their leaders' speeches in favour of European unity. Five years after the end of Europe's most catastrophic war, the way to make wars impossible seemed to have been found. The generation of French and German students of 1950, who ceremonially burned the frontier-posts between their two countries, were demonstrating support for their governments in their own dramatic way, but something of their excitement can be read even in the preamble of the Treaty setting up the Coal and Steel Community. The six governments

Considering that world peace may be safeguarded only by creative efforts equal to the dangers which menace it;

Convinced that the contribution which an organised and vital Europe can bring to civilisation is indispensable to the maintenance of peaceful relations;

Conscious of the fact that Europe can be built only by concrete actions which create a real solidarity and by the establishment of common bases for economic development;

Desirous of assisting through the expansion of their basic production in raising the standard of living and in furthering the works of peace;

Resolved to substitute for historic rivalries a fusion of their essential interests; to establish, by creating an economic community, the foundation of a broad and independent community among peoples long divided by bloody conflicts; and to lay the bases of institutions capable of giving direction to their future destiny; have decided to create a European coal and steel community.

The final reference to the basic ingredients of coal and steel may seem an anticlimax after the eloquent introductory paragraphs, but the six governments knew quite well that coal and steel, which had recently provided the sinews of war, could now be harnessed to ensure Europe's integration in peace.

The treaty, by referring to ' concrete actions ' more generally, also indicated that the principle known as ' sector integration ' might be applied in other areas too; plans for European pooling of agriculture and transport were by this time under active discussion, and the broader plan for a full European Economic Community was already present in the minds of Monnet and his colleagues. The actual document of the Schuman Plan Treaty, signed on 18 April 1951, symbolised the principle of integration: as we are told by one of Monnet's close collaborators, ' the document signed was printed in French by the National Printing Office, in German ink on Dutch vellum; the parchment of the cover came from Belgium, the ribbon from Italy and the glue from Luxembourg '.*

The ' institutions capable of giving direction ' to which the Treaty referred, consisted of a High Authority of nine men, a Council of Ministers representing the six national governments, an Assembly of 78 members, chosen from the national parliaments, and a Supreme Court charged with interpreting the Treaty and punishing breaches of it. These four institutions— the independent executive, the body representing governmental interests, the democratic element of parliamentary control, and the judiciary to provide legal sanctions—were all to be

* Richard Mayne, *The Recovery of Europe*, p. 196.

reproduced in the later Communities of Europe, most importantly in the European Economic Community established in
1957.

The High Authority of ECSC, over which Monnet presided
from its beginnings until 1955, was in fact endowed with more
independent powers of action than the later European Commissions were to be given. It was empowered quite simply to remove
all tariffs and other barriers on the movement of coal and steel
within the Community, making it, as far as these industries were
concerned, into one international market. The sweeping powers
given to the High Authority to achieve this end—the very name
'Authority' recalled the Ruhr Authority set up by the Allies
to control heavy industry in Germany—would have been hard
to accept if the scope of the Authority's action had been less
narrowly defined: in fact, in the Rome Treaty which later did
apply the principle of integration to broader sectors of economic
life, the powers of the European Commission, as we shall see,
were more carefully limited. The roles of the other three components in the ECSC's institutional system—national representation, democratic control and judicial sanctions – were fairly clear
and familiar: the true originality of Monnet's approach was the
device he had adopted in reaction against his frustrating years
in the service of the League of Nations, the independent Authority
with limited but real powers of action.

The Treaty was ratified by the summer of 1952, and the
High Authority held its first meeting at its headquarters in
Luxembourg in August of that year. Within two years, the principle of a common market for all categories of coal and steel had
been put into practice, and by 1958, when the transition period
ended—certain special concessions in the rate of tariff reductions
had been allowed, for instance to Italy—considerable progress in
intra-Community traffic had been achieved. The trade in coal
between members of the Six had grown by 21 per cent, in coke
by 14.8 per cent, in iron ore by 25.5 per cent, in scrap by 175
per cent and in steel by 157 per cent. Part of this increase of
course reflected the general rebuilding of Europe's heavy industry
after its devastation in the war—steel *production* in the Six rose
by 42 per cent from 1953 to 1957, an indication of the same
trend—but the new free market for the industries concerned
played a large part in making this recovery so rapid. It should

also be noted that the ECSC treaty provided funds for the re-training and rehousing of workers—for instance, from uneconomic coal-mines—whose jobs ceased to exist as a result of the rationalisation brought about by the Coal and Steel Community.

The High Authority also made use of its power to intervene to break up price rings and cartels, and the prices of coal and steel in the Six rose much less rapidly during the 1950s —by a mere three per cent—than in the United States and Britain.

The British Labour government, which remained in office until October 1951, maintained its firm opposition—expressed during the original Schuman Plan discussions of May-June 1950 —to British membership of the organisation. When Winston Churchill then returned to power at the head of a new Conservative administration, the Six hoped for a moment that the statesman who had made the Zürich and The Hague speeches only a few years earlier, and had condemned the short-sightedness of the Labour government's rejection of Europe, would lead his country into membership of ECSC. Churchill himself, and some of his Ministers (notably Sandys and Macmillan) were indeed sympathetic to British membership of the European Community, but the Foreign Secretary, Anthony Eden, was adamantly opposed (joining a European federation, he told an American audience in January 1952, 'is something which we know, in our bones, we cannot do ') and Britain's chief role in Europe remained limited to the Council of Europe and OEEC. By 1953, Britain had made an arrangement providing for ' association ' with ECSC, but there was no question of her entering it as a member.

One of the main aims of ECSC, clearly indicated in its Treaty, was to serve as the pioneer for other ventures in ' sector integration '; the sectors envisaged for the next step included agriculture and transport, but by an unforeseen turn of events, the sector that became the next testing-ground for integration was in fact the highly sensitive and delicate one of military defence. The unforeseen event that brought this about was the Korean War, which broke out in June 1950, while the first discussions of the Schuman Plan were still in progress, and which by October was to bring forth the Pleven Plan for a European Defence Community.

K

European Defence Community and European Political Community 1950-54

The Pleven Plan, as we have seen, was a French proposal for solving the problem of fitting Germany into the Western Alliance, devised in response to American pressure resulting from Washington's assessment of Soviet Russia's intentions. It thus provides a perfect illustration of the interpenetration between global and European politics, and of the pressures to which Western Europe was subjected—especially as the British government insisted throughout that Britain was not part of 'Europe' in the EDC sense: Britain would give general support to the EDC, but her membership of it was out of the question. In the end a revolt by sections of French opinion was to cause the project to be scrapped, and the problem of German rearmament was to be resolved in a different way.

From 1950 to 1954 the argument about the EDC—'The Quarrel of the EDC', to quote a leading study of the subject*— dominated the political life of France and Germany: as we have seen, both national systems were deeply divided on the issue. The interaction between these two national systems—other parties were of course involved, but the essential dialogue was the Franco-German one—first decided the shape of the new supra-national system that was proposed, and then decided that it should be rejected.

As soon as the Korean War broke out France was placed under very heavy American pressure to accept West German rearmament. The idea of an independent German national army would probably have been unacceptable under any circumstances —Jules Moch, one of the French Ministers who opposed German rearmament most strenuously, was by no means atypical in having fought in the First World War and lost a son in the Second—but the precise structure proposed in the Pleven Plan was certainly influenced by the fact that the problem arose at the precise moment when the details of the Schuman Plan were being worked out.

If it was sensible for Germany's coal and steel resources to be brought under the same authority as those of France, it was doubly

---

* '*La Querelle de la CED*', eds. R. Aron & D. Lerner; English edition *France Defeats EDC* (1957).

logical—assuming that German rearmament had to be accepted at all—for her future armed forces to be controlled by a similar system. The Pleven Plan of October 1950 thus followed the Schuman Plan very closely in providing for an executive ('Commissariat') in charge of the future European army, a Council of Ministers to control the work of the Commissariat (which was to report to it annually) and a Court of Justice to receive any complaints against decisions the Commissariat took.

It was relatively easy to design such a set of institutions on paper: it was much more difficult to believe that they could provide an effective system for running the armed forces of an alliance. Even among allies who on the whole saw quite closely eye to eye—the British and Americans during the Second World War, for instance—an allied command structure proved very hard to manage. To take the control of armed forces away from national governments in peace-time raised much more serious difficulties—particularly as the projected European army was to be formed from quite small units taken from each nation and merged together to create a genuinely integrated force. A further objection to the EDC—at least from the French point of view—was that the proposed European Commissariat would in effect be managing the European army on behalf of the supreme NATO commander, an American general. Even though the NATO supreme commander of the time was an unusually statesmanlike officer (within a couple of years he was to become President instead of General Eisenhower), and even though he wholeheartedly endorsed the idea of the EDC, the French politicians opposed to it were furnished with an additional argument by the fact of its subordination to NATO.

It was therefore with considerable reservations that the government of René Pleven persuaded the French parliament, on 25 October 1950, to accept the principle of a European army. Once that parliament had been replaced by the much less docile one elected in June 1951 (see Chapter 6), and once the projected EDC began to take more precise form, the chances of parliamentary approval being translated into formal ratification became continually more slender.

Even though the new French parliament ratified the Coal and Steel Community Treaty in December 1951 by 376 votes to 240, the EDC treaty, signed by the Pinay government on 27 May 1952, threatened to hand over a much more sensitive area of national decision-making to a rather dubiously constructed new authority, and the opposition it aroused was correspondingly greater.

Part of the problem of the EDC was that the sacrifices demanded of the potential partners appeared so unequal. In the case of the Coal and Steel Community, all the member states at least possessed a component to put into the pool: it could be argued that the international authority already governing Germany's heavy industry was simply being extended, in a new form, to France and the other members. With armed forces, however, the position was quite different. Not to speak of the technical difficulties, already mentioned, of controlling an army in the same way as the coal and steel industries, the EDC proposal raised the fundamental question of whether Germany should be rearmed at all. It was only five years since the Allies had resolved to abolish German militarism for ever, and the Germans themselves had to a large extent endorsed the decision that the new Federal Republic would have no armed forces. Now—whatever arguments might be advanced about a possible Soviet threat of the 'Korean' type, or the existence of heavily armed para-military police units in the Soviet Zone—the Germans were being asked to become soldiers again. Worse, from France's point of view, the French army was being asked to merge its proud and independent existence into an amorphous and distasteful coexistence with the Germans. Worse yet, France was being asked to accept this at a moment when, as we have seen, the bulk of her best military units were fighting an increasingly costly war in Indo-China, so that the European army would in effect be dominated by Germany. Faced with mounting resistance to EDC, the French governments of Mayer and Laniel tried to obtain more presentable terms from their allies. Just as Adenauer used against the Americans the argument that German domestic opposition to rearmament could only be overcome if Germany received fully equal status in the new structure, so French governments used their own domestic opposition to press for better terms on their side. One of the major issues in dispute between France and Germany was the future of the Saar territory. It was economically still part of France (though the ECSC was to make this factor of decreasing importance), but its political future —essentially the question of whether the majority of the population should have their way and be allowed to rejoin Germany—

remained in suspense. France now attempted to make a pro-French solution of this problem a condition for ratification of EDC, though her general bargaining position was weak, and the Laniel government saw that it had little chance of success on this point.

One positive aspect of the EDC debate was that—like the ECSC before it—the EDC came to be seen as the motor of European integration on a broader front. Even though the breakdown of this 'motor' in August 1954 was to lead to a serious setback for the European movement as a whole, the project for a European Political Community which grew directly out of the EDC proposal was later to prove of considerable significance. Partly because of the patently arbitrary nature of the decision to attempt an integration of Europe's military forces without an integrated political authority—a decision forced on the six partners by external pressures—they agreed to work out a project for a broader political community. For this purpose, the 78-member Assembly of the Coal and Steel Community was somewhat enlarged and was empowered to discuss the form of a European political authority. Under the dynamic presidency of Paul-Henri Spaak, this so-called 'ad-hoc Assembly' produced a draft constitution providing for close consultation between the six member governments on all aspects of economic and political decision-making, which was approved in principle by the six governments by the summer of 1953. The adoption of the EPC was in fact dependent on the success of the EDC, and the fall of the latter a year later was to consign the former to temporary oblivion. However, many of its ideas were to reappear, both in the supra-national provisions of the Treaty of Rome in 1957 and in the French proposals for inter-governmental collaboration (the so-called 'Fouchet Plan') in 1962.

A new international climate and the fall of the EDC
The first sign that the EDC treaty might not come to fruition was the emergence of a basically anti-'European' parliament after the French elections of 1951; a second indication was to be seen in the replacement of Schuman by Bidault in 1953; and a third was the arrival in power as Prime Minister of Pierre Mendès-France, in the midst of the Indo-China crisis, in June 1954.

These were all changes within the national political system of the European state whose decision must affect the outcome of the whole argument. They occurred, too, in an international environment—a climate of growing East-West *détente*—which made the whole need for West German rearmament appear much more open to question. It was the outbreak of the Korean War, in June 1950, which had given rise to American pressure for this rearmament. The ending of the Korean War, by a cease-fire in the summer of 1952, followed by a formal armistice agreement a year later, began to reduce the acute Cold War atmosphere of 1950 and 1951, and led to increased doubts—in France, in Germany, and in wide circles of opinion in Britain—about whether German rearmament was really necessary after all. Over Indo-China, too, although the fighting became increasingly bitter by 1953-54, there was an increasing feeling in Europe that the war was far away, that a French defeat was likely (or inevitable), and that the outcome of this struggle could not in any case directly affect the security of Europe. Stalin had died in March 1953, and his successors—once they had overcome their mutual struggle for power, and particularly once the sinister figure of the Secret Police Chief Beria had been removed—appeared much more amenable to East-West understanding. It is true that Stalin's departure occurred almost simultaneously with the arrival in office of John Foster Dulles, President Eisenhower's Secretary of State, whose attitude to East-West *détente* from 1953-1959 was to be almost the mirror-image of that adopted by Stalin from 1945 to 1953; still, the overall pattern of the mid-1950s was that of a distinct amelioration of the more acute tensions of the Cold War. From the Korean cease-fire of 1952 (accompanied, as we have seen, by new Soviet proposals for the neutralisation of Germany) to the renewed suggestions about German reunification made by Malenkov in 1954-55, and the agreement to neutralise and evacuate Austria in 1955, the general image of Soviet policy was to be much more placatory than in Stalin's time.

All this weakened the position of the American government in pressing for the EDC to be ratified, and strengthened the hand of the opponents of German rearmament in France, Britain and Germany itself. It was harder to argue that Soviet pressure represented a threat to Western Europe, and much easier to argue that the decision to go ahead with German rearmament would create insuperable barriers to the new East-West *détente* which appeared to be developing. If this analysis was accepted—as it increasingly was—then the general objection to West European integration, as voiced most loudly by German Social Democrats intent on reunification, became a very powerful one.

Two distinct arguments could be discerned, if the internal French debate and the broader European debate are considered together. For France, the basic question was whether German rearmament was still—in the light of the improving East-West climate—necessary at all. By the summer of 1954, the French opposition to EDC—caused partly, it must be repeated, by Britain's continued refusal to put her military weight into the balance together with Germany's—was to lead to a rejection of the supra-national structure of the EDC. On the other hand, the general Western desire to see West Germany rearmed—which was shared even by the Mendès-France government in France— was strong enough for agreement to be reached that Germany should be rearmed, within a less markedly supra-national structure, by the end of the same year.

The parliamentary skirmishing about the destiny of the EDC took the form of a series of *démarches* by Mendès-France—once the Indo-China issue was out of the way at the end of July— designed to remove the supra-national features of EDC which France found objectionable. (It will be remembered that Mendès-France presided over a French cabinet including several Gaullists, to whom the principle of integration in a European army was anathema.) In a series of dramatic encounters during August, Mendès-France first tried to persuade the five co-signatories of EDC (in conference in Brussels) to dilute the supra-national pro- visions of the treaty as far as the French army was concerned; he then attempted, in a weekend confrontation in England with Churchill and Eden, to get Britain to reconsider her refusal to join the EDC. Both endeavours were unsuccessful: France's Continental partners would accept no more delays, as Spaak and Adenauer firmly told Mendès-France in Brussels, and Churchill and Eden would do no more than warn Mendès-France that rejection of EDC would only mean the need to accept German rearmament in a different form. The French Prime Minister thus had no choice but to present the EDC treaty for ratification by the French Assembly. The debate was a curious one: as we have seen, Mendès-France's only option was to refrain from taking sides, and the debate was dominated by anti-German diatribes from Communists, Gaullists and the veteran Radical Edouard Herriot—the apostle of Franco-German reconciliation in the 1920s—who now vibrantly warned his compatriots of the fate which this reconciliation had suffered in the 1930s, and warned them not to take the risk again.

The Assembly predictably rejected EDC on 30 August 1954 by 319 votes to 264, and a further bout of diplomatic activity was needed to make arrangements for the inevitable rearmament of West Germany in a new and acceptable form. Mendès-France again took the lead in conferring with France's allies—this time to solve the problem which his country's rejection of her own 1950 proposal had caused. The outcome was the agreement signed on 23 October to enlarge the Brussels Treaty Organisation of 1948 (its members were France, Britain and Benelux) into a Western European Union into which Germany and Italy would both be admitted. They were also to become members of NATO, and the function of WEU was essentially to ensure that Germany did not create armed forces larger than twelve divisions, and that she kept to her pledge not to manufacture atomic, biological or chemical weapons. Britain also undertook, in token of a commitment to WEU which she had refused to make to EDC, to keep four army divisions and her tactical air force on the European continent.

The supra-national EDC was thus scrapped, after four years of intense European efforts, and with it went the plan for a European Political Community. The ECSC thus appeared no longer as the pioneer of an ever faster-moving process of integration, but rather as an island standing out amidst a tide of political power returning to the national capitals.

The re-launching of Europe: from Messina to Rome

This situation was to be dramatically reversed, and the trend towards integration unexpectedly revived, by the train of events started off by the Messina Conference which the governments of the Six held in June 1955. One of the first things they had to do was to agree on a successor to Jean Monnet, as President of the Coal and Steel Community's High Authority. Monnet had announced in November 1954 that he wished to give up this post when his term as President expired: this should have occurred in February 1955, but Monnet had agreed to stay in office until the Six agreed on a successor. The Messina Conference in June was to confirm the choice of René Mayer, a former French Prime Minister, but it was no secret that Monnet was already engaged in the diplomatic ' pressure-group' activity which marked the next phase of his contribution to European unification. He was in active contact with the governments—particularly those of the Benelux countries—whose proposals were the basis for the Messina Conference's work. These proposals—the Benelux one dated 20 May 1955, for instance, which called for ' a new stage in European integration', based on economic unity—bore the signs of Monnet's influence, in the period when he was discreetly trying to use his position at the head of ECSC to help Europe recover from the setback of the EDC crisis. He came out fully into the political arena in October 1955, when he announced the formation of the Action Committee for the United States of Europe. This body was a fairly select group—originally numbering thirty-three—of leading spokesmen of all the main shades of political and trade union opinion in the Six (and later in Britain too). It marked a significant progress that Monnet was able to enrol in the Action Committee not just the leaders of European Christian Democracy, already well known as ' good Europeans' but also spokesmen from other political forces which had been sceptical or hostile: the Committee included the SPD leader Erich Ollenhauer, the SFIO leader (and future Prime Minister) Guy Mollet, and Maurice Faure from the French Radical Party, who was to be Mollet's Minister for European Affairs. The meetings of the Action Committee, held normally at six-monthly intervals, were to provide a powerful stimulus to parliamentary and public debate on the next stages in the way to European unity, and an equally powerful support in ensuring the signature of the Treaty of Rome.

Another important factor in the success of the Messina Conference was that the Coal and Steel Community could be seen to be making a positive contribution to the development of the industries for which it was responsible. If the EDC failure had occurred in a situation in which the idea of European integration had been unable to show any positive achievements at all, the prospects for further steps forward would have been much worse.

The combination of Monnet's subterranean prodding and the

evident success of the ECSC, however, stimulated the governments
of the Six to put forward the new proposals which led to the
Messina Conference. As well as the document worked out by the
three Benelux governments, already mentioned, there was a
memorandum from the Italian government calling for greater
European efforts towards cooperation in the fields of social policy
and economic development, and a document from the Bonn
government putting forward among other proposals the idea of a
European university.

These documents were discussed by the representatives of the
Six at Messina: Luxembourg's Prime Minister Joseph Bech, the
Foreign Ministers of Belgium, France, Italy and the Netherlands
(Spaak, Pinay, Martino and Beyen), and the Permanent Under-
Secretary of the German Foreign Ministry, Professor Walter
Hallstein. They agreed to set up a working committee under
Spaak, where representatives of the six governments would sit
with experts from the ECSC's High Authority to examine the
ways to move towards closer European integration.

The Spaak Committee met between July 1955 and March
1956, at the Château de Val Duchesse near Brussels, and made
recommendations which were to lead directly to the treaties
setting up the European Economic Community and Euratom,
signed in Rome in March 1957.

Although the EEC later proved to have much greater importance
than Euratom—which was to languish during the 1960s while
EEC was to advance towards important integration policies—it is
striking that in the atmosphere of 1955-57, Spaak, and to a
certain degree Monnet and some of their colleagues, regarded the
coordination of Europe's nuclear energy policies as the first
priority. Here, it seemed, was a vital yet fairly clearly defined
field of national policy—like the earlier sector of policies for coal
and steel—which could logically be detached from national
decision-making and put under a European authority resembling
the ECSC. Atomic energy appeared to many Europeans at this
time as a source of power which would speedily provide a cheap
supplement to existing energy resources—one which needed
planning on a European level—and whose subjection to a European authority would provide a strong impetus towards further
steps in integration. This view persisted even in 1958—when
the French officials sent to join the staff of the newly established

EEC received the apologies of their superiors for the fact that they were being assigned to the 'unimportant' Common Market instead of to the Atomic Energy Authority which was regarded as more significant! The expectation was to prove false, however; partly because the member-states of Euratom kept large areas of nuclear research under national control; partly because this research did not in fact offer great quantities of cheap energy as early as expected; and partly because Britain, which might have contributed substantially to this area of European policy from her own fairly advanced research programme, chose not to join Euratom any more than the ECSC or the Common Market.

The British government showed an interest in the Messina Conference by sending a medium-ranking official of the Board of Trade as an observer, and continued to be represented in the work of the Spaak Committee until the autumn of 1955.

By November, however, the British representative had withdrawn from the Committee, since the Six appeared determined to pursue the 'supra-national' approach they had evolved in the ECSC and EDC negotiations, and Britain was unwilling to join any new organisation based on this attitude. The clash of views was less sharp than in 1950, since the Spaak Committee was in fact taking great care to avoid the public commitment to supranationalism which had brought the EDC to disaster. Their proposals for the institutions of the EDC and Euratom, as will be seen, allowed national governments a much greater say in decision-making than did the ECSC structure. Even this, however, went too far for the British government, now led by Sir Anthony Eden— who appears to have believed that the Six would not in fact succeed, especially after the collapse of EDC, in setting up an effective European Economic Community. British official attitudes towards the Six's attempts at unity during the winter of 1955-56 thus varied from scepticism to open hostility (for which Britain would later pay dearly), and the Six moved forward towards unity on their own.

The West European political climate of 1956-57, which produced the Treaties of Rome in March 1957, was in many ways favourable to a closer degree of integration. The French government led by Guy Mollet was better disposed to this course than those of Mendès-France or Edgar Faure; and Mollet— although a socialist—was on very good terms with Chancellor

Adenauer. (Their close working partnership, in fact, tended to disprove the view that European integration was the work largely of Christian Democrats, since Adenauer's relations with at least one French MRP leader—Georges Bidault—were distinctly worse than with Mollet.) The two governments reached agreement on the Saar—which was returned to Germany at the beginning of 1957—and they also saw Europe's need for general political cohesion in similar terms. The Soviet invasion of Hungary in October 1956, and the American action in opposing the Anglo-French invasion of Egypt at the same time, were seen by both Adenauer and Mollet as reasons for Europeans to move closer together.

The Treaty of Rome: aims and first stages
The Treaty of Rome, by which the six members of the ECSC agreed to go ahead with the integration of their economies on a much broader scale, was signed on 25 March 1957. As well as the treaty setting up the European Economic Community, the Six signed on the same day the treaty establishing the European Atomic Energy Authority or Euratom: as we have seen, this organisation failed to fulfil the high expectations of its founders and in the rest of this chapter the use of the term 'Treaty of Rome' will refer only to the EEC treaty. The EEC represented a development of the 'supra-national' principle of the ECSC, in contrast to the 'inter-governmental' or 'functionalist' approach of the OEEC and the Council of Europe: its operation produced before long a situation described by one writer as 'Europe at Sixes and Sevens', since the action of the Six in setting up EEC led a so-called 'outer-Seven' to form a looser European Free Trade Association (EFTA), based firmly on the principle of inter-governmental action. The story of EEC's relations with EFTA (whose members were the United Kingdom, Denmark, Norway, Sweden, Switzerland, Austria and Portugal) belongs to a later chapter (Chapter 13).

The provisions of the Treaty of Rome—an elaborate document of 248 articles—can be very roughly classified in two categories: those designed to achieve 'negative' and those designed to achieve 'positive' integration. In the first category belong all the proposed measures aimed at removing tariff barriers, abolishing obstacles to free movement of people and capital between the Six, and the merging of external tariffs of the members into one general tariff system *vis-à-vis* the outside world. These could be described very broadly as the measures designed to merge the six national markets into a ' common market ' in the strict sense—an economic union with no barriers to the internal movement of goods, people and capital, and a common external tariff.

The second range of measures, aimed at what was later called ' positive ' integration, were naturally more ambitious: in fact they were only laid down in very broad terms in the treaty itself, since the intensive negotiations in the Spaak Committee and subsequently had shown by early 1957 that quite large differences of view still existed among the national governments. The Germans were on the whole unwilling to adopt ' interventionist ' economic policies which appeared to go against the philosophy of Professor Erhard's ' market economy ', while the French negotiators brought with them the ideas of economic *dirigisme* which Monnet and his colleagues had originally developed in the postwar French Economic Planning Commission. In particular, France wanted assurances that her industrial competitiveness would not suffer because her systems of social security, paid holidays and equal pay for women were better developed than those of Germany; that provision would be made for the territories of her former colonial empire, mainly in Africa, to benefit both by trade and by aid from the new European Community; and that her farmers would have the benefits of a managed market for agricultural produce, guaranteeing minimum prices and reasonably predictable sales, in contrast to the free market which Europe was to adopt for industrial goods. The other members of the Six were in agreement with these points—Belgium also had her Congo in Africa, and in Germany itself a powerful peasant lobby supported the proposed Common Agricultural Policy—and they were duly written into the Treaty. On certain other aspects of ' positive integration '—the development of common European policies for industry and technology, or the harmonisation of legal and tax systems, the Treaty was deliberately vaguer, since these policies would clearly only be worked out in the longer term.

To carry the agreed objectives into effect, the Treaty of Rome set up a system of institutions very similar to that of the ECSC: the Council of nine members corresponded to the High Authority;

the Council of Ministers was, as before, the body where members of the six governments had their say on the development of policy; the Assembly—which consisted of the 78-man ECSC Assembly enlarged to 142 and with responsibility for all three Communities—represented the element of democratic control; and the Court of Justice provided legal sanctions for the carrying-out of the Treaty. There were, however, some important differences between EEC and ECSC, reflecting the fact that much broader sectors of economic life were not coming under a degree of supra-national control: the EEC Commission was given less power than the High Authority to impose its will on member states; the Council of Ministers was required to operate by a complicated system of weighted voting, so that member states did not have to fear being outvoted on matters of importance to them; the Council's hand was further strengthened by the establishment of a powerful Committee of Permanent Representatives—ambassadorial-ranking representatives of the Six in Brussels—who kept a continual check on the Commission's work in between the frequent meetings of the Council of Ministers; and the Assembly—even though it gave itself the imposing title of 'European Parliament' and took to debating the general policy of the Community—had relatively little control over the budget or functioning of the institutions. (The Economic and Social Committee of 101 members, again, had a purely consultative role.)

The EEC thus began its life as something more than a traditional inter-governmental organisation—the independent Commission, charged with the task of developing common policies, was to ensure this—but something much less than a full federal structure. The six governments, represented in the Council and the Committee of Permanent Representatives, were concerned not to allow the European Commission too much power: nonetheless, the programme entrusted to it was more ambitious than anything Europe had yet seen.

By the Treaty of Rome, the Six committed themselves to achieving full economic integration within 12 years—with a possible extension to 15 if any of the member states found the pace too fast. The 12-year period of transition was divided into three four-year stages, with a general commitment to dismantle a certain degree of tariff protection at the end of each one, as well as to reach agreement on certain critical sectors of policy, e.g. agriculture.

The Treaty of Rome thus contained a mixture of firm provisions—on which agreement had already been reached by the Six—and general commitments whose detailed working-out and implementation were left to the Commission and its staff. The Commission, which took office in 1958, had as its President Walter Hallstein, the lawyer and diplomat who had negotiated the ECSC Treaty for Germany and had represented her at Messina; its Vice-Presidents were the Italian Piero Malvestiti, the Dutchman Sicco Mansholt (a former Netherlands Minister of Agriculture who was to play a considerable part in developing the EEC's Common Agricultural Policy), and Robert Marjolin, a former colleague of Monnet's in the French Planning Commission. The Commission's other members were Hans von der Groeben, Robert Lemaignen, and Giuseppe Petrilli (respectively German, French and Italian), the Belgian Jean Rey (a former Minister for Economic Affairs and future President of the European Commission) and Michel Rasquin from Luxembourg.

The setting in which this European executive had to operate —the framework of the Treaty of Rome—was the product of a process of interaction between the national policies of the Six and the idea of a ' European ' interest represented by men like Jean Monnet. The Commission was now itself to take a hand in the game of shaping Europe's future; even though in the 1960s, as hitherto, the process was to be one of interaction between the ' European ' view and the interests of the various member states.

10 France Under de Gaulle 1958-69

Introduction: a new start?

General de Gaulle became Prime Minister of France on 1 June 1958 in circumstances which gave him a virtually free hand to design the kind of political institutions he had long argued that France needed. After the draft had been worked on for some time, during which the ideas of de Gaulle and his colleagues naturally predominated, the constitution of the new Fifth Republic was put to the vote on 28 September and received 79 per cent of the 22.6 million votes cast. A few weeks later, on 23 November, elections took place for the first Assembly of the new régime: the size of the Gaullist group in parliament increased dramatically from 16 to 187, and, together with their allies the conservative Independents, they formed an overwhelming majority of 331 members of the assembly of 465. In a further vote on 21 December, the representatives of the French people were asked to elect their President according to the rules laid down by the new constitution ('representatives', since the constitution provided for the election of the President not by direct popular vote, but by the votes of parliamentarians and local councillors): de Gaulle received 77.5 per cent of the votes, and his nearest competitor a mere 13.6 per cent.

By the end of 1958 a new set of institutions had thus been established and the holders of the main posts had duly been selected: de Gaulle as President of the Republic; Michel Debré as Prime Minister (Debré, a faithful follower of the General for many years, typified—like André Malraux, the novelist and Gaullist minister—a certain type of Fifth Republican leadership); Jacques Chaban-Delmas as President of the National Assembly (Chaban-Delmas typified a less doctrinaire kind of leader, in that he had been a Radical Party politician and colleague of Mendès-France in the Fourth Republic); Maurice Couve de Murville as Foreign Minister (here was a different type again—Couve de Murville was a high-ranking career diplomat, and thus one of de Gaulle's 'technocratic' ministers). The claim of the

' new men ' of the Fifth Republic was that their institutions would provide France with more stable leadership than the feeble Fourth Republic, which had indeed died without great mourning in May 1958.

The Gaullist critique of the Third and Fourth Republics, as we have seen, centred on the argument that the multiplicity of political parties, in an Assembly which was the main centre of power in the whole system, was incapable of sustaining governments enjoying any authority or continuity. Each cabinet had to regard itself—and was regarded by the outside world—as a mere committee to whom the all-powerful Assembly might delegate power for a limited period, only to withdraw it by a vote of no confidence when any governmental action incurred its displeasure. The central purpose of the changes involved in 1958 was thus to create the basis for a less fragmented party system, and also —since a change of such magnitude would take some time—to reduce the power of the Assembly over the executive branch of the government. The makers of the new constitution introduced several devices designed to achieve these objectives. The reduction of the number of political parties was to be encouraged by a reform of the electoral law which made it—paradoxically—more like that of the Third Republic than of the Fourth: instead of the unmanageable parliaments of 1951 and 1956, deputies would henceforth be elected in single-member constituencies, with the crucial proviso that, if no candidate received an absolute majority on the first ballot, a second would be held, in practice between the two leading candidates. The reasoning behind this reform was that while the first ballot would allow French voters to express a preference between the whole spectrum of competing ideologies, the second would compel them to concentrate their votes on candidates capable of sustaining a viable governing majority.

As for the powers of the Assembly, these were curtailed in two directions: first, the procedure whereby the Assembly could vote a government out of office was fairly drastically limited, by a more stringent specification of the circumstances in which a vote of confidence was authorised; secondly, a very large area of governmental decision-making was taken away from the Cabinet, and handed over to the President of the Republic.

The presidency—which was in fact tailored to fit the aptitudes and spheres of interest of General de Gaulle—became something

L

very much more than the ceremonial or brokerage office occupied
by Auriol and Coty, the Presidents of the Fourth Republic.
Although all the ceremonial functions remained, and although
the President was in theory to represent a national viewpoint
transcending that of political parties and economic interests, it
was clear that he was also empowered to take decisions over the
whole range of governmental policies. In practice, this meant
that in some cases, where President de Gaulle was not personally
interested (e.g. educational or industrial policy), the formulation
of policy was left to the Prime Minister and Cabinet; other affairs
of state—particularly the crucial areas of foreign policy, defence
policy and the Algerian problem—became known as the ' presidential domain ', and there decisions rested firmly in the hands
of President de Gaulle.

The General's powerful personality, combined with the overwhelming votes of confidence expressed in the various elections
of late 1958, naturally gave him a wide degree of latitude in approaching these questions; however he still had to exercise some
caution—particularly on the explosive issue of Algeria—in order
not to create irrevocable antagonism among important groups
among his supporters.

The Gaullist party, as we have seen, occupied a massively
strong position in the Assembly elected in November 1958. Its
spectacular achievement in winning nearly 200 seats out of 465,
even though this could be attributed very largely to de Gaulle's
personal prestige and to the general feeling that there was no
alternative, made the Union for the New Republic (as it com-
prehensively entitled itself) into France's first approach to a uni-
fied conservative party: it brought together many of the elements
hitherto dispersed among the Independent and Peasant Parties,
the Poujadistes and the right wings of the Radicals and Christian
Democrats. The Gaullist Party in fact repudiated any suggestion
that it was a party of the right—many of its leaders, such as
Soustelle and Malraux, had left-wing backgrounds, and it contained a not inconsiderable trade union element led by Louis
Wallon and others—but its basic philosophy was right-wing:
support for capitalist economics, French national interests (in
opposition to the supranational tendencies of the Common Market
and NATO) and above all the continuation of French rule in
Algeria, were widely held beliefs among Gaullist parliamentarians.

The political fortunes of the Gaullist Party fluctuated somewhat during the decade of de Gaulle's rule (its title fluctuated more severely, changing to 'Union for the New Republic—Fifth Republic', in the 1962 election, and 'Democratic Union for the Fifth Republic' in 1967): its parliamentary representation rose from 187 to 229 in 1962, dropped to 200 in 1967, rose again to 294 in 1968. The gains of 1962 meant that the Gaullist Party was no longer obliged to form a coalition government with the conservative Independents, with whom it had been allied in 1958. The Independents (133 seats in 1958; 48 in 1962; 40 in 1967; 64 in 1968) were led originally by Antoine Pinay, a former Prime Minister who joined de Gaulle's government as Finance Minister in 1958, and later by Valéry Giscard d'Estaing, a much younger man (born in 1926) but like Pinay an apostle of strictly orthodox financial policy. The Independents thus provided the Gaullist Party with the support of France's more traditional right-wing voters, but the two parties disagreed on some aspects of policy—a disagreement expressed in Giscard's celebrated phrase of 1965—'*Oui, mais . . .*'. The Independents, besides standing for traditional economics and mistrusting even the tentative notions of 'workers' participation' voiced by certain Gaullists, were strong supporters of European integration: the fact that this ensured that France did not withdraw from the EEC, which had come into effect at the start of the General's first year of office, 1958, was something, but the Independents also opposed de Gaulle's cavalier treatment of the Brussels organisation in 1965-66. They were also in disagreement with his negative policies towards the United States and NATO, and sceptical about his attempt at an 'opening to the East'.

The remaining political forces of the Fourth Republic now counted for very little. The Christian Democrats (formerly MRP, now known as Democratic Centre) won 57 seats in 1958 and 36 in 1962, but in 1967, even grouped together with various dissident conservatives and other centrists, they mustered a grand total of only 40. They were of course violently opposed to de Gaulle's negative views on European integration, but could do nothing but protest: in the course of the 1960s, some of their leaders (particularly Maurice Schumann, the former assistant of Robert Schuman) had reverted to their war-time Gaullist allegiance, and took up ministerial posts.

The same occurred among the Radicals, of whom a number —including Chaban-Delmas and Edgar Faure—joined de Gaulle's government in the years after 1958. (The Radical Party survived these defections, but won a mere 23 seats in 1958, 42 in 1962 and 24 in 1967.)

The Socialist Party, still led by Guy Mollet until late in the 1960s, was condemned to permanent opposition after 1958: its parliamentary representation was substantial—44 seats in 1958, 65 in 1962, 76 in 1967 and 57 in 1968—but its only hope of regaining power lay in alliance with the Communists. (Two of its leaders, Gaston Defferre and François Mitterand, were able to present de Gaulle with something of a challenge, on the basis of a Socialist-Communist united front.)

The Communist Party, finally, though reduced to 10 seats in 1958 (mainly by the functioning of the new electoral system rather than a drop in votes) recovered to 41 in 1962, 72 in 1967 and 33 in 1968. Its main dilemma was how far to compromise its Marxist programme in order to cooperate with the non-Communist left.

Algeria 1958-62

De Gaulle returned to power in June 1958 essentially as a result of the revolt by the army and local French residents against any idea of Algerian independence: by 1962 his government had signed the Evian Agreement with the Algerian National Liberation Front, which made Algeria an independent state. In June 1958, when the new head of government visited Algiers, he was acclaimed by a wildly enthusiastic crowd of European residents (many of the white population were third- or fourth-generation inhabitants of Algeria), and responded to their demonstration against independence by an expansive cry of 'I understand you' ('*Je vous ai compris*'): in 1962, his decision to give independence to the Algerians aroused bitter hostility among the same European population, and led to an irreconcilable breach with some of the General's most ardent supporters, including Jacques Soustelle and others who had worked most actively for his return to power in 1958.

It is uncertain whether de Gaulle already realised in 1958 that he would one day have to concede independence to Algeria, as previous governments had granted it to the neighbouring territories of Tunisia and Morocco. These two states had in fact been simply protectorates, under French rule only since the 1880s and the early twentieth century respectively, whereas Algeria had been legally part of France since the 1830s. Another reason why France's resistance to local independence had been stronger, for instance, than against the Indo-Chinese colonies, was because one-tenth of the population of Algeria—about a million people—were of European extraction. These were the crowds who acclaimed de Gaulle in the forum in Algiers in June 1958 and who became bitterly disillusioned as his government began, by late 1959, to move towards accepting an independent Algerian state in which their position could be weakened *vis-à-vis* that of the Arab majority.

As the war in Algeria wore on, engulfing ever more of France's military strength in a manner reminiscent of the Indo-Chinese war a few years earlier, it became clearer to de Gaulle, a supreme realist, that independence might be inevitable. It was, after all, in line with his general philosophy that a people who proved themselves to be a nation—as the Algerians were now doing—should win the reward of having their nationhood recognised in the form of statehood. The Algerian National Liberation Front and the Provisional Government of the Algerian Republic—established in Cairo and recognised by a growing number of countries of the ' Third World '—thus looked less like a band of terrorists and more like ' responsible spokesmen ' (' *des interlocuteurs valables* ') as de Gaulle began to express it at the time.

The prospect of peace-talks with the Algerian nationalists— even though the latter now controlled large parts of Algeria outside the major cities of Algiers, Oran and Constantine—was anathema not only to the European resident population but also to part of the leadership of the French army. The generals in command in Algeria, after all, were in many cases men who had fought for almost eight years in Indo-China, only to see their efforts end in failure, and who had then helped de Gaulle to return to power in 1958 in the firm conviction that he would help them to keep Algeria part of France. Even his careful attempts to carry the army commanders with him towards the inevitable granting of Algerian independence failed to convince them that he was right. In February 1960, when a group of right-wing extremists in Algiers put up barricades and demonstrated against the idea of Algerian independence, the local army command did nothing to hinder them. Much more serious, when de Gaulle's government began to consider serious negotiations with the Algerian National Liberation Front (eventually to start in February 1962, at the small French spa of Evian on Lake Geneva), some of the army commanders themselves openly revolted against Paris. The so-called '*putsch* of Algiers' of April 1961, when four generals defied de Gaulle (as they had defied the Fourth Republic in May 1958), ended in their humiliation. The situation was quite different from that of 1958, in that de Gaulle had the backing of the majority of Frenchmen in his view that old-style colonialism in Algeria was dead, and that France must cut her losses and withdraw. Although the rebellious generals made some attempt to organise a revolution in France against de Gaulle's government, the plotters there found no popular support—Algerian independence was supported by a large majority in a referendum—and the leaders of the rebellion in Algiers were arrested and placed on trial.

De Gaulle's successful resistance to this threat opened the way to the final negotiations for Algerian independence, and the Evian Agreement which granted this took effect in the summer of 1962. Most of the European minority left Algeria for metropolitan France. Here some of them continued an underground struggle against the government for some months, under the title of 'Organisation of the Secret Army', and a large number supported extreme right-wing movements up to the presidential election of 1965, when they gave a substantial vote to de Gaulle's neo-fascist opponent Jacques Tixier-Vignancourt. The majority of French Algerians, however, were absorbed into French life within a few years, and became politically more moderate—like the refugees from beyond the Oder-Neisse Line in West Germany.

De Gaulle between West and East 1962-68

The main effort of Algerian independence, as far as de Gaulle was concerned, was that it freed his hands for a more ambitious foreign policy. Although his challenge to the super-powers—the two 'hegemonial' powers of the 1945 Yalta settlement—was later to take on the spectacular form of journeys and speech-making in Latin America, Canada and Cambodia, the starting-point of his foreign policy was France's relations with Germany and with the Western alliance. During his ten years in office, from 1958 onwards, de Gaulle was to try each of the three classic variants of French policy towards Germany: the policy of close alignment with the maritime powers, America and Britain, to exercise joint control over Germany; the policy of close agreement with Germany herself, to keep any dangerous tendencies under control and to use Germany to some extent against the 'Anglo-Saxons'; and the policy of looking beyond Germany to her Eastern neighbours, to control her through understandings with the Soviet Union and the smaller Slavonic states. In the interdependent Western Europe of the 1960s, of course, none of these traditional French policies could be pursued with the simplicity attempted by Clemenceau in 1919, Briand in 1925 or Barthou in 1934, but the development of de Gaulle's relations with the West Germany of Adenauer bore distinct traces of these historical models.

The phase of the first kind of policy—the attempt to work closely with the maritime powers, i.e. to increase France's standing in NATO—was also the phase of the Algerian war. In September 1958, shortly after taking office as Prime Minister, de Gaulle addressed a letter to President Eisenhower in which he proposed a revision of the North Atlantic Treaty Organisation, so that the three nuclear powers—the United States, Britain and France—would be placed in the position of a permanent directorate making the basic policy decisions for the whole alliance. This proposal led to some discussions between Paris and Washington, but President Eisenhower was unwilling to upgrade France's status in the alliance as de Gaulle wished: seen from Paris, NATO remained an affair dominated by the 'Anglo-Saxons' (the British government of the time made a point of emphasising London's 'special relationship' with Washington), and the General began to move nearer to a position of withdrawing from the integrated alliance structure altogether.

The Berlin crisis of 1958 was in fact already providing a basis for de Gaulle to move towards the second main variant of France's German policy—the alignment *with* Germany *against* the Anglo-Saxon powers. France's strong verbal stand against Soviet pressure on Berlin, at a time when even Dulles was hesitant and Macmillan appeared a positive appeaser, impelled Adenauer even more closely towards Paris, and laid the foundation for the Franco-German Treaty of January 1963. The other main strand in the background leading to this was that the French government had been pursuing a line of European policy designed not so much to weaken EEC altogether—the Fifth Republic had inherited the Treaty of Rome already signed, and did not consider repealing it—as to ensure that the supra-national European Commission in Brussels was limited in its functioning and kept in check by a strictly inter-government body representing the six member-states. The Fouchet Plan (named after the French politician responsible for negotiating on the project) envisaged an elaborate political treaty to be signed by the six governments, providing for regular inter-governmental consultation at a variety of levels from heads of state downwards. It was rejected by France's partners, for reasons connected with the general development of EEC (see Chapter 13), but the nucleus of the proposal was then transferred to the bilateral Franco-German relationship, where it took the form of the treaty of January 1963. (De Gaulle's international position had in the meantime been greatly strengthened by the winding-up of the Algerian War, by a triumphal tour of West Germany in the autumn, and by victories both in the parliamentary elections and in a referendum in favour of electing the president by direct suffrage.)

The reason why this agreement may be regarded as marking a transition to the idea of a Franco-German bloc against the Anglo-Saxons is that it came within a few days of de Gaulle's rejection of Britain's application to join EEC, which the General saw as an attempt to submerge the European organisation in a vast Atlantic free trade area. President Kennedy had spoken of European-American ' interdependence ' in his Philadelphia speech of July 1962, but de Gaulle saw this only as a disguised form of American hegemony. A Franco-German bloc appeared to him to be the answer, and Chancellor Adenauer appeared to see the significance of Franco-German friendship in the same light. In practice, the treaty of January 1963, although symbolising a further reconciliation between two hereditary enemies, and doing much to favour educational and economic exchanges between the two countries, did not take on the anti-American or anti-NATO quality de Gaulle had expected, since this ran directly against Germany's wishes. The German government in fact became increasingly close to Washington in this period, as we shall see

(Chapter 12), and de Gaulle's disappointment was considerable. This led to the third period of his foreign policy, when he first stalled the machinery of the EEC in the great crisis of June 1965, then took France out of the integrated structure of NATO in April 1966, and finally embarked on a series of visits to Moscow and other Eastern capitals in an endeavour to break down Europe's division into two blocs.

De Gaulle's visits to Moscow, Warsaw and Bucharest did something to improve the climate of East-West relations in Europe, but it was hard to resist the impression that their main purpose was to rally the French people in support of a head of state whose popularity was beginning to drop once the immense problem of Algeria was out of the way. In December 1965, after seven years as President, de Gaulle stood for re-election and was given an unexpectedly hard fight by François Mitterand, the candidate of the left. In the first ballot, Mitterand's score of 32.2 per cent of the votes prevented de Gaulle from getting the absolute majority required for immediate election (the President got only 43.7 per cent), and a second ballot was needed, in which de Gaulle obtained 54.4 per cent of the votes against Mitterand's 45.5 per cent. This was very far from the triumphant election results of 1958 or 1962: it reflected an increasingly tense economic situation, when a policy of financial stringency was applied by de Gaulle's Finance Minister Giscard d'Estaing, and when the discontent of the working class was beginning to mount to the peak it was to reach in 1967-68.

It would be unfair to depict de Gaulle's spectacular foreign policy as motivated entirely by the desire to distract the French people's attention from this depressing economic and social situation. True, he had written in his war memoirs that the French people were prone to fissiparous tendencies and needed to be led into ' *vastes entreprises* ' in order to be truly themselves. The President's claim to be overcoming the Cold War division of Europe—leading a revolt against the ' two hegemonies ' in the hope that Roumania and Poland would shake off Soviet domination as he claimed to have thrown off that of America—was certainly a ' *vaste entreprise* ' of this kind, and part of its motivation must be sought in French domestic politics.

However, it corresponded also to de Gaulle's conviction that France really *could* play a leading part in creating a new and more

flexible Europe. The same applies to some of his other gestures
in foreign policy—the dramatic fashion in which he reopened
diplomatic relations with Communist China early in 1964, or
toured Latin America later the same year making eloquent
speeches in Spanish promising to help France's Latin cousins to
free themselves from American domination. The same mixture
of dramatic effect and expectations of real results characterised
the General's visit to Cambodia late in 1965, when he made a
magnificent speech attacking America's policy in Vietnam and
praising Cambodia's policy of neutralism; his attitude towards
the Arab-Israeli war in 1967—though here his pro-Arab line
antagonised large sections of French opinion, even though it corresponded with France's economic interests; and his visit to
Canada later the same year, when he created a sensation if not a
scandal by his support for the autonomist movement of French-
speaking Canada by his calculated cry of '*Vive le Québec
libre!*'.

De Gaulle's attempt at creating a new Europe, with a leading
role for France, as well as establishing a French presence on the
larger world scene, stood in striking contrast to the way France
under the Fourth Republic had so often been at the mercy of
external forces. His policy was in many ways a negative one—it
consisted of challenging or disrupting the structure of EEC or
NATO, or defying American domination, without being able to
offer any constructive alternative, at least in the short run. In
this way it resembled the policies practised—or at least preached
—by Britain during the 1950s and early 1960s, when Eden and
Macmillan claimed that Britain was still a world power, without
in fact having the strength to back this claim up. France, similarly,
did not have the economic resources to make good de Gaulle's
lavish promises to Latin America, and his policy outside the
central area of great-power confrontation in Europe remained
one of essentially empty gestures.

Within the central area, too, de Gaulle's vision of a Europe
liberated from the domination of the super-powers was rudely
shattered by the Soviet invasion of Czechoslovakia in August
1968. The General reacted to this by denouncing the Soviet-
American collusion of Yalta 23 years earlier as the cause of
Europe's division into spheres of influence, now brutally confirmed. His Defence Minister, Michel Debré, bravely wrote off

the Soviet invasion as a mere ' traffic accident ' on the road to a
new Europe. The harsh fact remained, however, that the Gaullist
hopes of the blocs giving way to a flexible diplomatic system were
now condemned to failure: France herself had no alternative
but to reaffirm her solidarity with the Western alliance—though
without rejoining the integrated command structures of NATO.

The ' events ' of May 1968 and the end of de Gaulle
Even before Czechoslovakia, de Gaulle's power-base inside French
society had been gravely damaged by the revolutionary explosion
known as the ' events ' of May 1968. In Paris, dramatic scenes
in the Latin Quarter, where thousands of students took over the
Sorbonne and fought nightly battles with heavily-armed riot police
(the CRS established by Jules Moch to deal with the Communist
strikers in 1947), were accompanied by a mass strike in which
millions of French workers took part. These outbursts of revolt
by students and workers were the culmination of growing unrest,
the origins of which stretched back for several years. As early as
1963 a large strike of coal-miners had been met by the government first with firm resistance, then with capitulation; in 1965,
a serious financial crisis had caused a tight budgetary policy and
general restrictions on economic growth; in 1967, after a General
Election in which the Gaullist party only with difficulty managed
to keep its absolute majority, a series of cuts in the social services
were announced, which were to be implemented not by parliamentary legislation but by administrative decrees.

There was thus a considerable groundswell of public discontent
by the spring of 1968, when the students of Paris set off the
train of events which nearly brought about de Gaulle's immediate
downfall, and gravely weakened his régime. A series of incidents,
beginning with protests against disciplinary measures at the new
University of Nanterre at the beginning of May, led within a few
days to widespread rioting in Paris: on the night of 10 May
armed police stormed 60 barricades erected by the students and
the night's fighting resulted in 367 badly injured being taken to
hospital, the arrest and detention of 468 students as well as the
destruction by fire of 60 cars. Within a few days, the Sorbonne
was occupied by revolutionary students and by 18 May—when
de Gaulle had to cut short his visit to Roumania to return to
Paris—strike action had been taken by motor workers, transport

services and the Post Office. Massive demonstrations in favour of higher pay and workers' control took place throughout French industrial centres; the state-controlled radio and television services, protesting against the obligation to give only the official version of events, joined the strike; and in Paris, in a symbolic gesture against the capitalist financial system, a group of insurgent students attempted to set fire to the Stock Exchange.

The Communist-led trade union federation (CGT) at this stage revealed what a profoundly un-revolutionary or even counter-revolutionary force it was by embarking on wage negotiations with the government, and concluding an agreement which was repudiated by the great majority of its members. The Catholic union federation (CFDT) in fact appeared closer to the revolutionary mood of the masses, by demanding much larger pay rises and also—more significantly—the right of workers to manage their own factories. President de Gaulle was clearly uncertain how to react to these pressures, and to the statements by the spokesmen of the political opposition—Mitterand and Mendès-France—that they would form a new government if they had the support of all the left-wing forces. The President of the Republic disappeared for several hours on 29 May: it afterwards transpired that he had visited General Massu, the commander of the French military forces stationed in Germany, and had obtained an assurance of the army's support in the crisis—though only at the price of liberating General Salan, one of the imprisoned rebels of April 1961, and of allowing Georges Bidault, another supporter of 'Algérie française' to return to France after six years in exile.

President de Gaulle and his Prime Minister, Georges Pompidou, disagreed on what tactics to adopt to mobilise the Gaullist sections of public opinion against the left. De Gaulle favoured a referendum—the device which had won him overwhelming support for his policies in 1958 and 1962—whereas Pompidou argued that a parliamentary election, which was certain to reinforce the slender Gaullist majority elected in 1967, would be more in tune with the spirit of the time. De Gaulle's personal magic was indeed fading and he had to accept the advice of Pompidou and the majority of the Cabinet. The ensuing election campaign, during which the first ballot was held on 23 June and the second a week later, confirmed the correctness of Pompidou's judgement: the majority parties—Gaullists and their independent allies—won 358 of the 485 seats, inflicting on the opposition the loss of 118 seats, including that of Pierre Mendès-France.

De Gaulle's position was greatly strengthened, and the wage-increases awarded to the striking workers were kept within fairly strict limits. The effects of the May-June events on the French political system took a little time to become apparent: the first outward sign was that Georges Pompidou, the Prime Minister whose advice had in fact saved de Gaulle, was removed from office and replaced by Maurice Couve de Murville (whose place as Foreign Minister was taken by Michel Debré). Pompidou, who had been Prime Minister since 1962—the longest term of office of any French Prime Minister since Guizot in the 1840s—appeared to have been ill-rewarded by de Gaulle, but his moment of triumph was not in fact to be long delayed.

The position of the French government, and de Gaulle's personal standing, were severely shaken by the events of May and June 1968. In particular, the immense gold reserves, which had allowed de Gaulle to challenge the dominant position of the dollar in the world monetary system, were drastically reduced, and the voice of France in world affairs was strikingly muted; the new situation was underlined by the Czech crisis in August, which dealt a massive blow to the Gaullist vision of the future of East-West relations in Europe.

At home, also, it was increasingly felt that the General no longer represented the wishes of the majority of Frenchmen as he certainly had done a few years earlier. True, he spoke in forward-looking terms of promoting workers' participation in industry, and his new Minister of Education, Edgar Faure (a Radical Prime Minister of the Fourth Republic, with a pronounced gift for political survival) carried out reforms which met many of the student demands of May 1968. However, the General's departure from office was clearly not far off. The manner of his going was characteristically imposing, and almost certainly he desired the end to come about as it did. Early in 1969 he announced that, as part of the programme of institutional reforms provoked by the events of 1968, he would ask the French people to vote on a project introducing powerful regional assemblies in the main provincial centres of France, and abolishing the Senate in its existing form. The proposal in itself seemed a progressive one—the excessive centralisation of political power in France had long seemed a barrier to effective local democracy and economic initiatives—but the authoritarian manner in which the project was imposed provoked very strong resistance. In the referendum on 27 April 1969 de Gaulle—who had not campaigned with his old vigour on behalf of his project—received only 52.41 per cent of the 'yes' votes, and although this was larger than the total of 'noes' (47.58 per cent), de Gaulle announced his resignation as President the next day.

In the presidential election that followed, in June, Georges Pompidou was elected as de Gaulle's successor: he chose Jacques Chaban-Delmas as his Prime Minister. With de Gaulle's departure, a new era in French political life had begun, even though Gaullism remained a powerful force and the new President and government were at pains to stress the themes of continuity and fidelity.

Under the Fifth Republic, France had certainly attained a position of influence and prestige—to use favourite Gaullist terms —which the Fourth had not known. Material prosperity had greatly increased (though much of the credit for this should go to the planning of investment under the maligned '*ancien régime*' of the Fourth Republic); the political system had been simplified, in the sense that the right wing—if not the left—had at last developed a moderately coherent and united political party; and France's standing in the world had in some ways benefited from de Gaulle's audacious if fundamentally ephemeral diplomacy. President Pompidou and his colleagues now faced the challenge of adapting de Gaulle's France to the new world scene of the 1970s.

11 Germany from Adenauer to Brandt

The Berlin Wall and the departure of Adenauer 1961-63
The barriers put up by the East Germans and Russians on the night of 13 August 1961 did more than seal off the Eastern from the Western sectors of Berlin: they also marked the end of the policy Adenauer had officially proclaimed ever since 1949, that the reunification of the two German states would one day take place through 'negotiation from strength'. By making clear the determination of the East German government to survive and no longer to allow its best-trained and most talented citizens to escape to the West through Berlin, the Wall closed off a whole line of approach to 'the German problem'—the line marked 'reunification'. Adenauer was clearly disorientated by the events of August 1961: even though the Western allies reacted with strong protests to the East German action—President Kennedy sent both Vice-President Johnson and General Lucius Clay (the hero of the 1948-49 blockade) to Berlin as special envoys in sign of solidarity—there was no question of any force being used to get the Wall taken down again. The West German government had to face the fact that its allies would not take any risks to rectify this weakening of West Berlin's position.

Worse still for Adenauer, his main ally, the United States, now showed dangerous signs of supporting his Social-Democratic rival, Willy Brandt, in the Federal elections due on 17 September —a month after the building of the Wall. Since its term began in January 1961, the Kennedy administration had in fact developed increasing impatience with Adenauer's negative and legalistic attitude towards East-West relations—or so the new men in Washington saw it—and the President flatly refused to give Adenauer the constant stream of assurances of American support that Dulles had tactfully provided. To a politician like Kennedy, the youthful and apparently flexible figure of Willy Brandt was much more appealing than that of the stony-faced Cold War veteran Adenauer—even though Brandt himself had shown himself resolutely opposed to the Russians as Mayor of

Berlin—and the American Embassy in Bonn strikingly failed in the 1961 election to provide the support for the CDU that had been readily available in 1953 and 1957.

In the 1961 election, for many reasons—of which tacit American support was only one—the SPD reaped the reward for the changes in programme, leadership and image which, as we have seen, it had carried out in the aftermath of the 1957 defeat. The Godesberg programme of moderate social reform had much greater public appeal than the doctrinaire and sterile Marxism of the past, and the dynamic figure of Willy Brandt appealed to many more voters than that of the worthy party bureaucrat Erich Ollenhauer had done. The CDU/CSU lost the absolute majority of votes and seats it had gained in 1957 (its share of the vote dropped from 50.0 to 45.3 per cent), and the new-style SPD gained more than a third of the votes for the first time in its history, going from 31.8 to 36.2 per cent. This meant that Adenauer was forced to engage in long negotiations with the FDP before being able to form a new cabinet in November, and that it now included three FDP members (like his cabinet of 1953) instead of being entirely composed of Christian Democrats (like the cabinet of 1957-61).

Adenauer was thus in a weaker position to deal with the crisis over Berlin, which developed to alarming proportions in the winter of 1961-62 as the Western allies attempted to work out a collective response to the building of the Wall. By the spring of 1962 it appeared fairly clear that, while France under de Gaulle was standing resolutely by the West German position (which denied the East German government any say in controlling access from the West to West Berlin), the British and even the American governments were prepared to negotiate with the Russians on the basis of allowing some East German representation on a body controlling the access-routes to the city. Adenauer was deeply alarmed by this prospect—the idea of recognising East Germany as a party to an international agreement, even tacitly, looked like a dangerous betrayal of a fundamental Western position—and resolved to take action to limit the likely damage. After encouraging press leaks in Bonn which gave away the essential points of the American negotiating position (as these had been discussed during talks in Washington between the Secretary of State Dean Rusk and the Soviet Ambassador Dobrynin), Adenauer made a well-publicised speech in Berlin on 8 May 1962, in which he violently denounced this American position as a potential sell-out of Germany's interests.

This episode had the desired effect of making a Soviet-Western agreement on Berlin at Bonn's expense unattainable for the moment. It also helped to cement Adenauer's close relations with the one Western ally he regarded as totally reliable: President de Gaulle. From the latter's point of view, as we have seen, the Franco-German treaty of January 1963 was a device to enlist West Germany in an anti-American front; Adenauer's fellow citizens, however, were not willing to see the treaty in the same light, and the Bundestag insisted on adding a preamble to the treaty specifying that close consultations with France should not conflict with any existing treaty commitment—i.e. essentially with the American alliance. Though somewhat reassured by this proviso, the Kennedy administration was still alarmed at the prospect of Germany being dragged into an anti-American position by de Gaulle's baneful influence, or even worse, developing a wish to possess, like France, her own nuclear *force de frappe*. There had in fact been occasional claims from Franz-Josef Strauss, Adenauer's Defence Minister since 1956, that Germany had a right to a greater share in NATO strategic policy-making, though even he had been careful not to do more than hint at any departure from the non-nuclear status agreed for Germany when rearmament began in 1955. The nightmare of Germany demanding nuclear weapons, however, came to preoccupy a number of leading officials in the Department of State in the months after the Franco-German treaty, and, as will be seen, the idea of German participation in a NATO multilateral force (MLF) was actively developed to counter the presumed danger.

President Kennedy himself took a calmer view of what was needed to reassure Germany of America's continued support. In June 1963, shortly before his assassination, he made a tour of Germany, paying a demonstrative visit to West Berlin in the course of which he had made a widely reported speech that included the celebrated phrase ' *Ich bin ein Berliner* '.

Adenauer naturally welcomed this support (even though it was accompanied by clear warnings that the Germans could not count on American help in reunifying their country by the ' official ' means of the 1950s: the simple absorption of East Germany).

M

By this time, however, the Chancellor's shaky position had been further weakened by the ' *Spiegel* affair ' of late 1962, when Strauss had been forced to resign from the government for having lied about his responsibility for the arrest of a journalist who had published an official document concerning military manoeuvres.* His ministerial colleagues, dismayed at Adenauer's inept handling of the *Spiegel* incident, were able to persuade him at last that the time had come for him to retire from office, and he reluctantly agreed to resign in October 1963.

Under the 14 years of Adenauer's Chancellorship Germany had developed a certain political stability. It was true that certain reactionary elements had been allowed to exercise influence at high levels (including Hans Globke, Adenauer's chief adviser, who was an ex-Nazi), and the Chancellor's somewhat contemptuous treatment of the Bundestag had not encouraged parliamentary debate to develop in full freedom. There had also been notably authoritarian episodes like Adenauer's attempt to exchange the Chancellorship for the Presidency at Heuss' retirement in 1959 (which he abandoned after discovering from careful scrutiny of the Federal constitution that the German President enjoyed nothing like the powers of de Gaulle in the Fifth Republic). However, the German people had many reasons for gratitude to Adenauer, who had led them—during a period of exceptional economic prosperity—to a smoothly-functioning and democratic political system and to the recovery of an international status which—even though it was due in part to the West's need for the German ' wedge ' in the Cold War—was truly remarkable.

Adenauer's successors 1963-65

Dr Erhard, who succeeded Adenauer as Chancellor in October 1963, appeared outwardly well placed—in terms of political popularity—to make a success of the Chancellorship, especially as it was generally agreed that Adenauer's last years had been marked by a decline in his ability and judgement and that a change was overdue. Ludwig Erhard had been Adenauer's Minister of Economic Affairs ever since 1949 and could even claim to have contributed to the very beginning of the ' economic

---

* *Der Spiegel*—the Hamburg left-wing weekly—was a regular critic of Strauss, and his attempt at revenge misfired.

miracle ' by bringing about the currency reform in 1948: he was thus associated with the most successful and popular aspect of Adenauer's policy—the transformation of the ruined Germany of 1945 into the prosperous and powerful state of the 1960s. However, Erhard as Chancellor suffered from several handicaps. The first was the continued opposition of Adenauer, who had in fact made it plain for several years that he regarded Erhard as unfit to succeed him, and who now continued to use his position as party Chairman to join in intrigues aimed at undermining his position. Erhard was further disabled by his own lack of political expertise: almost his whole professional career before 1949 had been in economic research and, as Minister for Economic Affairs, he had been able to continue as something of a technician, with responsibilities which did not call for the expertise of any particular political skill or judgement. This—and his personal disinclination to make decisions—weakened his position in dealings both with his rivals in the CDU/CSU and with his cabinet colleagues of the FDP.

Although Erhard's final breach with the FDP's leader Erich Mende was to occur on the issue of economic policy (which was to lead to Erhard's fall in 1966), many of the political disputes of his unhappy period as Chancellor revolved around issues of foreign policy. This indeed illustrated how Germany was still to a great extent at the mercy of developments in the outside world—in a manner somewhat reminiscent of France under the Fourth Republic—and how her resulting concern with security (i.e. defence against Soviet pressure on Berlin and on Germany more generally) was something quite basic and perfectly genuine. The Soviet threats against Berlin had, it is true, been toned down after the Cuban crisis of autumn 1962—in January 1963, Khrushchev had made it quite clear to the East German leadership that the Soviet share of four-power control over Berlin was not going to be handed over to them as he had suggested in 1958—but these threats might be renewed at any time. West Germany alone could never defend herself against any serious Soviet action against Berlin. She was in fact in the humiliating position of being economically Europe's most powerful state, yet politically and militarily still in a most exposed and dependent position: in the Bundestag election campaign of 1965 the Opposition leader Willy Brandt was to make the telling point that

Germany was ' an economic giant but a political dwarf ', to which Erhard found it hard to reply. Germany's industrial output had now comfortably overtaken that of France and of Britain, yet she remained completely dependent on her allies for the defence of West Berlin, and was herself still in the front line of any military challenge to which the Russians might—perhaps as a result of East German provocation—be tempted.

The factor which made this situation particularly tense and difficult for Erhard was that Germany's allies were now divided to an unprecedented degree, and Bonn was being forced to make choices of a kind that had never confronted Adenauer. In the 1950s, all of the Federal Republic's alliances and undertakings had appeared mutually compatible: integration into Western Europe (based on a growing *entente* with France) had seemed fully reconcilable with membership of NATO (implying a close link with Washington) and although the other main Western ally —Britain—had held rather curious views about its relations with Europe, she had played a friendly role in a network of German relationships which all fitted into a coherent pattern. In other words, the first Berlin crisis of 1948-49 had acted as a catalyst in promoting Western solidarity, both European and Atlantic, and in ensuring that West Germany was promoted into equal membership of the resulting Western structures.

The second Berlin crisis of 1958-63 had the opposite effect: that of bringing to light several points of serious divergence between the aims and interests of the Western allies; while de Gaulle's France appeared willing to stand behind Adenauer in refusing to parley with the Russians over Berlin, the United States and Britain—more concerned than France at this stage about overall East-West *détente*—were willing not just to negotiate about Berlin, but even to sign the Nuclear Test Ban Treaty of August 1963, on which they allowed an East German signature to appear too.

Although the United States, at the same time as signing the Test Ban agreement, was pressing the Germans to join a multilateral force (MLF) which would have given them a greater stake in NATO's nuclear deterrent (even a share in the so-called ' hardware '), great damage had been done by the conflict between Kennedy and de Gaulle. Bonn now found it much harder to reconcile her ' European ' and ' Atlantic ' policies, since her nearest ally, Gaullist France, was insisting that a good European policy must almost by definition be anti-Atlantic: the EEC was to be used as a device to protect the interests of continental Europe against the 'Anglo-Saxons' (and this naturally meant that Great Britain must be kept out of it).

Erhard's government was thus placed under pressure to adopt either the French view of the Western alliance or the American (including British) view, and the resulting strain on the German political system was considerable. On the one hand Chancellor Adenauer had accepted the Franco-German Treaty of January 1963: yet the Bundestag had deliberately redressed the balance by adding a preamble reasserting Germany's commitments to NATO and to America. This symbolised Erhard's dilemma as he tried to steer a course in foreign policy that would satisfy both the so-called 'German Gaullists' and the strong 'Atlanticists' in his cabinet. The former group in fact were not strongly represented within the cabinet itself: Adenauer had resigned and Strauss (the other firm supporter of a pro-French alignment) had been forced out of office in the *Spiegel* affair a year before Erhard became Chancellor. However, both still wielded considerable power—Adenauer was able to hold the post of Chairman of the CDU until early 1966 (he had previously combined this post with the Chancellorship, and it was a measure of Erhard's weakness that the two were separated for most of his term as Chancellor), and Strauss was re-elected to the chairmanship of the Bavarian CSU without any difficulty, even in the depths of the *Spiegel* crisis.

Adenauer and Strauss (with one or two powerful supporters in Erhard's cabinet, and the help of able pamphleteers including Baron von und zu Guttenberg) were able to keep up a running attack against Erhard for deviating from the former's policy of giving priority to the French alignment. Their label of 'German Gaullists' was in some ways ill-deserved—though they shared de Gaulle's views about possible American unreliability they were completely out of sympathy with his growing flexibility towards the Soviet bloc—but it served to contrast them with the opposing group of 'Atlanticists'. The latter included the Chancellor himself—Erhard had never been a strong friend of an EEC based on a Franco-German 'special relationship' and had even sympathised with Britain's Free Trade Area proposals of 1957-58—

and also many of his leading colleagues. Gerhard Schröder (who in 1961 had succeeded Adenauer's close follower Heinrich von Brentano as Foreign Minister), and Kai-Uwe von Hassell (who had replaced Strauss as Defence Minister) were both North Germans with a Protestant background, and this in itself made them less disposed to favour alignment with France, and more inclined to support NATO and to welcome the American proposal for a multilateral force.

The MLF proposal—after being actively 'sold' to the Germans during 1963 by a faction in the American State Department—ran into such strong opposition from France, and from Harold Wilson's Labour government elected in Britain in October 1964 (not to mention the United States Senate) that it was quietly shelved by President Johnson at the end of that year. The Erhard government was naturally embarrassed by this, and the hand of the 'German Gaullists' was thus considerably strengthened: with Adenauer and Strauss suggesting that Erhard was putting too much faith in an American administration which was not wholly reliable, and with a mounting feeling that the Chancellor's general competence in the management of affairs left much to be desired, Erhard and the Christian Democrats went into the 1965 election in a very disunited and demoralised condition.

Erhard's fall and its consequences 1965-66
The election of 1965 was by no means a disgrace for Erhard: the CDU/CSU increased its vote from 45.3 to 47.6 per cent and its seats from 242 to 245. The SPD opposition, however, increased their strength from 36.2 to 39.3 per cent and from 190 seats to 202. The main losers were Erhard's coalition partners, the FDP, whose vote dropped from 12.8 to 9.5 per cent and who now held 49 seats instead of 67. Their leader, Mende, renewed the coalition with Erhard, but the strains within the government increased.

Foreign policy remained the main focus of dissent, and Erhard was again criticised for becoming excessively dependent on the United States. It is true that he and President Johnson shared a common approach to social and economic problems, as well as a common dislike for General de Gaulle: when Erhard visited Johnson shortly after the 1965 election, the communiqué reporting their conversations observed that President Johnson's ideal of a free society with greater opportunities for all—the 'great society'—was similar to Chancellor Erhard's vision of a 'formed society' based on socially responsible capitalist economics. The point on which Germans criticised Erhard was when the communiqué spoke of the Vietnam War and expressed, on the Chancellor's behalf, 'the determination of his government to continue to assist in this effort for the cause of freedom'. Even though America's willingness to fight in the name of treaty obligations to South Vietnam could be seen as a symbolic guarantee of the safety of Berlin, many Germans criticised Erhard's 'subservience' to Washington.

The same accusation was to be made in a sharpened form in the autumn of 1966, when the Chancellor, again in Washington, attempted to obtain an alleviation of Germany's burden of contributing 'offset costs' for the American troops stationed in Germany. The year 1965-66 was marked by German's first serious economic recession since the war, due in part to the deflationary measures pursued by the powerful and ultra-conservative Federal Bank in 1964-65. As the number of unemployed rose to three-quarters of a million (affecting not only immigrant 'guest workers' but hundreds of thousands of Germans as well) the popularity of Erhard—himself an originator of the 'economic miracle'—declined further. This was confirmed in the Landtag elections of June 1966. Erhard's attempt to get Washington to alleviate the burden of offset costs was a complete failure—not surprisingly, since the Vietnam War was becoming ever more costly—and this was the occasion for a further weakening of his position. His unpopularity within his own party made it difficult for him to withstand the defection of the FDP ministers, who resigned—technically on a question of the budget estimates for the forthcoming year—on 27 October 1966.

The ministerial crisis which followed Erhard's rift with the FDP lasted several weeks, and was marked by bargaining of a fairly hard-headed kind between the three parties represented in the Bundestag: CDU/CSU (245 seats), SPD (202) and FPD (49). In theory, any one of three combinations was possible: a renewal of the CDU-FDP coalition (though this was unacceptable to the FDP under Erhard, and the FDP was perhaps unacceptable to most CDU members under any leadership); a coalition between the SPD and the FDP (by no means to be ruled out, since the left-wing elements in the FDP, led by Walter Scheel, were increasingly in revolt against the right-wing leadership of Erich Mende); or the so-called 'Grand Coalition' of the CDU and SPD, holding the overwhelming majority of 447 seats in a parliament of 496. In the end it was the last of these three possible coalitions that emerged. Observers of the political scene in Bonn were divided in their views on whether the prolonged triangular bargaining was a sign of political maturity—evidence that the German parties had outgrown their old attachment to sterile ideologies— or else of deplorable cynicism. All agreed, however, that the fact of the SPD's being considered a suitable coalition partner both by the CDU and by the FDP was evidence that it had undergone a considerable change.

After the defeat of 1965—the party's second under Willy Brandt's leadership—the Opposition leader had seemed gravely disheartened and had spoken of going into retirement. The party, however, re-elected him as Chairman at its Dortmund Congress in June 1966 (by 324 votes out of 326), and also re-elected as joint Vice-Chairman Fritz Erler and Herbert Wehner. These two men, who had both helped Brandt in the task of modernising the party programme at Bad Godesberg in 1959, had had conspicuously different political careers: born in 1913, Erler had been a Social Democrat for some time before the Nazi régime —under which he had spent many years in prison—and since 1945 he had made a name both in Germany and abroad as the SPD's leading expert on defence policy (his death early in 1967 was a great loss to his party); Herbert Wehner, who was seven years Erler's senior, had joined the Communist Party in 1927 and only left it in 1946, after spending part of the Nazi period in exile in Moscow. Wehner's Communist past naturally made him even more of a bogy-man to the German right than Willy Brandt's period as a Norwegian citizen during the war, but Wehner was in fact the SPD leader who was most insistent—from the early 1960s onwards—that the party's best hope of gaining power was through a coalition with the Christian Democrats. This after all was the formula which had brought success to the SPD in many German *Land* governments—the city of Berlin, for instance, had been ruled for years by an SPD/CDU coalition—and Wehner argued that a similar alliance at the Federal level would reassure hesitant middle-of-the-road voters that the SPD was a party not of dangerous ' reds ' but of responsible statesmen.

Wehner's chance to implement this policy came in the crisis following Erhard's fall: although the majority of the 202 SPD members of the Bundestag and the Party Executive finally accepted the view that a coalition with the CDU was the correct course, the argument was not an easy one for Wehner to win, particularly as his opponents had at least two powerful counter-arguments to offer. The first was that since the CDU was responsible for the economic recession which had overthrown Erhard, the same party should be made to take the responsibility for trying to right matters, and that a further spell in opposition would only put the SPD in an even stronger position for the next federal election, due in 1969. The other objection was that it was particularly inopportune for the SPD to come to the aid of a Christian Democratic party led—after Kurt-Georg Kiesinger replaced Erhard on 10 November—by an ex-Nazi. Kiesinger had not in fact been a particularly zealous member of the Nazi party: born in 1904, he had trained as a lawyer and joined the Nazi party, as had many of his colleagues, in 1933. He had spent the war years in the Foreign Ministry and—after Allied internment in 1945—had only started on a political career after some delay. An influential member of the Bundestag and Chairman of its Foreign Affairs Committee in the mid-1950s, he had also been Vice-President of the Council of Europe's Consultative Assembly. An able and persuasive debater, Kiesinger had been deeply hurt at Adenauer's refusal to reward his loyal support by giving him ministerial office, and had retired in 1958 to his native Württemberg as Minister President of the *Land* government in Stuttgart. This temporary exile from Bonn allowed him to avoid the increasingly acrimonious disputes within the CDU leadership during Adenauer's last years and through those of Erhard, and to emerge as an acceptable compromise candidate for the Chancellorship in 1966.

The Grand Coalition formed by Kiesinger on 1 December 1966 represented a strikingly broad cross-section of German political life. Beside the ex-Nazi Kiesinger were his Vice-Chancellor and Foreign Minister, Willy Brandt, an ex-émigré; and, as Minister for All-German Affairs, Herbert Wehner, an ex-Communist. The other SPD members of the government were Karl Schiller, a former professor of economics (Minister for Economic Affairs),

Gustav Heinemann, a CDU Minister of Adenauer's in 1950, who had left the CDU for the SPD in protest at German rearmament (Minister of Justice), Georg Leber, a trade union leader (Minister of Transport) and four others. Not the least remarkable thing about this participation of SPD ministers in a German national cabinet (for the first time since 1930) was the fact that they joined Franz-Josef Strauss, the right-wing CSU leader whom they had violently criticised for his authoritarian behaviour in the *Spiegel* episode only four years before and who now became Kiesinger's Finance Minister. The Grand Coalition government took office at a critical moment for the Federal Republic—as well as the economic difficulties, there was an ominous rise in the popularity of the neo-Nazi National Democratic Party—and both new and old Ministers faced heavy responsibilities. Although quite good working relationships developed between the leaders of the two parties—notably between Rainer Barzel and Helmut Schmidt, the powerful parliamentary whips respectively of the CDU and the SPD—inevitably the period of coalition government was marked also by rivalry between the two parties, as the critical Federal election of 1969 drew nearer.

The Grand Coalition 1966-69

The initial achievement of the Grand Coalition was principally in the field of economic policy: a modification of Erhard's explicit *laissez-faire* policies by Schiller's moderate degree of socialist planning led within a year or so to a resumption of industrial growth and a drop in unemployment. Despite this, a considerable amount of political discontent persisted, reflected in the substantial votes given at Landtag elections to the neo-Nazi NPD. The creation of a national coalition between the two major parties in the Bundestag would in any case have sent a number of 'protest' votes in the direction of other parties—and the FPD now the only opposition party in the Bundestag, also gained in strength in the *Land* elections—but the NPD reflected something more than either a protest at the Grand Coalition or lingering resentment at the considerable recession. Founded in 1964, the NPD was the latest in a series of neo-Nazi parties and organisations —numbering almost a hundred in all—which had appeared and disappeared throughout the history of the Federal Republic. It was inevitable that some voters in a nation so thoroughly in-

doctrinated with Nazism for twelve years would, almost by
compulsion, continue to support an organisation reflecting the
ideas of the Third Reich to a small extent, and such parties had
enjoyed varying degrees of success: the strongest, before the
NPD, had been the Socialist Reich Party, which had been represented by a handful of members in the parliament of 1949 before
being declared illegal in 1952.

In the Bundestag elections of 1965, the NPD won 2.1 per cent
of the votes: it got no seats because it failed to gain the necessary
minimum of five per cent of the votes and, as the election of
1969 drew near, interest centred on the question of whether it
would gain more than five per cent (thus getting 40 or 50 seats)
or not. In a series of Landtag elections from 1966 to 1968 the
NPD's vote rose ominously: in November 1966 it won 7.4 per
cent in Bavaria and 7.9 in Hessen; in October 1967, 8.8 per
cent in Bremen; and in April 1968, 9.8 per cent in Baden-
Württemberg. The party's leader, Adolf von Thadden, a member
of the Landtag of Lower Saxony, stood for a programme marked
by a crude nationalism: it demanded an end to foreign aid payments by Germany, an assertion of her national interests against
domination by 'territorially alien powers', and the recovery of
the lost Eastern territories. In November 1967, as the party
gained in support, a new and less vehemently worded programme
was adopted, but it still demanded the restoration of the Sudetenland, Austria and South Tirol, and other 'German' territories,
and its tone remained highly nationalistic and authoritarian.

The NPD's voters were mainly disgruntled small tradesmen or
white-collar workers feeling the pressures of big business and
organised labour: in some of the party's biggest Landtag polls
in 1967 and 1968, these were joined by SPD voters disappointed
at the minimal results achieved by the coalition government, and
there appeared to be a serious risk that the NPD would be well
represented in the Bundestag in 1969. As will be seen, however,
the SPD voters returned to their normal allegiance and the NPD
failed to pass the five per cent barrier.

Another group of Germans who opposed the Grand Coalition
were the left-wing students at the universities of Berlin, Frankfurt
and elsewhere, who began an increasingly turbulent series of
demonstrations at this time. The subjects of student protest varied
from overcrowding in universities to the state visit of the

reactionary Shah of Iran (this visit, in June 1967, led to riots in Berlin in which a student, Benno Ohnesorg, was needlessly shot and killed by a plain-clothes policeman). The riots were also in part directed against the so-called Emergency Laws of 1968, which provided for the Federal government to take special powers in case of national crisis, and which was denounced by the left as a revival of Hitler's Enabling Act of 1933; one underlying cause of the whole student movement, however, was the disgust of the student left (including Willy Brandt's own son) at the SPD's ' betrayal ' in entering a coalition with the CDU ex-Nazi Kiesinger.

The force of the student protest movement was largely spent by 1969—its size was also provoked in part by excessively brutal police reactions against originally quite small demonstrations— and one of the factors which helped to weaken it was certainly the Russian invasion of Czechoslovakia in August 1968. Although many of the young left-wingers denounced Soviet ' state capitalism ' as violently as they did its Western variant, and condemned the Soviet action of 1968 as the worst kind of traditional power-politics, the invasion made it harder for an extreme leftist movement to win support.

The Soviet invasion of Czechoslovakia also put an end to a new phase of *Ostpolitik* (' policy towards the East ') which had been cautiously developed by Willy Brandt as Foreign Minister in Kiesinger's government. Bonn's old hard line of the 1950s— the so-called ' Hallstein Doctrine ' (which forswore any dealings with Communist countries and punished by severance of relations any foreign state which recognised the DDR) had in fact progressively softened during the 1960s. Adenauer himself had explored the idea of commercial dealings with Poland, and the Erhard government had taken a further step ahead by issuing a ' peace note ' early in 1966 which envisaged closer relations with the Eastern bloc. By the time Kiesinger and Brandt took office, the view was established that states that had been ' obliged ' to recognise the DDR at its inception, i.e. the Socialist states of Eastern Europe, should not be penalised by deprivation of diplomatic relations with Bonn, as had states in the Third World who voluntarily recognised the DDR in subsequent years. In application of this principle, the Roumanian Foreign Minister visited Bonn in January 1967, and an exchange of ambassadors with Bucharest was announced; with Yugoslavia, also, Bonn resumed the diplomatic relations which had been instituted in 1955 and broken off by virtue of the Hallstein Doctrine in 1957.

Relations with the DDR naturally presented more problems than those with other Communist countries, but the Kiesinger government took some steps forward by proposing official talks on economic, commercial, technical and scientific exchanges; in June 1967 Chancellor Kiesinger made an unprecedented move by addressing his East German opposite number, Willi Stoph, as 'Chairman of the Council of Ministers' in an official letter. The East German response to these advances, however, remained negative, and the whole process of East-West dialogue in Europe was brutally interrupted in August 1968 by the Soviet invasion of Czechoslovakia.

Although the Soviet allegations that West Germany had been plotting with the Dubcek government were false (the claim that depots of arms had been found were never proved), there was something in the argument that West German policy towards Eastern Europe had contributed to the crisis. By pushing ahead with diplomatic and economic negotiations with the Soviet satellites—without thinking systematically about the political repercussions these might have—the Bonn government had probably helped to increase the fears of the rulers in Moscow (and East Berlin) that these Western activities must encourage subversive forces in Eastern Europe. Even though Dubcek himself might have had no intention of leading Czechoslovakia away from the Warsaw Pact, there was a risk that he would be supplanted by someone less cautious, and his policy was therefore 'objectively' one that the Soviet Union was obliged to stop by intervention.

The West Germans were to draw their conclusions from the events of August 1968 in formulating the next phase of their *Ostpolitik* when Brandt became Chancellor a year later.

The 1969 election: Willy Brandt becomes Chancellor

The 1969 election campaign, fought between the members of a coalition government whose cooperation had hardly concealed deep differences of opinion, was more bitterly contested than any before in the history of the Federal Republic. Whichever government emerged would have to deal with considerable problems both domestically and internationally: with the discontent expressed by the NPD's growing strength, as well as with the uncertainties resulting from Soviet-American negotiations on strategic weapons and other issues, which continued with only a temporary break caused by the invasion of Czechoslovakia.

The electors were asked to decide whether the CDU leadership, after guiding Germany for the entire twenty-year history of the Federal Republic, should be removed from office in this hour of uncertainty; whether the SPD, for three years the CDU's coalition partner, should be entrusted with a larger share of power on the strength of its current performance; whether the FDP, now appearing as a fairly radical opposition party under its new leaders Walter Scheel and Ralf Dahrendorf, should be given a new lease of life; and whether the NDP, having scored nearly ten per cent of the votes in the *Land* election in Baden-Württemberg, would get the ten per cent it needed to enter the Bundestag.

In the event, the CDU/CSU got slightly fewer votes than in 1965 (46.1 per cent instead of 47.6 per cent) and 242 seats instead of 245; the SPD increased its vote from 39.3 per cent to 42.7 per cent and its seats from 202 to 224; the FDP's vote fell drastically from 9.5 per cent to 5.8 per cent so that it narrowly missed total exclusion from the Bundestag and now held only 30 seats instead of 49; and the NPD, with 4.3 per cent, in fact failed to win any representation, although most of the opinion polls had predicted that it would.

The CDU/CSU was thus, as always, the largest party, but the combination of SPD and FDP was just strong enough—with a combined total of 254 seats—to give the SPD leader Willy Brandt a majority of 12—in fact reduced to nine by FDP defections—over the CDU/CSU. The persisting hostility between the CDU and the FDP, combined with the leftward move of the latter since 1966, had ensured that the SPD/FPD coalition was the most likely outcome, rather than a revival of either Erhard's CDU/FDP alliance or the Grand Coalition of the two bigger parties.

For the SPD, the unprecedented score of 47.7 per cent of the votes was more than just the culminating effort of the ally known to the party tacticians as ' Comrade Trend ' (in the elections since 1953 the SPD vote had grown steadily: 28.8 per cent; 31.8 per cent; 36.2 per cent; 39.3 per cent). It also reflected the undeniable success of the SPD ministers in the Kiesinger government. The voters were able to see the SPD leaders—Brandt,

Schiller, Leber, Heinemann and Ehmke (Heinemann's successor as Minister of Justice when the former was elected President of the Republic in April 1969) no longer merely as politicians with a good record in city and *Land* government, but in their new capacity as Ministers of the Federal Republic. The emphasis in the Party's campaign was on the argument that the SPD was already contributing to the modernisation of Germany. The poster slogan 'we are building modern Germany—we have the right men' was projected, with visual illustrations of booming steel-plants and sun-drenched beaches, against an exciting background of orange.

In contrast, the CDU/CSU tried but failed to conceal a deep inner uncertainty by using the slogan 'safely into the seventies' —an unsuccessful echo of Adenauer's slogan 'no experiments'. The CDU had still not recovered from its setbacks of the years since Adenauer's decline and fall: the ineffective leadership of Erhard, the economic recession, and the undignified scramble for the chancellorship won by Kiesinger, were recent enough memories to inflict serious damage on the party's electoral appeal.

Not realising how weak their true situation was, the CDU leaders became complacent after their victories in the 1967 and 1968 Landtag elections, which suggested—together with the SPD's losses—that all the credit for the Grand Coalition's successes would go to them. Their election campaign was marked by too little effort by Chancellor Kiesinger, and probably too much ebullience by Franz-Josef Strauss. Although the party's election posters made great use of Kiesinger's portrait (with such slogans as 'everything depends on the Chancellor') his electioneering efforts were surpassed by those of Strauss, who addressed packed meetings—of supporters, but also of opponents who were pro-voked by Strauss's aggressive style to redouble their own campaign efforts—in towns far removed from his native Bavaria. Like Kiesinger, such former 'stars' of CDU election campaigns as Ludwig Erhard and Gerhard Schröder failed to make the expected mark on their audiences and even newer men like Ernst Benda and Gerhard Stoltenberg (respectively Minister of the Interior and Minister for Scientific Research) were disappointingly unimpressive. The CDU held the bulk of its older electors, but failed to win over new voters, particularly young ones. Strauss tried to convince the German public that an SPD/FDP coalition would imperil Germany's national interests by making dangerous agreements with the East, but this failed to carry conviction against the evident determination of Willy Brandt and Helmut Schmidt to stand firmly by the Western alliance. On economic issues—which, as usual, weighed more heavily with the electorate —a vote of general confidence was given to Economics Minister Schiller, against Finance Minister Strauss.

The FDP was clearly revealed by the 1969 election campaign as a party of the left—on some issues, speaking in more radical terms than the SPD. The views of the party's new spokesman, Ralf Dahrendorf—on educational reform, effective workers' participation in management at factory level, and a 'facing of the facts' about Germany's relations with the East—appeared to find considerable support among the younger professional people who formed the bulk of the FDP's active membership. Although some of the party's leaders—notably Erich Mende, who had been Vice-Chancellor under Erhard until 1966—tried tactically to keep the way open for an alliance with either the CDU or the SPD, the main emphasis of the party's policy went in the direction of the SPD/FPD coalition, which was the eventual outcome. If the election results as a whole are considered, FDP candidates who supported Dahrendorf's reforming views came off distinctly better than the supporters of Mende, and the FDP appeared to have lost many of its more right-wing votes to the CDU.

The negotiations between the SPD and FDP on the formation of the new government went ahead with a speed that broke all the records for German cabinet-forming, even in Adenauer's heyday. Kiesinger and the CDU did no more than utter a few resentful statements to the effect that the voters' wishes were being disregarded, since the CDU/CSU was still the largest party. The main elements of the SPD/FPD coalition's programme soon became fairly clear. On foreign policy questions, the two parties agreed on a programme of cautious but firm development of the lines of action laid down by the Grand Coalition: that is, to the immediate signature of the nuclear Non-Proliferation Treaty (though with the proviso that the delay between signature and ratification should be used to clarify some matters of importance to Germany, particularly the Soviet right to inspect nuclear installations); to the stepping-up of diplomatic negotiations with

the Soviet Union, leading to an exchange of declarations renouncing the use of force; to the abandonment—at least in
practice—of the 'Hallstein Doctrine'; to the signature of a
'general treaty' with the DDR to provide a basis for the settlement
of intra-German questions—i.e. a recognition of the East German
government in fact if not in international law; and—in the still
fundamental area of West European affairs, not forgotten amid
all the activity in the field of *Ostpolitik*—to new proposals for
the reform of the EEC's agricultural policy and for the enlargement of the European Community to include Britain and the
other candidates.

On economic policy, there was more difficulty in bringing
Socialist and Liberal points of view together. The SPD had to
withdraw its demand for the immediate extension of workers'
co-determination (of the rather bureaucratic kind supported by the
party since the war) to cover the overall direction of industrial
firms. The FDP also secured a commitment by the new government to reform the tax structure in such a way as to help the
building-up of private savings by the middle classes; and the
appointment as Minister of Agriculture of a right-wing FDP
politician, Josef Ertl, signified the abandonment of the SPD's
policy of encouraging small peasant farmers to leave the land.
On other reforms in domestic policy—for instance, the reduction of the voting age to eighteen, and the strengthening of
the Federal Ministry of Science into a full Ministry of Education,
with real powers over *Land* governments—the two parties agreed
without difficulty.

The government led by Willy Brandt—which was in fact to
be remarkable in its first two years of office for its foreign rather
than its domestic policy—marked a distinct turning-point in the
history of the Federal Republic. The SPD led the government for
the first time since 1930 (the party also provided, in Gustav
Heinemann, the first SPD President of Germany since the death
of Friedrich Ebert in 1925), and the CDU went into opposition for
the first time in its history.

The part the new government would play in the development
of West European affairs—in which it would have to work with
the French government under Georges Pompidou—appeared
likely to be a combination of Bonn's traditional 'European'
policy, with some special additions from the policies of the new

N

governing parties: the proportions in which old and new policies would be blended, however, was only to become clear with time.

12 Italy and Benelux in the Sixties

The 'opening to the left'

As we have seen, the late 1950s had witnessed a dual trend in Italian politics—the leftward evolution of Christian Democracy and the rightward movement of the Socialists under Nenni—which together prepared the way for the 'opening to the left', the main feature of Italian government in the 1960s.

The Christian Democrats were ready to accept the idea of extending the coalition to the Socialists as early as October 1959, when the Party's new Secretary-General Aldo Moro joined his predecessor Fanfani in giving a left-wing emphasis to the debates at the party congress in Florence. As a result of pressure by Moro and Fanfani, the existing centre coalition led by Antonio Segni was placed under increasing strain, as its Liberal members reacted with alarm to any prospect of an alliance with the Socialists. Segni resigned in February 1960 and, in the long crisis that followed, a number of underlying realities of Italian politics became clearer. In particular, although the centre coalition of Christian Democrats, Liberals, Republicans and Social Democrats might be revived for a further brief spell, its inner cohesion was broken, and the 'opening to the left' now preached strongly by Moro represented the way ahead. Although this trend was strongly resisted by the Vatican and by the right wing of the Christian Democrats—particularly Tambroni, who headed a short-lived government in the spring and early summer of 1960—it was increasingly hard to withstand. Nenni's Socialist Party now appeared to be decisively breaking its links with the Communists: it pointedly refrained from voting against Fanfani when he attempted to form a government in August 1960, and the *de facto* collaboration between Socialists and Christian Democrats was a marked feature of the local election campaign of November.

January 1961 saw the creation of the first centre-left municipal coalition, in the city of Milan: it was followed in February and March by similar experiments in Genoa and Florence. By the summer of 1961, 40 such centre-left coalitions had been formed, always in towns where the local Christian Democrats held left-wing views and the Socialists were open-minded enough to accept that to govern in conjunction with the Christian Democrats was not to betray the interests of the working class: there were still far more towns where the Socialists remained faithful for the moment to their long-standing alliance with the Communists.

The Roman Catholic Church, also, was divided in its attitude towards the leftward evolution of Christian Democracy. On the one hand, the traditionalists represented by the Catholic Action movement vigorously condemned any alliance with the Marxist and materialist Socialist Party; on the other hand, Pope John XXIII, who succeeded Pius XII in the autumn of 1958, was a man of very progressive views. In 1957, as Patriarch of Venice, he had wished success to the Socialist Congress held there; by 1961 he was warmly praising the work of the left-wing Christian Democrat Fanfani, and in his first major encyclical, *Mater et Magistra* (Mother and Teacher), he spoke out for a mixed economy, more social justice and more control over the forces of market economics, and a generally leftward orientation. The right-wing forces of Catholic Action were placed on the defensive, and by January 1962 the Christian Democratic Party Congress was ready to welcome the general principle of an ' opening to the left' which Moro and Fanfani manoeuvred the party into accepting.

From the Socialist side, Nenni made their task easier by publishing an important article in the January 1962 issue of the American review *Foreign Affairs* in which he affirmed that although the Socialist Party had originally opposed Italian membership of NATO, it would be opposed to Italy's leaving the alliance now, partly ' because to withdraw under present conditions would jeopardise the European equilibrium, which, though it is dangerously unstable, does contribute to the maintenance of a truce between the two opposing blocs '.

The next move in the complicated *rapprochement* came during February, when Fanfani formed a new three-party government (Christian Democrat-Social Democrat-Republican) which for the first time enjoyed the open support of the Socialists: Nenni and his followers abstained rather than positively voting for Fanfani, but Nenni's support for the new government's programme was quite unequivocal. This programme included the development of regional governments throughout Italy; administrative and educational reforms; an improvement of peasant conditions; better economic planning, including urban improvements; public ownership of the electric power industry; and continued membership of NATO. These lines of policy were to be more or less effectively carried out during the ensuing years. There was a revival of animosities between the Socialists and Christian Democrats in the spring of 1962, when the term of office of President Gronchi expired, and a battle for his succession developed between the Social Democrat Saragat and the conservative Christian Democrat Antonio Segni. The election of Saragat would have helped the ' opening to the left ' not only by bringing a man of the left to the post of head of state, but also by removing him from the leadership of the Social Democratic Party, thus clearing the way for a reunification of the two Socialist parties under the unchallenged leadership of Nenni: however, these developments were to be postponed since in 1962 it was Segni who won the presidential election.

The nationalisation of electricity brought together the parties of the centre and left in the summer of 1962: even a majority of Christian Democrats and Republicans agreed with the argument of the Socialists and Social Democrats that the private owners of the power industry were not cooperating effectively in the development of the South, and were fixing high prices in defiance of governmental policy. Before the end of the year, nationalisation was approved by a parliamentary vote of 404 to 74.

This was the context in which Nenni announced his party's readiness to join a centre-left coalition, as a full partner, after the parliamentary election due to be held in April 1963. The offer was rejected by the Christian Democrats—still hoping to keep even their right-wing electoral clientèle intact by formally refusing any pacts with the Socialists—but the outcome of the election in fact made the centre-left coalition the logical next step. The Christian Democrats dropped—in comparison with the election of 1958—from 42.4 per cent of the votes to 38.3 per cent, and from 273 seats to 260; both the Socialists and Social Democrats slightly increased their representations; and the Communists—aided, perhaps unwittingly, by Pope John's dramatic action in receiving Khrushchev's daughter and son-in-law in audience—increased their strength from 22.7 per cent to 25.3 per cent of the vote, and from 144 seats to 166. The Christian Democratic Party—now firmly under the leadership of Moro, since Fanfani was blamed for the election losses—took a few months to orientate itself fully towards coalition with the Socialists, but by August the party's National Council had come out firmly for this policy. The international climate—the post-Cuban *détente* symbolised by the Nuclear Test Ban Treaty and the ' hot line ' linking Washington and Moscow—helped both Christian Democrats and Socialists to take the final steps towards coalition; so also did the active urgings of one of President Kennedy's personal advisers, Professor Arthur Schlesinger.

In December 1963, Moro formed the first of a series of four-party coalitions—together, these were to last until the next election in June 1968—in which Pietro Nenni joined him as Deputy Prime Minister. After 16 years in what Nenni had called ' the ghetto of isolation ', the Socialists had returned to power, and Nenni promised to carry out a programme of economic and social reforms, enlarging those promised by Fanfani the previous year, as well as pledging Italy's fidelity to her undertakings to NATO.

The centre-left coalitions of Moro and Nenni were not notably successful in carrying out the promised reforms, taken as a whole: the governing parties failed to overcome the problems of inflation and economic stagnation, and they disagreed on issues affecting religious principles, particularly education and divorce.

It is true that various reforms were attempted. Between 1963 and 1968, the sum of £800 million was allocated for school buildings and the training of teachers. By a law passed in 1968, £120 million was to be spent on university buildings and university reform. A commission was set up in 1963 to attack the problem of the Mafia, and by the late 1960s the police were at least making a serious effort to rid Sardinia of bandits. A five-year economic plan was approved in 1965, but the success of this was slowed down by the delay in instituting regional government and by the resistance of the working class (particularly the trade unions) to a wages and incomes policy.

The Moro-Nenni coalition, although it had certain achievements to its credit, in fact failed to live up to the expectations it had originally aroused.

Thus, although the experiment of a centre-left coalition suited the mood of the Italian people in the early part of the 1960s—particularly under the reforming Papacy of John XXIII—a reaction towards the right had developed by the end of the decade. The Communist Party, representing a quarter of the electorate, remained excluded from the governing coalition, although its collaboration with the Socialists at the local level continued to exercise a powerful pull on the latter party. The influence of the Communists also helps to explain the failure of the attempt, made during this period, to reunite the two Socialist parties which had separated in 1947.

Socialist unity and European integration
One of the main causes of Italy's immobile political system in the 1950s and early 1960s—particularly the continuous domination by the Christian Democrats, with the attendant problems of complacency and corruption—was the persistent disunity of the left. In a situation where the Communist Party regularly polled between one-fifth and one-quarter of the votes, the political balance was automatically tilted towards the right, and the situation was aggravated by the split between Nenni's Socialists and Saragat's Social Democrats after 1947. As part of the ' opening to the left ' in the 1960s, it seemed possible that the two Socialist parties would at last merge, possibly even providing the basis for a strong left-wing party which would succeed in attracting some elements of the Communist Party itself, and thus bringing them back into the arena of political cooperation.

The election of Giuseppe Saragat to the Presidency of the Republic in 1964 made unity easier, since his personal relations with Nenni were not good, and a reunification of the two parties under their joint leadership (one or the other would inevitably have taken precedence) was out of the question. The two parties came together in November 1966, forming the United Socialist Party (PSU) under Nenni's leadership, with a programme strongly influenced by the ideas of the Social Democratic Party—many of which, especially on foreign policy, Nenni had by now accepted. The fusion was not complete: both parties maintained a degree of autonomy within the PSU, and the situation was further complicated by the refusal of a substantial part of the left wing of the old PSI to accept fusion at all. This group formed a new party, the Italian Socialist Party of Proletarian Unity (PSIUP), which remained close to Nenni's previous alignment with the Communists.

The section of Italian political opinion between the Communists and the Christian Democrats thus remained divided and unable to exercise its full political weight. The parties entered the elections of May 1968 in a state of strong mutual antagonism, which was reflected in the weakening of all of them except the solid ranks of Communists and Christian Democrats. The former increased their vote from 25.3 per cent to 26.9 per cent and their seats from 166 to 177, while the latter rose from 38.3 per cent (260 seats) to 39.1 per cent (266 seats). The Socialist Party under Nenni, meanwhile, dropped from 19.9 per cent and 120 seats (this was the combined total of the PSI and PDSI in the 1963 election) to 14.5 per cent and 91 seats in 1968. Nenni's position in the centre-left coalition was thus seriously weakened: although a new Christian Democratic Prime Minister formed a further coalition including the Socialists, which lasted from December 1968 to August 1969, a further split in the PSU made the situation untenable. Rumor's Cabinet resigned, and the centre-left experiment of the 1960s appeared to have come to an unhappy end.

It is hardly surprising that Italy, in view of her unstable political situation and pressing economic problems, had little energy left to spare for making major contributions to European unity during the 1960s. Her representatives in Brussels worked hard to make a success of the newly established EEC, in which hard bargaining on the Italian side had ensured an advantageous position for Italy's exports, especially agricultural produce and wine. The governments of the 1960s, however, produced no Italian statesman in a position to make a contribution on the European scene comparable with that of De Gasperi in the early 1950s.

Towards the end of the 1960s, Pietro Nenni took an active interest in developing the European Community in a democratic direction, and during his spell as Foreign Minister in Mariano Rumor's first government (December 1968 to August 1969), he made proposals for direct elections to the European parliament, and for more active social and economic policies by the Brussels authorities. The adviser who worked out these proposals was the veteran Italian federalist Altiero Spinelli, who was to play a leading part in the further development of the EEC when he joined the European Commission at the beginning of the 1970s.

The Benelux countries in the 1960s

The most striking feature of Belgian politics during the 1960s was the continued worsening of relations between the French-speaking and Flemish-speaking communities. The divisions between the linguistic groups within each major political force that had come to the surface during the 1950s became more pronounced and the Liberal Party, which came out openly in favour of a decentralised federal structure for the country, gained in strength at successive elections.

The country continued to be governed by a series of coalitions, normally between the Christian Social Party and the Socialists: the Prime Ministers, all members of the former party, were Théo Lefèvre (1961-65), Pierre Harmel (1965-66), Paul van den Boeynants (1966-68), and Gaston Eyskens (1968 onwards). Each of them had to preserve within his coalition not only the balance between Christian Socialist and Socialists, but also that between French- and Flemish-speaking politicians.

The long series of coalition governments, all forced to take constant account of the Flemish-Walloon tension, made several attempts at constitutional reforms designed to take more account of the linguistic problem. In 1965, for instance, after several years of committee-work, a draft reform was produced which would have written the linguistic frontier into the constitution, and would have made it obligatory for any piece of legislation to obtain at least one-third of the votes of each linguistic group before passing into law. The Lefèvre government, which had devised this proposal, in fact failed to win a two-thirds majority in the 1965 election—the Liberal Party, standing for more radical decentralisation, doubled its vote at the expense of the coalition parties—and the proposal was thus not implemented.

This deadlock was characteristic of the way in which the linguistic conflict increasingly dominated every aspect of Belgian life—social, administrative, cultural and educational—and produced a situation in which extremists came to despise the official political process and the recognised political parties, and took to direct action by violent demonstration.

The other issue which occupied the attention of Belgium's

people and their leaders in the early 1960s—unexpectedly, this time—was the crisis in the Belgian Congo. The Belgians had not considered the possibility of preparing the Congo for independence, which was precipitated in 1960, partly by de Gaulle's unexpected offer of independence to the neighbouring French Congo two years earlier. In June 1960, Belgium suddenly granted independence in response to local pressures, and the Congo, with virtually no trained local leaders, fell into disunity and near-anarchy. Cohesion of a kind was restored by United Nations forces, and Belgium was criticised for her ' neo-colonial ' attempt to retain the richest part of the country—Katanga—under her control, so as to keep her hands on the minerals owned by the Belgian Union Minière.

Many Belgian families suffered losses of life or property, and many more had members of their family injured, during the Congo crisis, and the public found the Congolese ' ingratitude ' and the condemnation by world opinion hard to forget. Although Belgium and the Congo concluded agreements about technical and educational aid in the years after independence, Belgian opinion remained cool towards the ex-colony, and many Belgians favoured cutting off economic aid altogether.

The frustrations of Belgian domestic politics, as in the 1950s, made Belgian political leaders of both linguistic camps turn towards European integration as a larger unit within which factional quarrels might be forgotten. The additional frustration of the sudden end of colonial rule in the Congo provided a further impetus for a focus of attention on Europe, which had in any case been the chosen field of activity of Paul-Henri Spaak and Belgium's other post-war leaders.

In 1961 Spaak returned to Belgian politics after his four-year spell as Secretary-General of NATO—he occupied the post of Foreign Minister in the Lefèvre government—and was very active in the attempt of 1961-63 to bring Britain into the EEC. His opposition to the French veto of January 1963 was echoed by his successor Harmel when President de Gaulle again blocked Britain's entry in 1967. In the meantime, the Belgian government had stood strongly by the European Commission in its attempt to strengthen its powers against French resistance in 1965-66. One of the leading members of the Commission was Jean Rey, who had been a Belgian Liberal parliamentarian since

1939 and a Minister in 1949-50 and 1954-58, before becoming the member of the European Commission responsible for external trade matters: his success in this capacity, particularly his effective negotiation of the Kennedy Round of tariff reductions, led to his appointment as President of the EEC Commission as Hallstein's successor in 1967.

In the affairs of NATO, too, Belgium played a leading part, especially after de Gaulle's withdrawal of France from the Organisation led to the transfer of its headquarters to Brussels in 1966. Harmel, the Belgian Foreign Minister, was responsible for a programme of rethinking of the military, political and economic objectives of the alliance in 1966-67, which produced a report advocating a balanced combination of military deterrence and diplomatic *détente* with the Soviet bloc. Belgium herself set a quiet example of the new style of NATO diplomacy, by establishing quite close links with a number of the smaller East European countries, notably Poland.

The pattern of Dutch political life in the 1950s—a plethora of small parties, combined with an underlying stability and continuity—was disrupted in the 1960s by a number of new political forces. The first of these was the Farmers' Party, which was founded in 1958 by peasants who felt that the existing parties failed to represent their interests adequately, but which spread as a protest movement of town workers dissatisfied with the political consensus too. (In the municipal elections of 1966 it received 10.9 per cent of the votes in The Hague and 9.4 per cent in Amsterdam.) The five major political parties, conversely, dwindled in support from 91.5 per cent of the vote in 1956 to 78.8 per cent in 1967; this was a further sign that the public were increasingly disillusioned with political parties whose endlessly deadlocked coalitions appeared unable to produce answers to the fundamental problems of Dutch society. By the end of the 1960s, in response to this pressure, reforming left-wing movements had arisen within each of the three main religious parties— one Roman Catholic and two Calvinist—and the Socialist Party was also faced with a revolt by its left-wing and youth sections.

A number of social, economic and educational reforms were introduced by the coalition governments by the end of the 1960s, but not before Amsterdam and to some extent other cities had been the scene of anarchist demonstrations by the so-called

' provos ' who denounced the materialist abuses of capitalist society in the same style as the ' hippies ' of California.

The basic stability of Dutch political life remained unaffected, particularly in the sphere of foreign policy. Here continuity was guaranteed by the presence of Joseph Luns as Foreign Minister throughout the 1960s. Under his guidance, Dutch foreign policy firmly supported NATO, and also the enlarging and strengthening of the European Economic Community. On the question of enlargement, the Dutch had strong commercial motives as well as those of sentiment for wishing to see Britain and other trading nations admitted to the Community: they therefore resisted to the utmost the French vetoes of 1963 and 1967, and refused to give their support to the French Fouchet Plan, since this was not linked with British membership. On the strengthening of the Community, while the Dutch felt strongly that the Commission in Brussels should be given more power, they also argued that this should be combined with greater democratic control, and in the course of the great EEC crisis of 1965-66 they pressed hard for an upgrading of the powers of the European Parliament.

Neither the enlargement nor the strengthening of EEC was to become a reality during the 1960s. However, the tenacious support of these objectives by the three Benelux countries—who had realised the advantages of union more easily and much earlier than their more ambitious larger neighbours—made a powerful contribution to keeping the European idea active during the 1960s, and prepared the way for a further move ahead as that difficult decade came to an end.

The political life of Luxembourg continued during the 1960s in the same generally uneventful pattern that had prevailed in the 1950s. The country was closely linked to Belgium in many ways, the sister of King Baudouin being married to the Grand Duke of Luxembourg, and the Belgium-Luxembourg Economic Union providing an even closer form of financial integration than Benelux or the EEC.

This agreement provided for the pooling of all Belgium's and Luxembourg's currency reserves, and for complete freedom in the transfer of capital—still not achieved in EEC as a whole—since Belgian currency was valid in Luxembourg. The agreement was limited in duration—unlike EEC—but included no ' escape clause ' and in fact led to a total integration of the Belgian and Luxembourg monetary systems.

In the broader field of European integration, Luxembourg figured in the 1960s partly in the somewhat sad role of a theatre stage in the process of being abandoned by the actors. When the Commissions of the EEC, Euratom and the ECSC were merged in 1967, the headquarters of ECSC were transferred from Luxembourg to Brussels: Luxembourg insisted on delaying the merger until she received adequate compensation in the form of the installation of part of the legal and other departments of the Communities in a large and expanding office-block in Luxembourg.

13 European Institutions in the 1960s

The EEC and EFTA

The changes in the political and economic circumstances of France and Germany and of the rest of the Six between the late 1950s and the late 1960s naturally had a direct bearing on the way the institutions set up under the Treaty of Rome functioned in practice (see Chapter 9). A few examples will illustrate this interdependence between national policies and Community institutions. When the government of the French Fifth Republic began to insist that the Communities should be limited essentially to carrying out the minimum functions laid down in the treaties, rather than developing supra-nationalism further, the French Chairman of the Euratom Commission, Monnet's colleague Etienne Hirsch, proved to be too 'European' for the Paris government, and his tenure of office was not renewed when his first term expired at the end of 1961. Again, when the French government persisted with President de Gaulle's idea of using the European Community in support of a policy of Franco-German collaboration fairly clearly directed against the United States and Britain, the Community's negotiations about how to develop political union and whether to admit Britain to membership were—as we shall see—profoundly affected. In the mid-sixties a conflict developed between France and the other members about the powers of the European Commission, and the ensuing crisis nearly destroyed the Community altogether. Finally, at the end of the 1960s, as West Germany became stronger, it was noticeable that the Bonn government's commitment to West European integration, while it did not decline, at least failed to grow at the same rate as German interest in relations with the East.

These large issues involving the diplomatic interests of the member states did not at first affect the working of the new institutions very seriously. Once the major conclusion had been reached that the new Fifth Republic of France would not take the country out of the European Community—as 'Europeans' had feared any future Gaullist government might do, from the tone of the Gaullists' remarks about Europe—the European Commission and the Community's other organs were able to get on with the tasks laid down for them in the Treaty of Rome.

As early as 1958, the Six reached agreement on a joint system of social security for migrant workers. By May 1960, they began a series of measures designed to free the movement of capital between the member countries. The following month saw the publication of the first rules against discrimination in transport, and the Commission's first proposals for agricultural policy (approved after hard bargaining in January 1962) were also put forward at this stage. In 1960 the European Social Fund was brought into being, with an initial budget of $30 million. By the end of 1961 the European Investment Bank had provided loans totalling $120.5 million, more than two-thirds of which was invested in Italy. In October 1961 the Community adopted the principle of an elaborate system of regulations designed to enable citizens of any Community country, and any firm established within it, to do business, exercise a profession or supply services, throughout the area. Two months later, in December 1961, the first Community regulations dealing with cartels were published, and in the same month the Community began to tackle the immensely long and hard task of harmonising regional policies among the Six.

Another difficult area of policy was that concerned with Europe's energy resources: this was a matter on which the EEC obviously had to collaborate both with the Coal and Steel Community and with Euratom, and a joint working party of the three Communities proposed a programme for immediate action early in 1961. The implementation of this was interrupted by the crisis of Euratom already mentioned, involving Etienne Hirsch's replacement by a more docile French President, Pierre Châtenet, but the longer-term aspects of Europe's energy requirements were still the subject of close study by the Communities. On more general aspects of economic policy, the Six set up not only the Monetary Committee provided for in the Treaty of Rome, but also a trade-cycle policy committee—the latter despite some German reservations about a device which smacked of economic 'planning'.

In the field of external relations, the Six gave active

consideration to their relationship with the United Kingdom and the other members of the European Free Trade Association—to be described shortly—and also laid down the principles of the Association between the Community and the developing countries of French-speaking Africa—now mainly granted independence by the Fifth Republic.

Perhaps the most important of all, the Six had been able, by the beginning of 1962, to agree to go ahead to the second phase of the transition period, precisely at the end of the four-year time-scale originally agreed. The most difficult issue needing to be resolved before this decision could be taken was the problem of the common agricultural policy on which an all-night session of the Council of Ministers reached agreement in the early hours of 14 January 1962. Once this agreement was achieved—and a precedent set for many all-night sittings at the end of each year's work for the Community—the first series of internal tariff cuts and the first levelling-out of external tariffs between the Six went ahead without difficulty. The latter operation was even carried out *ahead* of the original schedule, while inter-Community quantitative restrictions on trade in industrial products was abolished almost completely.

By January 1962, the Six had thus successfully completed the first of the three stages which were designed to lead them from separate national economies (except for the already integrated sector of coal and steel) into full economic union. In the meantime, the so-called 'outer Seven'—Britain, Denmark, Norway, Sweden, Austria, Switzerland and Portugal—had set up the European Free Trade Association, which was to liberalise trade among its members in the course of the 1960s. The background of EFTA was a British proposal of 1957—Britain having dropped out of the negotiations of the Spaak Committee during 1956 (see Chapter 9)—that the nascent EEC should be joined in a broader trade arrangement, or European Free Trade Area. This proposal—whereby EEC would remove its tariff barriers to all trade with the entire membership of OEEC—reflected the British view that the more ambitious EEC proposals for economic union and common policies went too far. With this in mind, the British proposal for a Free Trade Area concentrated entirely on the freeing of industrial trade among the members: it differed from the EEC project in making no provision for agriculture, in not covering the trade of member states with outside partners, and in not providing for any institutional framework like that of the EEC.

The member states of the emerging EEC negotiated seriously about the British proposal from mid-1957—when the British first put it forward in what appeared to be a counter-move to the signing of the Treaty of Rome—until late 1958. The Six regarded the proposal with mixed feelings: on the one hand, many influential Germans (including Dr Erhard, the Economics Minister) were sympathetic to a broader and looser trade grouping than the Six, but on the other hand there were serious technical objections to the British plan on the grounds that it would allow Commonwealth and other imports too easy access into the EEC via the European Free Trade Area.

At President de Gaulle's meeting with Chancellor Adenauer at Bad Kreuznach in November 1958, the French President won West Germany's support for his view that the British proposal should be rejected, and the decision was announced by Jacques Soustelle, de Gaulle's Minister of Information.

The British reaction—after initial surprise and dismay—was to set up the European Free Trade Association, approved by the governments of the 'Outer Seven' in July 1959. The EFTA secretariat, established in Geneva, was a much smaller organisation than the massive EEC staff in Brussels—reflecting the relative simplicity of the task of setting up a Free Trade Area, contrasted with the planning of an economic union. The timing of tariff cuts between the Seven was arranged to coincide with the cuts the Six were due to make, and there was general talk of 'bridge-building' between the Six and the Seven: in the short run, however, Western Europe's two economic groupings went along very separate ways.

The crises of 1962-63: political union and the British application
Between 1960 and 1962, an important series of negotiations took place among the Six on a proposal for creating closer links between the national political systems of the six capitals and the activities of the Brussels institutions at the European level: the proposal for spanning the gap, however, was not equally welcome to all of the parties concerned.

o

The plan discussed between the six governments was a French one, launched after a meeting between de Gaulle and Adenauer at the end of July 1960. In its original form it provided for close ' political union ' between the Six, to be achieved by political cooperation along the following lines:

(1)   there were to be regular meetings of the heads of state or of government of the Six and/or their Foreign Ministers, supplemented by periodic meetings of Ministers with more ' technical ' responsibilities;

(2)   a permanent inter-governmental secretariat was to be established;

(3)   four permanent inter-governmental committees were to be set up, dealing respectively with foreign policy, defence, economics and cultural affairs;

(4)   a new European assembly was to be set up, whose members were to be appointed by the national parliaments.

The establishment of these new forms of European political consultation was to be confirmed, according to the original French proposal, by a popular referendum in each of the six countries.

This last idea—a characteristically Gaullist suggestion—was received negatively in Germany, where Chancellor Adenauer pointed out that it would be unconstitutional (the Federal Republic having reacted strongly against the idea of plebiscites as practised under the Weimar system). More fundamental objections were, however, raised to the French proposal, which looked at first sight like an attempt to proceed from the economic union of EEC to a new form of political union, just as the European Political Community in 1953 would have been built on ECSC.

The most serious objection to the French proposals in the ensuing debate in the ' Fouchet Committee ' (named after the French Gaullist who presided over the Committee established by the Six) was the emphasis they gave to inter-governmental, as opposed to supra-national forms of action: this applied both to the 1960 proposal and to two later ' Fouchet ' Plans.

The Six had in fact proceeded fairly actively with both forms of action: as we have seen, the institutions of the EEC, though supra-national to some degree, also gave the national governments great weight in the decision-making process, and this weight had been further supplemented by a growing volume of inter-governmental consultation, particularly through regular meetings of the Foreign Ministers of the Six. What displeased the Dutch government and some others, in the new French proposals, was that by institutionalising certain aspects of inter-governmental consultation (by, for instance, regular meetings of heads of state and a permanent inter-governmental secretariat), this procedure would tilt the balance too far against the supra-national institutions of Brussels. The Dutch and Germans were also wary of any scheme which might set up a European grouping of a kind opposed to the United States and Britain, and the French proposal for European discussions of defence appeared to challenge NATO. Adenauer had accepted de Gaulle's original proposal in July 1960 at a moment when he was concerned that the American election campaign might weaken United States leadership of the alliance, and in early 1961 he found the new Kennedy Administration difficult to deal with, but in the course of the year he realised the need for trying to maintain the closest possible contact with Washington. On the question of Britain, the Dutch and other critics of de Gaulle's plans argued that it was illogical to propose the kind of loose European institutions congenial to Britain (as her Ministers made clear during the negotiations of 1962 for British membership of EEC) while in fact taking a critical view —as Paris did—of Britain's application to join. The fundamental objection to the Fouchet Plan, however, was that it decisively weakened the Brussels institutions to the advantage of the national capitals of the Six: on these grounds, the plan was rejected by France's partners by the spring of 1962, only to reappear, as we have noted (see Chapter 10) in the Franco-German treaty signed the following January.

Like the earlier interchanges in the Fouchet Committee, this treaty came to play a role in the parallel series of negotiations —originally unconnected—on Britain's application to join the EEC. This, submitted after the Prime Minister, Harold Macmillan, had announced a decisive change of policy in July 1961, reflected a number of new factors in the international scene as perceived from London. Firstly, growing integration among the Six was an undeniable fact, and Britain's attempt to participate in the process of European economic growth through EFTA was not proving completely successful. Secondly, Britain's hopes of playing an independent diplomatic role in the world—for instance, Macmillan's visit to Moscow during the Berlin crisis of 1959—had ended fairly ignominiously with the abortive Paris summit conference of May 1960. Thirdly, the new American administration of President Kennedy clearly had less patience with Britain's attempt to keep aloof from Europe than had been shown by President Eisenhower, and Macmillan was made clearly aware of this when he visited Washington in April 1961. Fourthly, the Commonwealth—the other non-European pillar of Britain's policy alongside her ' special relationship' with Washington—had been seriously shaken by the Suez crisis of 1956, and its inability to provide a coherent view on world problems was demonstrated by its conflicts on race relations, leading to South Africa's withdrawal in 1961. It should be added that Macmillan and some of his leading colleagues—for instance, Duncan Sandys, the Secretary of State for Commonwealth Relations—had for some years been convinced ' Europeans' on grounds not dissimilar to Jean Monnet's: however, the factors that brought the bulk of Britain's political, industrial, and official leadership to share their views were essentially the negative ones of a foreclosing of non-European options.

To overcome the considerable remaining hesitation in Britain, as well as the objections of the Commonwealth, the British spokesmen in the early negotiations in Brussels in 1961-63 (led by Edward Heath, Macmillan's Lord Privy Seal) took a tough line on many points, particularly the terms of the Common Agricultural Policy and the prospects for continued Commonwealth imports into Britain and Europe. This tough line was opposed by equal toughness on the part of France—very often speaking for the Six as a whole, despite the current disagreements on the Fouchet Plan—and the negotiations dragged on until January 1963.

President Kennedy's public support for the British application —for instance in his Philadelphia speech of 4 July 1962, where he spoke of ' interdependence' between the United States and a united Western Europe—was designed to help Britain, but had the opposite effect in the eyes of the French government. When Macmillan signed the Nassau Agreement with President Kennedy in December 1962 (providing for the purchase by Britain of American Polaris nuclear missiles, to replace the Skybolt rocket the American administration had abandoned), de Gaulle saw this as formal proof that Britain—despite Macmillan's protestations of 'European' faith—was still in the pocket of the United States. In his press conference of 14 January 1963, which announced France's refusal to continue the negotiations with Britain, de Gaulle underlined her continuing dependence on America and condemned President Kennedy's 'Grand Design' as a device for perpetuating America's control over Western Europe.

More generally, de Gaulle argued that Britain was still not ready to become truly European, but remained a maritime power with a powerful inclination to turn her back on Europe in moments of crisis.

He also argued—correctly—that many of the most important issues in the Brussels negotiations (notably agriculture and the Commonwealth) were still far from being settled. Even though the other five governments, and the EEC Commission, issued statements deploring the unilateral breaking-off of the negotiations, there was no way for them to be continued until a new approach was made by a new British government four years later.

NATO and the MLF crisis 1963-64
The British and American governments were also concerned with a further problem which critically affected relations between the West European governments, and also the working of the European institutions, during the early 1960s. In some ways the history of the MLF (multilateral force) up to its abandonment at the end of 1964, was similar to that of the European Defence Community up to the rejection ten years earlier. In each case a military command structure was devised as a way of solving a political or psychological problem; in each case a variety of different responses among the allies made relations worse rather than better; and in each case the scheme put forward was abandoned because of a change of mind by the state that had first proposed it.

The idea of an Allied nuclear force had been discussed in NATO circles since the late 1950s, but the precise notion of a mixed-manned or fully-integrated force including West Germany, as suggested by the Kennedy Administration in 1961, was a response to specific new elements in the situation. In the first place, some American strategic planners argued that Western Europe's growing economic and political weight would lead to demands for a greater share in alliance decisions; secondly, it was feared in Washington that Germany might be tempted to follow the British and French examples of nuclear independence if she were not given some other form of share in NATO's nuclear ' hardware '; thirdly, the credibility of the American nuclear shield was thought to be undermined by the onset of strategic parity between the USA and the USSR; fourthly, it was recognised that Western Europe ought to develop a new force, more under its own control, to offset the new threat from Soviet medium-range ballistic missiles; and finally, it was hoped that the MLF would provide a means for Europeans to pay a greater share of the costs of Western defence.

The proposed MLF at first received only the most general blessing of the American Administration: for instance, in a speech by Mr McNamara, the Secretary of Defence, at the NATO Ministerial Council meeting in May 1962, it was made clear that the proposal was one which the Europeans were entirely free to accept or reject, without American policy being engaged on either side. However, de Gaulle's dramatic attack on British and American policy in January 1963, combined with his determined wooing of West Germany, greatly strengthened the hand of the ' MLF lobby ' in Washington. This group—mainly leading officials of the European section of the State Department—was able to convince President Kennedy that a more active pursuit of the MLF was needed, as it offered a way of inoculating Germany against Gaullist infection, and a vigorous ' sales campaign ' was mounted. The American advocates of the plan met with their greatest success in Bonn: Paris remained stonily hostile, and London was divided (the Foreign Office welcoming the project for diplomatic reasons, and the Ministry of Defence disliking it for strategic and economic ones), but in Bonn—particularly after Erhard had replaced Adenauer at the end of 1963—the proposal was very warmly received.

By the end of 1964, in fact, it appeared quite likely that the MLF would come into existence, if at all, essentially as the result of a German-American agreement, since the other governments were more opposed to it than ever: President de Gaulle was openly accusing Chancellor Erhard of adopting the American view on MLF in breach of the spirit, if not the letter, of the Franco-German treaty of January; and the British Labour government under Harold Wilson, elected in October 1964, made a scarcely veiled bid to destroy the MLF altogether by proposing that the Allies instead discuss the new idea of an Atlantic Nuclear Force (ANF) on quite different lines—the integrated approach of MLF being replaced by joint allied planning for nuclear forces that remained basically national (and not German).

The American government, in its eagerness to retain German support for the proposal, had by now backed Germany's refusal within the Six to accept a lower price for agricultural products—a refusal based on the hopes of the CDU and FDP to keep the farmers' votes in the 1965 election. In this way, as well as in matters of military strategy, the MLF was exercising an increasingly divisive influence within the Six. In the face of mounting evidence of its unpopularity and inefficacy, President Johnson quietly shelved the proposal in December 1964 by making it clear that his administration no longer attached great importance to its success.

Within a year or so, the MLF discussions had shown the way to a much more effective method of associating the Germans with NATO's nuclear strategy: the Nuclear Planning Group, or so-called 'McNamara Committee', of which Germany was a full member. (In this respect of giving birth to something better, the MLF again resembled the EDC: the frenzied debates preceding the latter's demise in 1954 had paved the way for German membership of WEU in 1955.)

In the short run, the MLF's untimely end greatly embarrassed the Erhard government, which had reaffirmed its support for the project until the end. It also enhanced the position *vis-à-vis* Germany of de Gaulle, who was strongly placed to take a further initiative relating to Europe's institutions during 1965.

The EEC crisis of 1965 and the Luxembourg 'Compromise'
The aftermath of the break-off of negotiations with Britain in January 1963, combined with the renewed strains caused by the MLF negotiations, produced great difficulties for the EEC institutions. As the President of the Commission, Walter Hallstein, joined the Dutch and other member governments in criticising the high-handed manner of France's veto of January 1963, tension between the Brussels Commission and the French Government began to build up towards the dramatic clash which was to come in June 1965. During 1963 and 1964, it was already apparent

that the Brussels machinery no longer functioned as smoothly as in the previous years: decisions were reached by a process of overt bargaining between the member states—known as the 'synchronisation' of, for instance, a French and a German interest—with the Commission's rôle as a mediator and proposer of solutions seriously reduced.

The crisis of June 1965 came after some preliminary warning signs: in March, the French Gaullist party was allowed to stretch the rules of the European Parliament, where it wished to form a parliamentary group of its own (although it was smaller than the officially permitted minimum size) rather than to sit with the Liberals or Christian Democrats; at about the same time, the French Government indicated its displeasure at the European Commission's increasing tendency to adopt the style of a government, with President Hallstein receiving ambassadors in formal dress, to the accompaniment of champagne and red carpets.

These issues of style were highly symbolic: for de Gaulle, the European Commission was a body of civil servants, exercising certain functions delegated to them by national governments who remained the real masters. The French Government objected even more profoundly to a linked series of three specific proposals put forward by the Commission in June 1965. These proposals attempted to combine three items in a package deal: the completion of the farm finance regulations agreed in principle in January 1962; the Commission's wish to have its own independent sources of revenue; and the demand for greater control over the Community's budget by the European Parliament.

The link between these proposals was a logical one: if the Community was to replace the 1962 agricultural financing arrangements—due to expire on 30 June 1965—by a gradual increase of direct Community income from levies on farm imports, it made sense for the same principle to be applied to the Community's budget as a whole. (This would mean that the Community, instead of depending on contributions from the member states, would be able to increase the proportion of its income derived directly from the common external tariff on industrial imports.) If, in turn, the Commission were to be thus endowed with the power to raise its own revenue, then it made sense—this point was particularly stressed by the Dutch Parliament, and later by the Bundestag—for this budget to be subjected to democratic control by the European Parliament (imperfect though the latter body was).

The Commission made a tactical error in assuming that France's interest in the first of the three items—the signing and sealing of the agricultural policy—would make her willing to accept the rest of the package, which ran directly against the Gaullist view of the primacy of nation-states. The French Foreign Minister, Couve de Murville, who was Chairman of the EEC Council of Ministers in June 1965, objected first to the manner in which the Commission had publicly announced its proposals in the European Parliament without first referring them to the national governments, and then to the attempt to link farm finance with the other two issues. When the Council of Ministers failed by 30 June 1965 to settle the first issue in isolation, as France demanded, Couve de Murville brought the meeting to an end, despite the protestations of his colleagues that the over-running of time-limits was a standard Community procedure.

For seven months after this critical meeting, France virtually absented herself from the Council's sessions, sending only junior representatives to carry out routine business, and refusing to take part in any meetings designed to give new strength to the Community. In de Gaulle's view—which he expounded at a press conference on 4 September—the Commission had transgressed against the Treaty of Rome by trying to absorb too much power from the member governments, and France would have nothing to do with the Council of Ministers until such aberrations were clearly renounced. The French President also issued a stern warning against any further progress from the unanimity rule towards majority voting in the Council of Ministers itself— this was a separate issue from that of the Commission's powers, and majority voting was in fact provided for in the Treaty of Rome itself—and Couve de Murville alarmed the supporters of European integration still further by calling in October for a general ' overhaul ' of the Community's institutions.

The French Government was impelled towards a compromise by the presidential election of December, in which de Gaulle was forced into a second ballot by the combined strength of two opponents, Mitterand (Socialist) and Lecanuet (Christian

Democrat), and emerged victorious but somewhat deflated. In January 1966 the compromise between France and her partners —the so-called 'Gentlemen's Disagreement'—was signed in Luxembourg. In the seven main points of this document, the Commission agreed, in essence, to take care to consult member governments at all stages of its proceedings, to refrain from acting like a government in publishing its projects and receiving ambassadors, and to coordinate its work more closely with the Council of Ministers and the Permanent Representatives of the member states. In exchange for this, France agreed to return to her place in the Council, and to accept in principle that certain decisions be taken there by majority vote. However—and in this sense the Luxembourg compromise was not complete—the document records that 'the French delegation considers that where very important interests are at stake, the discussion must be continued until unanimous agreement is reached'. Even more ominously, the next paragraph reads:

> The six delegations note that there is a divergence of views on what should be done in the event of a failure to reach complete agreement.*

Despite this agreement to disagree, the Six recognised that they had enough interests in common—to start with, the interest in reaching a satisfactory settlement of the problem of agricultural financing—for the work of the Council to be resumed on the old basis. What the Luxembourg agreement registered, essentially, was the fact that progress towards the idea of a supra-national authority—whether a majority of member states, or the Commission—overruling a member on a matter of vital interest, was still not acceptable. Even though France took the lead in insisting on the reaffirmation of this principle, it was clear that in practice none of the other member states would submit to being overruled on matters of vital interest, and *in practice* the Commission would not have tried to carry out or condone such overruling. The peculiarity of de Gaulle's style was that he insisted on such restraints being spelt out in black and white—in reaction against the incautious steps of the Commission in trying to increase its own rôle too fast in 1965.

* Quoted in Richard Mayne, *The Institutions of the European Community* (Chatham House/PEP, 1968) p. 47.

After the crisis of 1965-66, decision-making in the Community placed much greater and more explicit emphasis on the part to be played by national governments, and the real power of the Committee of Permanent Representatives increased very considerably. Under French pressure, the term of office of President Hallstein was not renewed when it expired in 1967, and he was replaced as President by the Belgian Commissioner Jean Rey, whose attempt to increase the supra-national element in Community decision-making was pursued more tactfully than Hallstein's. The 1965-66 crisis was a reminder that the European Community, while it was already something more than a grouping of sovereign states, was still a good deal less than a federal United States of Europe. This ambiguity was to be apparent in several important undertakings of the Community in the next few years.

From the Kennedy Round to The Hague Summit 1967-69
The choice of Jean Rey as Hallstein's successor was due in part to his effective conduct of the Kennedy Round of tariff reductions on behalf of the Community, which he represented as the Commissioner responsible for external relations. The Kennedy Round, within the framework of the General Agreement on Tariffs and Trade, aimed at an all-round reduction of tariffs on both industrial and agricultural products. The negotiations lasted from 1964 to 1967, and were largely unsuccessful in the difficult field of agriculture. For trade in industrial goods, however, a significant reduction in tariff barriers was achieved, and a good deal of the credit for this rightly went to Jean Rey's persistent efforts to secure a coordinated EEC position. This was an area of policy in which—despite the grave tensions of the 1965-66 crisis—the Community could effectively function as a unit in international affairs.

There remained, however, many other matters on which the members still disagreed. One of these was the question of British membership, which was raised again in 1967. The Labour government had attempted since 1964 to play a leading part in world politics, and the Prime Minister, Harold Wilson, had begun by aspiring to influence American policy, and even to strengthen the effectiveness of the Commonwealth as a political force; by late 1966, however, Wilson had decided, for essentially the same negative reasons as the Conservatives in 1961, that membership of EEC offered Britain the best chances both of economic prosperity and of political influence. He accordingly renewed Britain's application for membership, and made a tour of the Six capitals early in 1967, accompanied by his Foreign Secretary, George Brown. Even the French government appeared to welcome this British approach, but President de Gaulle was now at the height of his influence on world affairs, and by the end of 1967 he had again decreed that negotiations for British membership were not to be pursued. As in 1963, this provoked protests from the other members of the Community, but they appear to have realised that even de Gaulle was not eternal, and that the commitment of all Britain's political parties to EEC membership made this simply a question of time.

A further development within the Community, during this period, marked a consolidation and strengthening in preparation for the next phase. It had become clear that the existence of three separate communities—ECSC, EEC and Euratom—was anomalous, and a source of weakness. Instead of being able to work out a coherent policy for Europe's energy requirements, for instance, the authorities concerned—ECSC, Euratom and the energy policy department of EEC—had been defending sectional interests, and had thus been unable to defend even these at all effectively against national governments: both Euratom and ECSC had been weakened and defied by the member states in the course of the 1960s. It was thus agreed to merge the three communities into one: the first stage was the merger of the Executives—the 14-member Commission headed by Jean Rey took over the functions of the ECSC High Authority and the EEC and Euratom Commissions—and the full merger of the Communities themselves was due to follow a few years later.

This change took place without notable opposition from any of the member states—it was a much less direct challenge to their power than the Hallstein Commission's move of 1965— and represented a strengthening of the Community under the skilful guidance of Jean Rey.

As the 1960s drew to a close, having survived the major clashes of 1963 and 1965-66, the European Communities appeared to be pursuing their task of European integration in a more realistic fashion and with a slower timetable in view than Monnet and the other pioneers had perhaps envisaged in the

1950s. The economic revival of Europe had given new vigour to the nation-states—though not all of them used it as aggressively as de Gaulle's France—and the 'Europeans' in Brussels and elsewhere were forced to some extent to mark time. They needed a new political impetus, and this could only come from a collective decision by the governments of the member states: such a decision was to be made at the summit conference at The Hague in December 1969 by a new political leadership of the main states of Europe, whose attitudes and policies have now to be described.

14 Europe Enters the Seventies

France after de Gaulle

Although de Gaulle had dropped him as Prime Minister in the crisis of 1968, Georges Pompidou had no serious rival for the presidential succession. As the Gaullist nominee, he was opposed, in the first ballot of the election of June 1969, by the centre politician Alain Poher (who received 23.30 per cent of the votes to Pompidou's 44.46 per cent) and by the Communist Jacques Duclos (who obtained 21.27 per cent). In the second ballot, Pompidou beat Poher by 58.21 per cent to 41.78 per cent, although this time the latter did as well as François Mitterand had done in 1965 by collecting both Communist and 'European' votes.

When Jacques Chaban-Delmas took office as Prime Minister, later in June, he announced that his government would be one 'of reconciliation and of action', and promised a number of reforms designed to overcome the grievances that had produced the crisis of 1968. In August, faced with the evident weakness of French exports in a competitive world market, the government devalued the franc, and this laid the basis for a programme of economic reforms introduced in the autumn.

The government included a number of men who had served under de Gaulle—for example, Michel Debré as Defence Minister —but also some new faces, amongst them Maurice Schumann, who took over the Foreign Ministry with the fairly clear intention of continuing the 'European' policy he had begun as Under-Secretary to Robert Schuman twenty years earlier. The non-Gaullist party in the coalition—the Independents led by the Finance Minister Giscard d'Estaing—clearly had more influence under General de Gaulle's successor than before. The régime headed by Pompidou and Chaban-Delmas thus combined innovation with continuity: while it was clear, for instance, that defence policy would scarcely deviate from a classical Gaullist position of national independence so long as Debré could preserve this, a new spirit in French diplomacy was soon to follow on Maurice

Schumann's return to the Quai d'Orsay, and the financial policy of Giscard d'Estaing had nothing specifically Gaullist about it.

The political forces of the left remained gravely weakened and divided, as the public support they had apparently enjoyed in May 1968 had evaporated and did not return. The Socialist leader Gaston Defferre was discredited by his very poor showing in the presidential contest against Pompidou—he received barely five per cent of the votes in the first ballot—and in July 1969 Alain Savary took over the leadership of the party. The victory of Savary—a left-wing Socialist who had criticised the Fourth Republic's policy in Algeria—marked the eclipse not only of Defferre but also of Guy Mollet, who was at last persuaded to hand over to Savary the general secretaryship which he had held since 1947. The new leader's overall policy was to seek an agreement with the powerful Communist Party to the left of the Socialists, rather than with the surviving Radical and centre party fragments to his right. The Communist Party was not easy to deal with: early in 1970 it demonstrated its doctrinal intransigence by expelling Roger Garaudy (one of its most original thinkers and leaders) for criticising certain aspects of Soviet policy. However, by May 1970, talks on joint action between the Socialist and Communist parties had progressed fairly well, and in the traditional May-day parade in Paris, leaders of both left-wing parties and of their respective trade union federations marched together for the first time since 1947.

By 1971, however, it was open to doubt whether Savary's tactics of unity with the Communists would bring success after all. Both in the municipal elections in the spring, and in the senatorial elections in the autumn, the Gaullist party was able to hold and to improve its position, and the policy represented by Savary appeared to have failed. He was replaced in 1971 by François Mitterand, who seemed capable of offering a stronger challenge to the Gaullist régime—as he had done as presidential candidate even in 1965.

The government itself undoubtedly appeared less monolithic than in de Gaulle's heyday: although for the moment it had little to fear from the Socialist/Communist alliance, and lost only the occasional by-election seat (for instance, the town of Nancy to the Radical Jean-Jacques Servan-Schreiber), it was undermined by internal dissent and in particular by the incipient defection of the Independents, who by late 1971 seemed to be trying to take a more distinct position *vis-à-vis* the government, with an eye to the parliamentary election of 1973. The serious weakness of the left-wing opposition parties, however, suggested that there was very little chance of the Gaullist-Independent coalition being defeated, provided that it retained at least a moderate degree of cohesion.

The changed position of France, between the mid-1960s and the end of the decade, was most clearly reflected in her foreign policy: perhaps it would be more accurate to say that de Gaulle, by the force of his personal dynamism, had been able to raise France to a higher standing than her true economic and political resources justified, and that Pompidou's judgement of what she could do reflected the realities more accurately. Many of the more ambitious aspects of de Gaulle's foreign policy were quietly abandoned. France no longer aspired to liberate Latin America from the United States, and no longer appealed to the states of Asia and Africa to adopt neutralism. When President Pompidou visited North America in February 1970, it was to proclaim his friendship for the United States rather than to call on the people of French-speaking Quebec to free themselves from Anglo-Saxon domination. France, instead of courting a world rôle, concentrated her attention more modestly on areas where she could still exercise real influence: that is, in Africa, the Middle East and Europe. In Africa, the policy of developing close economic, cultural and political links with French-speaking ex-colonies was pursued further (some of the economic aid now coming from France's partners in the European Community), and these ties survived even France's considerable trade in weapons with the South African Republic. In the Middle East, President Pompidou continued the essentially pro-Arab stance taken up by de Gaulle, which benefited France in terms both of oil imports and of arms exports to Libya and other Arab states. In Europe, there was a considerable change of emphasis: instead of attacking the European Community's institutions and preaching the idea of European cooperation extending from the Atlantic to the Urals, Pompidou gave up at least the grandiloquence of de Gaulle's dealings with the Soviet Union (if not their economic substance) and, within a few months of taking office, helped to bring about the 'summit conference' of the Six in The Hague. This conference of December 1969, as we shall see, marked a great step forward in the consolidation of the Community and its enlargement to include new members. The change in French policy was due only in part to de Gaulle's departure: it is likely that a further reason for Pompidou's willingness to accept Britain's entry into the Community was apprehension about the growing weight of Germany. There was also the evidence of the Strategic Arms Limitation Talks (SALT) held between the United States and the Soviet Union from 1968 onwards that the two super-powers could, acting together, take decisions which might affect the future of Europe. Like the other states of Western Europe, France increasingly realised that a further development of European unity was necessary as a way of influencing events within Europe itself, not to mention the world outside.

Germany 1969-71: Willy Brandt's first two years
The SPD/FPD coalition that took power in Bonn at the end of 1969 was, as we have seen, something new in the history of the Federal Republic: the post of Chancellor, as well as that of President, was now in the hands of the SPD and for the first time the CDU was banished to the opposition benches. There was some talk of a radical break with the past, and many observers expected the government to introduce substantial legislative reforms. In practice, the work of the new government was to build on that of its predecessor: Brandt, Schiller, Schmidt and the other leading SPD Ministers had, after all, worked as coalition partners of the CDU for the previous three years; and their FPD colleagues, such as Walter Scheel (now Vice-Chancellor and Foreign Minister), had also served in coalitions with the CDU in earlier years.

Chancellor Brandt announced that his government would concentrate its main attention on domestic reform, and a number of new measures were introduced in the fields of tax and family law, in the educational system and in other areas. In economic policy, although it caused difficulties in the European Community's agricultural policy, Professor Schiller's revaluation of the mark during the election campaign was generally welcomed and he continued the policy of mildly socialistic economic planning he had begun under the Grand Coalition. A series of disagreements between Schiller and the Finance Minister, Alex

P

Möller, led in 1971 to the latter's resignation, and to the absorption of the Finance Ministry into Schiller's Ministry of Economics.

More serious were the disagreements between the SPD and the party's coalition partner the FDP. There were a number of aspects of economic policy—notably codetermination in industry, and policy on incomes—where the two parties disagreed, and where the easiest course was to avoid taking any decisive action at all.

This was one reason for the unexpected dynamism of Brandt's ' government of domestic reform ' in the field of foreign affairs. The other reason was that it proved unexpectedly easy both for the new Chancellor to get the German people to face the facts of Germany's division and to get the Russians to do something to make the facts less unpalatable. The Brandt government will certainly go down in history as the one which took decisive steps in creating a new system of relations with the Federal Republic's Eastern neighbours—particularly the Soviet Union, Poland, and the DDR—but it should not be forgotten that this Eastern policy, or *Ostpolitik*, was firmly rooted in Bonn's attachment to the West. The Chancellor and his Defence Minister, Helmut Schmidt, made it absolutely clear that they still regarded the alliance with America through NATO as the fundamental basis of Germany's security, and Brandt himself took an active part, three months after taking office, in the summit conference at The Hague that re-launched the movement towards West European integration.

What was new in the Brandt government's approach to foreign policy was a determination to look Eastwards as well as Westwards, and to accelerate the movement for *rapprochement* with the East that had been started under Erhard and Kiesinger earlier in the decade. As government spokesmen put it, reconciliation with France and Israel—two of Nazi Germany's outstanding victims—had been the great achievement of Adenauer's foreign policy, and the time had now come to give equal attention to the third victim, Poland. A basic principle of Brandt's Eastern policy was, however, to make it quite clear both to the Russians and to the East Germans that this did not aim at changing the *status quo* in the immediate future (or indeed ever using force to destroy the GDR in the name of German reunification), but rather that it accepted the territorial division of Germany as the irreversible basis for a better relationship. Brandt and his closest advisers (notably Egon Bahr, who had worked with Brandt in the municipal government of Berlin and who shared his views on the need for a new relationship with the East) drew from the invasion of Czechoslovakia in 1968 the conclusion that any German *Ostpolitik* that approached the Soviet satellites directly—without first clarifying relations with the Soviet Union and the GDR—could only end in disaster.

Brandt therefore began by approaching the GDR, taking good care to inform both the Russians and his Western allies what he was doing. During the first half of 1970 he met his East German counterpart Willi Stoph on two occasions—at Erfurt in East Germany, and at Kassel in the west—and although no dramatic agreements were then reached, the scene was set for a closer working relationship between the two German states. The East German demand for full diplomatic recognition was rejected by Bonn: its acceptance would in fact have raised serious problems for East Germany, since it would certainly have put an end to the European Community's readiness to recognise trade between the two Germanies as 'internal', and hence not subject to the EEC's external tariff. But West Germany went so far as to accept the existence of two German states on the territory of the German nation. The ground was thus cleared for detailed negotiations between officials of the two states on a number of matters, including an agreement on the position of West Berlin, which was achieved by the end of 1971.

Having demonstrated his peaceful intentions towards the GDR, Chancellor Brandt turned his attention to Moscow. A treaty renouncing the use of force was signed between the Federal Republic and the Soviet Union in August 1970, and Brandt's visit to Moscow for the occasion was a general sign of Soviet-German *détente*. The declaration on the renunciation of force did not in itself alter things greatly (it had been evident for years that the two states would not use force against one another) but the signature symbolised a will to cooperate, and it paved the way for closer relations in trade, technology and other matters of common interest.

The agreement with the Soviet Union also made it easier for Brandt to approach the satellites without arousing Russian suspicions. He did this most notably by visiting Warsaw in December 1970, to sign a further treaty of friendship. This time the document contained some extremely important provisions—in particular, the German government practically accepted the Oder-Neisse Line as their country's Eastern frontier—but its most important aspect was probably the symbolic impact of the Chancellor's visit to Warsaw. The sight of the German Chancellor—who had himself been driven into exile by the Third Reich—kneeling on the site of the Warsaw Ghetto in atonement for the killing of the Jews by the Nazis was striking evidence that a new Germany indeed existed.

The Chancellor's policy of seeking agreements with Moscow, Warsaw and East Berlin naturally provoked criticism at home from the Christian Democratic Opposition—notably from the right wing led by Franz Josef Strauss—but the general popularity of the policy with the German public, confirmed by the results of the *Land* elections in Hessen and Bavaria in November 1970, soon led to a damping-down of the violent accusations current in the middle of the year of selling out German national interests. Brandt also made a point of keeping his Western allies closely informed on the progress of his Eastern negotiations, and the Western capitals on the whole welcomed the contribution of the Federal Republic to the overall process of East-West *détente* in Europe.

In order to placate domestic critics, as well as to ensure that Germany's new relations with the East were based on genuine compromise and not on one-sided concessions, Brandt insisted that his treaties with Moscow and Warsaw would only be submitted for parliamentary ratification when a satisfactory 'arrangement' on the problem of Berlin had been made. Such an arrangement was reached (the more sweeping word 'settlement' was carefully avoided) when the Western powers and the Soviet Union signed an agreement in August 1971. This document, which had the approval of both German states (although the GDR made difficulties right up to the moment of signature), provided in essence for West Berlin's links with the Federal Republic to be recognised by the East, in exchange for Bonn's acknowledgement that West Berlin was not legally *part* of the Federal Republic. (West Germany's acceptance of this point brought her into line with her allies' interpretation of the constitution of 1949.) With the signature of this agreement, confirmed by the two German governments in December, the way seemed clear for the ratification of West Germany's treaties with Moscow and Warsaw, and for the further stage of a multilateral Conference on European Security.

Her devotion to East-West relations did not, however, prevent West Germany from being an active partner in the process of Western European integration. After the leading part played by Brandt at The Hague came the negotiations on European economic and monetary union leading to the Werner Plan of early 1971; and when the financial crisis of that spring led to the abandonment of the plan, Germany worked assiduously side by side with her partners to find a new solution. She also played an active part in overcoming France's scruples about admitting the United Kingdom to the European Community. The SPD's original scepticism about European integration seemed to have been so far overcome that it was hard to believe Germany would have pursued a different policy under a CDU government.

Italy and Benelux 1969-71
As we have seen (Chapter 11), Italy ended the 1960s with a centre-left coalition under Rumor and Nenni (from December 1968 onwards) which failed in a disappointing way to solve the great economic problems facing the country. The newly united Italian Socialist Party again fell apart at this stage, with a powerful group in between the Socialists and Communists—the PSIUP—that refused to collaborate in governing, and that drove even such erstwhile left-wingers as Nenni back towards an alliance with the old Social Democrat party.

A temporary solution to the political crisis of the summer of 1969 was found in the creation by Rumor of a one-party Christian Democratic government—backed tacitly by the other former coalition parties. But in February 1970 Rumor resigned, unable to cope with the combination of economic stagnation, wild-cat strikes, heavy wage claims and demands for large and expensive reforms in health services, transport, housing and taxation.

A new coalition was formed—again under Rumor—and in the important regional election of June 1970 (regional councils having at last been established in belated pursuance of a provision of the constitution of 1948), the coalition parties increased their strength. The Communist vote stayed stable at 27.9 per cent—this was the first major election since the war when this vote had not risen—but the influence of the Communist Party was increased by renewed dissent within the Socialist Party. If a section of the PSI were to follow the PSIUP into alliance with the Communists (which seemed possible by the end of 1971), the centre-left coalitions (from the Christian Democrats to the PSI) would be out of the question. In the meantime, when Rumor resigned in July 1970, a new centre-left coalition was in fact assembled by Signor Colombo, a dynamic, younger Christian Democrat leader who appeared potentially capable of leading this positional combination to new success in the 1970s. One possibly ominous event in the course of 1971 was the success of the neo-Fascist MSI—a reaction to the centre-left movement —in the local elections held in June.

At the end of the year, with Italy's internal situation unstable and her external security potentially threatened (both by the growth of the Soviet fleet in the Mediterranean and by the weakness of Yugoslavia), political attention was focused on the contest for the presidency, won by the Christian Democrat Leone. Italy continued to be interested in the process of European integration—Mariano Rumor made a contribution to the Conference of The Hague, and Pietro Nenni's proposals for direct elections to the European Parliament continued to be actively propounded by Altiero Spinelli (a member of the European Commission from 1970)—but her position was inevitably subordinate to that of France and Germany.

The same applied even more strongly to the Benelux countries. In Belgium, the language problem continued to dominate political life. In response to separatist pressure from both the Flemish- and French-speaking communities, various schemes for a devolution of power to federal units were considered, and in 1970 the coalition government of Gaston Eyskens worked out an elaborate constitutional reform giving wide economic and cultural powers to new regional authorities. These proposals—passed by the Social Christian-Socialist coalition with the support of the Liberal Party—failed to satisfy the demands either of the French- or of the Flemish-speaking factions, and in the general election of November 1971, the political parties representing the extremists made notable gains. In particular, the 'Franco-phone Front' in the capital (largely a French-speaking city, but within the Flemish-speaking part of Belgium), together with its associate the 'Walloon Rally', increased their votes from six per cent to 10.5 per cent. These gains, and those of the Flemish Federalist Party (now 11 per cent) seriously weakened the Liberal Party, and left a renewal of the Social Christian-Socialist coalition the only course possible. The new government of Eyskens was, however, subject to internal pressures on the language issue, as the French-speaking wing of each party felt obliged to make considerable demands on the Flemish wing in order to avoid being outbid by the French-speaking federalist opposition. In forming his new government, Eyskens thus had to give the usual close attention to the delicate balance both between linguistic and between party groups in the distribution of Ministries. The constitutional reform of 1970 (with its considerable devolution of power to the new regional authorities) appeared to offer a reasonable hope of containing the pressures towards total disintegration of the Belgian state. If it failed, the only alternative appeared to be a more radical form of decentralisation along federalist lines.

The Netherlands, in contrast, remained free of divisive social conflicts. Although religious influences remained very strong in political and social life, at the beginning of the 1970s the government represented an impressively tolerant degree of compromise: in the coalition of five parties, the Prime Minister (Barend Biesheuvel) belonged to the Calvinist Anti-Revolutionary Party, and the Foreign Minister (Norbert Schmelzer, J. H. Luns having given up the post after nineteen years) was in the Catholic People's Party. The government devoted considerable attention to domestic affairs: there were serious problems on the economic front, and also reforms were carried out in 1971 to the laws on divorce and abortion; but the Netherlands remained more open than most other states to influences and pressures from the outside world. As a merchant economy, doing a good deal of trade outside as well as inside the European Community, the Netherlands had strong reasons for wishing to extend the Community to the United Kingdom and other European states.

As all three Benelux countries saw their economic and political future closely bound up with that of Western Europe as a whole, they took a keen part in re-launching the ' European ' idea which was signalled by the Conference of The Hague of December 1969.

The European Community: The Hague and after

As the European Community entered the 1970s, lively activity was to be seen on a number of fronts. The Community was not merely disposing of well-worn and difficult issues like the long-term arrangements for agricultural financing (settled at the end of 1969); it was also embarking seriously on lines of policy which, though often discussed in the past, had never led to effective action. These included the development of political consultation between the Foreign Ministers of the Six, the commitment to press ahead from a customs union to full economic and monetary union, and—perhaps the most significant of all—the agreement to negotiate seriously with Britain and three other applicants for the enlargement of the Six to Ten.

The impetus towards all these new developments of policy came from the summit conference of the six heads of government (or heads of state) which took place in December 1969 in The Hague. This important meeting, held in the city where the European movement had first been launched in 1948, was facilitated by the change of government in France—Pompidou had replaced de Gaulle as President six months earlier—and by Chancellor Brandt's determination to prove that his new *Ostpolitik* was firmly rooted in Germany's commitment to her partners in the Six. At certain critical stages of the conference at The Hague, and particularly on the difficult issue of negotiations with Britain, there is no doubt that the German Chancellor pressed the French President in the direction of accepting new lines of policy.

One of the striking things about the background of The Hague Conference, however, was that each of the statesmen taking part tried to take for himself the maximum credit for initiating and promoting the ' re-launching of Europe '. The world had changed since de Gaulle had been able to defy his European partners and still win the support of the French people. Europeans were uncomfortably aware that the two super-powers were negotiating (if not behind their backs, then at least over their heads) on a number of issues which must inevitably include the future of Europe, as well as the technicalities of arms control and the problems of the Middle East. Within Europe itself, the growing weight of Germany was making itself felt, and although post-Gaullist France had general confidence in the intentions of Chancellor Brandt, the countervailing force of a new member—Britain—was a welcome prospective addition to the Community from France's point of view.

The main points agreed at The Hague were as follows: the future agricultural financing arrangements should be settled immediately (i.e. by the end of 1969); the negotiations with Great Britain and the other applicant states should be taken up and actively pursued; in the field of economic and monetary policy, the Community should develop plans for short-term cooperation in establishing a European Reserve Fund, and longer-term plans for creating a full economic and monetary union by 1980; in the field of political consultation, plans should be worked out for regular discussions between Ministers of Foreign Affairs and also senior officials of the Foreign Ministries of the Six; progress also needed to be made on a number of other issues, including technological cooperation, development aid, social policies and the establishment—after many years of delay —of a European University.

The decisions of the Conference of The Hague reflected the usual series of compromises: in particular, France's agreement to the resumption of negotiations with Britain—despite her own growing interest on this point, already mentioned—was dependent on the agreement of her partners to the French wish for the agricultural financing arrangements to be signed and sealed as early as possible.

The heavy programme of work for European officials that resulted from the decisions reached at The Hague in fact began with the agricultural item and, by late December, agreement had been achieved on a system to replace the existing provisional scheme. It was agreed that by the mid-1970s the Commission would directly receive the proceeds of the levies on food imports from outside the Community, and that the main beneficiary from the Common Agricultural Policy, France, would be assured of receiving income on a continuing basis.

The second big area for decisions by the Six after The Hague was that of economic and monetary policy. The conference

endorsed the proposal that the Community should develop into a
full economic and monetary union by the year 1980, and a committee was set up under the Prime Minister of Luxembourg,
Pierre Werner, to work out detailed plans and a timetable. The
Six were, however, divided in their approach to this problem.
On the one hand the so-called 'economists', Germany and the
Netherlands, pressed—as they had before—for the coordination
of economic policies as an essential and early stage of the progress towards unity; on the other, the 'monetarists'—notably
France—argued that unity in the field of monetary policy must
be the first step. In the winter of 1970-71, agreement was reached
on the so-called 'Werner Plan'—a compromise whereby economic and monetary policies were both to be synchronised in
a combined programme—but in May 1971, an acute monetary
crisis (provoked by the flow of surplus dollars into Germany) led
to serious divergences between the Six. Germany's policy led to
criticism by France to the effect that unilateral actions in the
field of interest-rates were contrary to the spirit of monetary
union embodied in the Werner Plan, and the whole prospect of
the latter being implemented was cast into doubt. The state of
tension between Paris and Bonn on monetary matters was
aggravated by the renewed crisis of August 1971, when President
Nixon's unilateral action, in imposing an import surcharge and
renouncing the gold exchange standard for the dollar, provoked
contrasting responses in France and in Germany. By the end
of the year, although the Six were closer to working out the
lines of a common response to the problems revealed by the
American action, the necessary degree of cooperation between
France and Germany was still not fully established.

In the meantime, the Community had undergone a further
institutional change: in May 1970, the 14-member Commission
presided over by Jean Rey had been replaced—according to the
provisions of the treaty merging the three communities—by a
Commission of nine members headed by the Italian politician
Franco Malfatti. The two French members, Raymond Barre and
Jean-François Deniau, had both served on the earlier Commission: the two most dynamic new members were the German
Ralf Dahrendorf (a Professor of Sociology turned FDP politician
and a junior Minister in the Brandt government) and the veteran
Italian federalist Altiero Spinelli.

One of the tasks of the new Commission—again arising from the decisions of The Hague—was to promote consultation on political affairs, particularly on questions of foreign policy, between the six governments. The committee set up to explore the means to achieve this was headed by the senior permanent official to the Belgian Foreign Ministry, Jean Davignon; and the so-called Davignon Report of July 1970 made provision for regular six-monthly meetings of Foreign Ministers and for more continuous consultations at the level of officials. The first of the regular meetings of Foreign Ministers was held in Munich in November 1970, and the second in Rome in May 1971: on the latter occasion, the Six broke with precedent by agreeing on a subject which was quite outside the economic matters officially covered by the Treaty of Rome— the lines of a possible peace settlement for the Middle East. These discussions of the Six on foreign policy matters—somewhat in the manner envisaged by the Fouchet Plan of the early 1960s, though this time the consultations meant a consolidation rather than an undermining of the EEC's institutions—were later enlarged to discussions of Ten, as Great Britain and the other applicant states were invited to take part in a special session after each meeting of the Six. This process of working out an embryonic European foreign policy in the political field—economically, the Community was already a power in the world system—was thus related to the remaining main field of operations resulting from the Conference of The Hague—the enlargement of the Community.

Once the Conference of The Hague had given the signal, negotiations were quickly taken up between the Six and Great Britain—first with Harold Wilson's Labour government, and after June 1970 with the new Conservative government of Edward Heath. There were some difficult points in the bargaining—particularly over the size of Britain's contribution to the Common Agricultural Policy—but by mid-1971, the essential problems had been successfully resolved.

The terms of the agreement were approved by the British parliament on 28 October 1971, and the signature of the accession treaty on 22 January 1972 meant that Britain and her co-applicants, the Irish Republic, Norway and Denmark, were at last to rejoin the mainstream of European political and economic developments, reversing the decision they had made when they rejected the Schuman Plan 21 years earlier.

The political structure of the Europe they were to help in making, and its relations with the rest of the world, were vital matters that remained very much in doubt as the year 1972 began.

15 The Way Ahead: Europe in Tomorrow's World

In 1965 Willy Brandt described West Germany as 'an economic giant, but a political dwarf'. The same remark applies to the European Community of Ten which is now struggling to define its identity and its rôle in the world of the 1970s. Economically, the status of a giant is undeniable: the Community is larger than the United States in population, trade and monetary reserves and, taken as a whole, its output (already 60 per cent of America's) shows a markedly faster rate of growth. In the aspects of external policy not concerned with economics, however, the European Community gives the image of a dwarf—and a schizophrenic one at that. Although the main states in the Community of Ten—France, Britain and West Germany—increasingly agree on the main lines of their foreign policies, there are still a number of issues on which they differ: France takes a different attitude towards NATO from that of Britain or Germany; West Germany is understandably more preoccupied than her allies with reshaping her relationships with her Eastern neighbours; while Britain's legacy of post-imperial concerns, from Singapore to the Caribbean, can hardly be shared in full by her European partners.

There is thus a considerable gap between the rhetoric of politicians about 'Europe's rôle' in world politics and world peace, and the realities of persisting differences of perspective between the major capitals of Europe. The evidence of the quarter-century of history surveyed in this book suggests that those differences of perspective will be eroded in time—the British have given up their world-power pretensions of the fifties and early sixties, and the France of Pompidou is much less assertive than that of de Gaulle—but this history also shows that the nation-states are far from dead.

A further reason why Western Europe will take some time to evolve an effective foreign policy is that the enlarged Community faces an extremely heavy agenda of matters concerned with putting Europe's own house in order. The institutions of the

European Community were designed primarily to deal with the economic and social policies of the area itself, and not with external relations; both the institutions and the national governments of the Ten will have considerable tasks to accomplish in adapting themselves to a Community much larger in size and more diverse in membership. Governments will of course have to give some attention to Europe's relations with the outside world but, in the short run, at least, there is no doubt that the harmonisation of economic, industrial and agricultural policies— by the well-established procedures of interaction between national and Community authorities—will absorb a great deal of Europe's energies. In this process, the member-states of the Community will doubtless begin by asserting their national interests as distinctly as possible—to take an important example, the British government is likely to adopt the French interpretation of the Luxembourg Agreement of 1966, rather than the Five's interpretation—but the habit of cooperation, and the pressures to adopt common policies, are likely to lead in time to the development of closer integration. The institutions of the European Community of the sixties may either be strengthened or give way to a new set of institutions capable of embodying this higher degree of integration: one possibility would be a European Commission reduced in size (its increase to 14 members in 1973 being only temporary), but strengthened in its links with the national governments through the appointment of a Minister for European Affairs in each national cabinet.

So far as the European Community's present external relations are concerned, it could without exaggeration be said to have acquired a world rôle in a fit of absent-mindedness. Beginning with the association agreements with France's former colonies in Africa, and continuing with special arrangements with most of the Mediterranean countries, the Community found itself by the early seventies in some form of commercial agreement with over seventy countries—more than half the states in the world. From trade agreements with Latin America to the special relationship with East Germany, the Community's network of international links makes it the most widely connected trading unit in the world system. In many ways, this position has begun to create problems for the United States: American exports into Europe have been made more difficult, particularly in the agricultural sector; Japanese goods, barred from Europe by the high Community tariff, are being diverted in dangerously large quantities to America; and the Community's agreements with third countries limit American exports there too. This was the background against which President Nixon's introduction of import surcharge and other measures in August 1971 attempted to cure America's balance of payments deficit, a problem only partially resolved by the monetary agreements of December.

The main substance of Europe's external policy is thus economic, and even here, much remains to be done before agreed policies can be worked out: the divergence between the French and German responses to the international monetary problems of 1971-72, though not irreconcilable, is only one example of national differences impeding the development of a Community viewpoint.

The sheer weight of the European Community in the world economic system, and the commitment to common external trading arrangements, however, mean that a European policy— in the general direction of trade liberalisation—can be expected to emerge in due course.

The outlines of a European foreign policy in diplomatic and strategic matters are harder to envisage: the tenacity of divergent national interests is certainly less marked than in the 1950s and 1960s, but they persist all the same. It is important to distinguish between parts of the world where Europe is *not* likely to play an important political rôle—however substantial her economic and other interests may be—and areas where she can hardly help developing a foreign policy of her own, whether she wishes to or not. The area where Europe *must* have a foreign policy is that of East-West relations in the central power balance which spans Europe itself: in an age when the two super-powers are engaged in dialogue on strategic force-levels and other matters, it will be essential for the Europeans to coordinate their own views on such things as the development of a European grouping within NATO, the mutual and balanced reduction of military forces, the tasks and procedures of a European Security Conference, or the possible creation of a standing Commission on East-West relations in Europe. The increasingly intimate economic dealings between the European Community and the members of Comecon—in striking contrast with the Cold War period described in the earlier chapters of this book—is creating the basis for a closer political relationship which appears certain to bring the two halves of Europe together again. This process will, of course, be slow: even though the Soviet Union's grip on Eastern Europe has become less obviously oppressive since the worst days of the Cold War, her invasion of Czechoslovakia in 1968 was a reminder that she would allow no undermining of her influence, and progress towards a new system of security for Europe will be arduous and difficult. Nonetheless, the European Community will certainly add a strategic dimension to the close economic relationships which its members have already developed with their neighbours to the East. The main task of a European foreign policy will inevitably be the development of the structure of Europe itself, between the two super-powers.

The area, in contrast, where Europe will probably *not* develop an active foreign policy is, in effect, the rest of the world, outside the central power balance. The construction of Europe marks, in a sense, the ending of the phase of history in which European colonial rule spread throughout the world; and the Europeans will not easily, in this post-colonial phase, become involved in political initiatives or military peace-keeping operations in the Far East or Africa. The Mediterranean and Middle East will certainly remain areas of concern to Europe, both because of their oil resources and on account of the strategic threat potentially posed by Soviet naval strength. Farther afield, however, the prospects of active European political involvement are much more limited.

It is worth repeating that Europe's *economic* commitments to the under-developed countries of the world are very considerable. In terms of economic aid, the EEC countries in recent years have been devoting a larger proportion of their resources to the 'have-not' countries than Britain. In the complementary field of trading arrangements, the Community's policy has been less liberal than that of Britain, but Europe has made significant concessions in trade preferences in the last few years, and the enlarged Community will certainly continue to make a considerable contribution to the development of poorer countries.

Europe is therefore likely to develop as a 'regional' rather than a 'global' power. It is sometimes argued that Europe's greatest contribution to world peace and stability will henceforth be not through her capacity for exercising military force, but as a 'civilian' power: a grouping of states that—having learnt to resolve their differences and merge their rivalries in a new form of international relationship—set an example of engagement in purely economic and social terms with the rest of the world.

It is doubtful whether such an example, even if Europe were to set it, would in the short run alter the tendency of other parts of the world to continue with conflicts and even wars: the 'learning process' in international relations works very slowly, if at all. It is, however, certain that the European Community of the 1970s, by overcoming historic enmities between European nations, represents a profoundly significant historical development in its own right, whose influence is bound to be felt in one way or another in every part of the world.

Richard Mayne's *The Recovery of Europe* (Weidenfeld and Nicolson, 1970) gives an extremely full and valuable analysis of the political and economic forces at work in the early post-war years, though it is disappointingly thin on the 1960s. It has a comprehensive bibliography, which makes it unnecessary to include one here. *Europe since Hitler*, by Walter Lacqueur (Weidenfeld and Nicolson, 1970) is a more discursive work, dealing with the major trends—political, social, cultural—without any particular focus on European integration. *Western Europe since 1945* by D. W. Urwin (Longmans, 1968) gives a clear short account of the period up to the early Sixties. See also F. Roy Willis, *France, Germany and the New Europe, 1945-1963* (OUP/Stanford UP, 2nd ed., 1968).

On post-war French politics, the standard works are by Philip Williams: *Crisis and Compromise: Politics in the Fourth Republic* (Longmans, 1964), and (in collaboration with Martin Harrison) *Politics and Society in de Gaulle's Republic* (Longmans, 1971).

The best study of Germany is by Alfred Grosser, *Germany in Our Time: A Political History of the Post-War Years* (Praeger, 1971), which summarises the author's numerous earlier writings and contains an admirable bibliography.

English-language studies of Italy are less satisfactory than those of France or Germany: the best are *A Political History of Post-War Italy*, by Norman Kogan (Praeger, 1966), and *Italy since 1945* by Elizabeth Wiskemann (Macmillan, 1971).

On the Benelux countries, general political surveys, and guidance to further reading, are given in two comparative studies: *Six European States: the Countries of the European Community and their Political Systems* by Stephen Holt (Hamish Hamilton, 1970) and *European Political Parties* edited by Stanley Henig and John Pinder (Allen & Unwin for PEP, 1969).

The development of the European institutions has been described by Miriam Camps in *Britain and the European Community, 1955-1963* (Princeton UP/OUP, 1964); the crisis of 1965-66 is analysed in *Collision in Brussels* by John Newhouse

(Faber, 1968), and the Community's political system as a whole in *Europe's Would-Be Polity* by Leon N. Lindburgh and Stuart A. Scheingold (Prentice-Hall, 1970).

A collection of essays on various aspects of policy will be found in *Europe Tomorrow: 16 Europeans Look Ahead*, edited by Richard Mayne (Fontana/Collins for RIIA and PEP, 1972). Students of European affairs should also consult the following periodicals: *European Community, International Affairs*, and *The World Today*.

Index